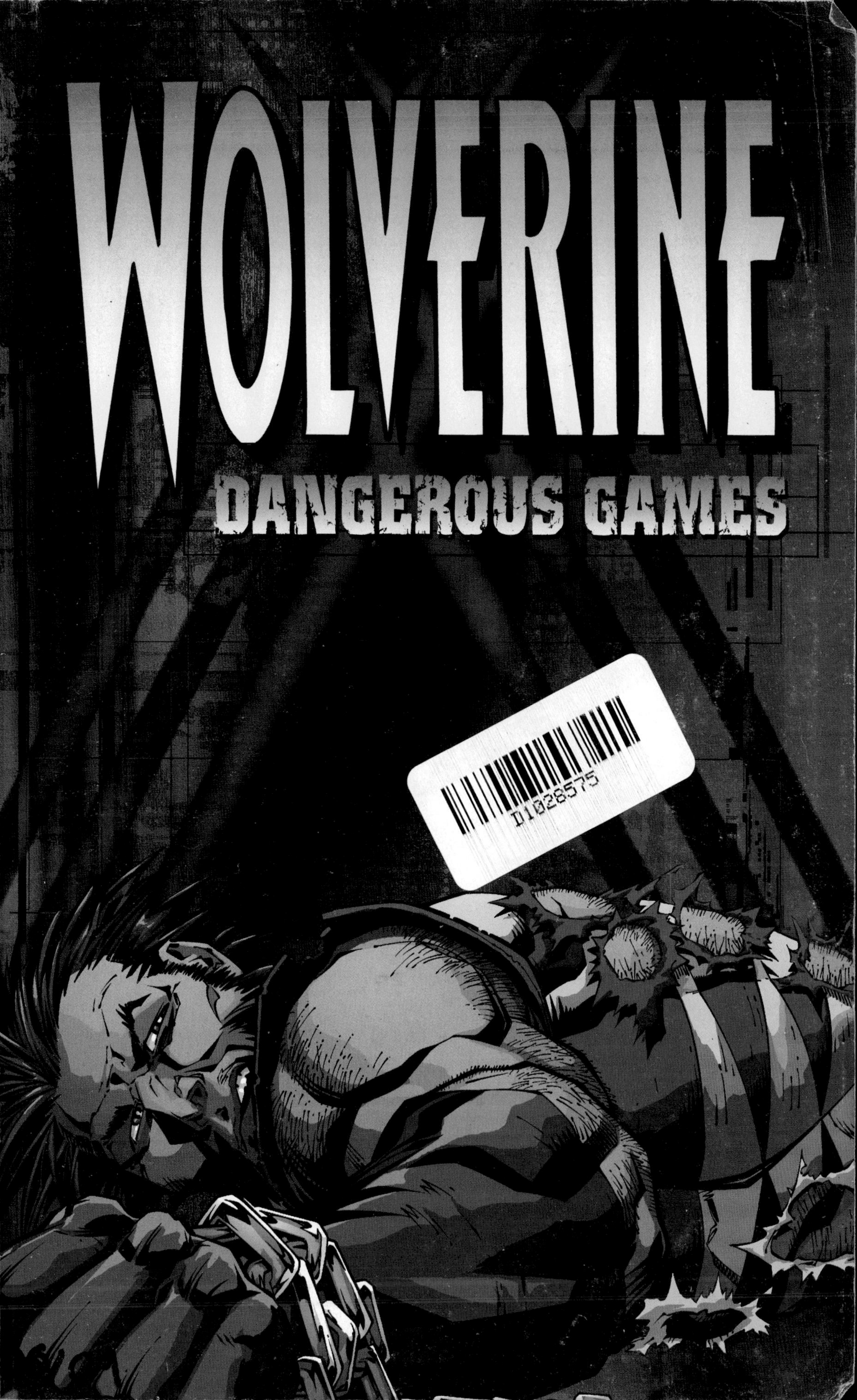
WOLVERINE
DANGEROUS GAMES

WOLVERINE

DANGEROUS GAMES

"THE DEATH SONG OF J. PATRICK SMITTY"
WRITER: GREGG HURWITZ
ARTIST: MARCELO FRUSIN
LETTERS: TODD KLEIN
ASSISTANT EDITOR: AUBREY SITTERSON
EDITOR: AXEL ALONSO

"TALLY HO!"
WRITER: SIMON SPURRIER
ARTIST: BEN OLIVER
COLORS: NESTOR PEREYRA
LETTERS: BLAMBOT'S NATE PIEKOS
EDITOR: AUBREY SITTERSON

"PURITY"
WRITER: RICK REMENDER
ARTIST: JEROME OPENA
COLORS: MICHELLE MADSEN
LETTERS: BLAMBOT'S NATE PIEKOS
EDITOR: AUBREY SITTERSON

"KILLING WOLVERINE MADE SIMPLE"
WRITER: CHRISTOPHER YOST
PENCILER: KOI TURNBULL
INKER: SAL REGLA
COLORS: BETH SOTELO
LETTERS: VIRTUAL CALLIGRAPHY'S CORY PETIT
ASSISTANT EDITOR: MICHAEL HORWITZ
EDITOR: JOHN BARBER

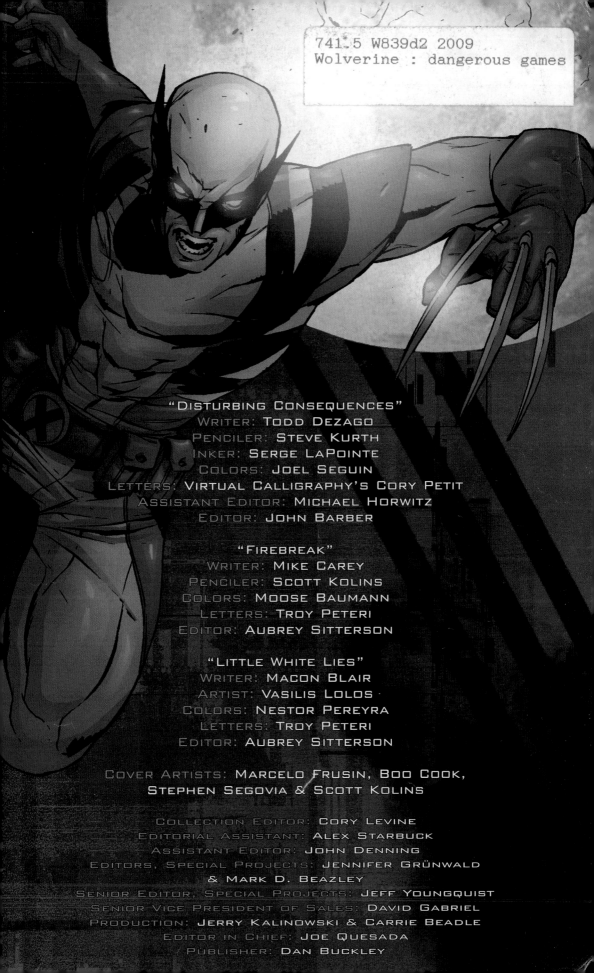

"DISTURBING CONSEQUENCES"
WRITER: TODD DEZAGO
PENCILER: STEVE KURTH
INKER: SERGE LAPOINTE
COLORS: JOEL SEGUIN
LETTERS: VIRTUAL CALLIGRAPHY'S CORY PETIT
ASSISTANT EDITOR: MICHAEL HORWITZ
EDITOR: JOHN BARBER

"FIREBREAK"
WRITER: MIKE CAREY
PENCILER: SCOTT KOLINS
COLORS: MOOSE BAUMANN
LETTERS: TROY PETERI
EDITOR: AUBREY SITTERSON

"LITTLE WHITE LIES"
WRITER: MACON BLAIR
ARTIST: VASILIS LOLOS
COLORS: NESTOR PEREYRA
LETTERS: TROY PETERI
EDITOR: AUBREY SITTERSON

COVER ARTISTS: MARCELO FRUSIN, BOO COOK,
STEPHEN SEGOVIA & SCOTT KOLINS

COLLECTION EDITOR: CORY LEVINE
EDITORIAL ASSISTANT: ALEX STARBUCK
ASSISTANT EDITOR: JOHN DENNING
EDITORS, SPECIAL PROJECTS: JENNIFER GRÜNWALD
& MARK D. BEAZLEY
SENIOR EDITOR, SPECIAL PROJECTS: JEFF YOUNGQUIST
SENIOR VICE PRESIDENT OF SALES: DAVID GABRIEL
PRODUCTION: JERRY KALINOWSKI & CARRIE BEADLE
EDITOR IN CHIEF: JOE QUESADA
PUBLISHER: DAN BUCKLEY

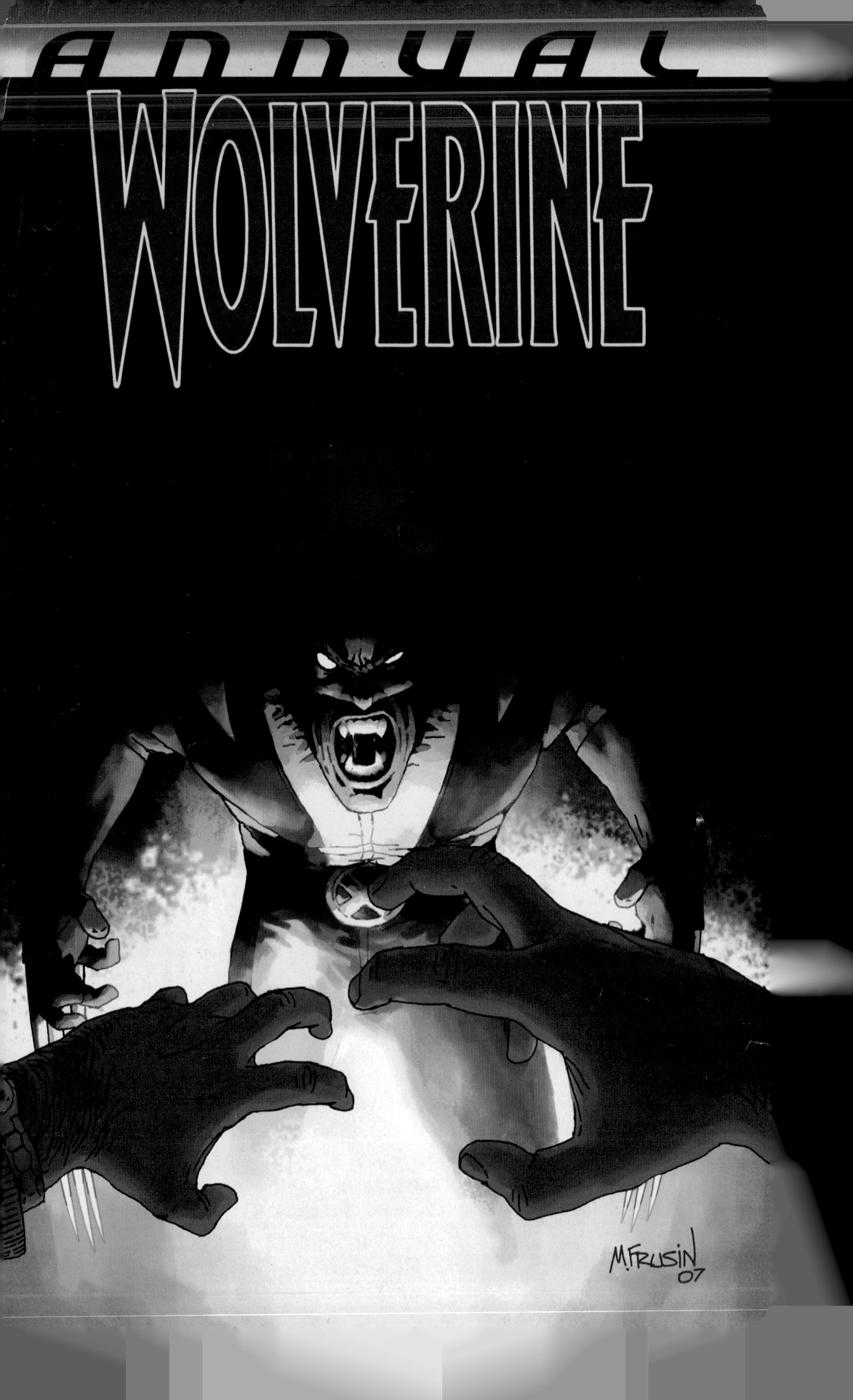

ANNUAL
WOLVERINE
M. FRUSIN 07

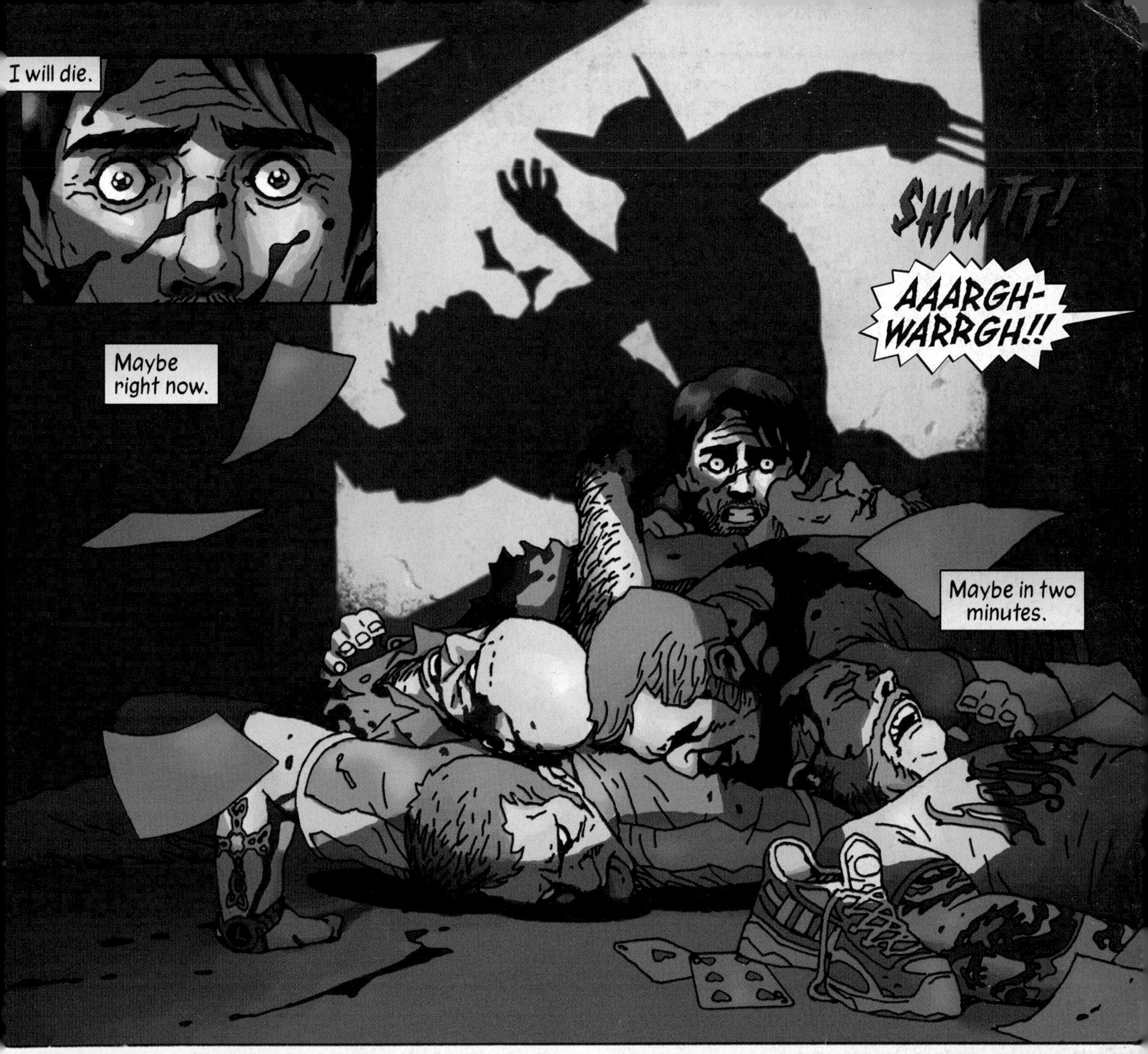
I will die.
Maybe right now.
SHWTT!
AAARGH-WARRGH!!
Maybe in two minutes.

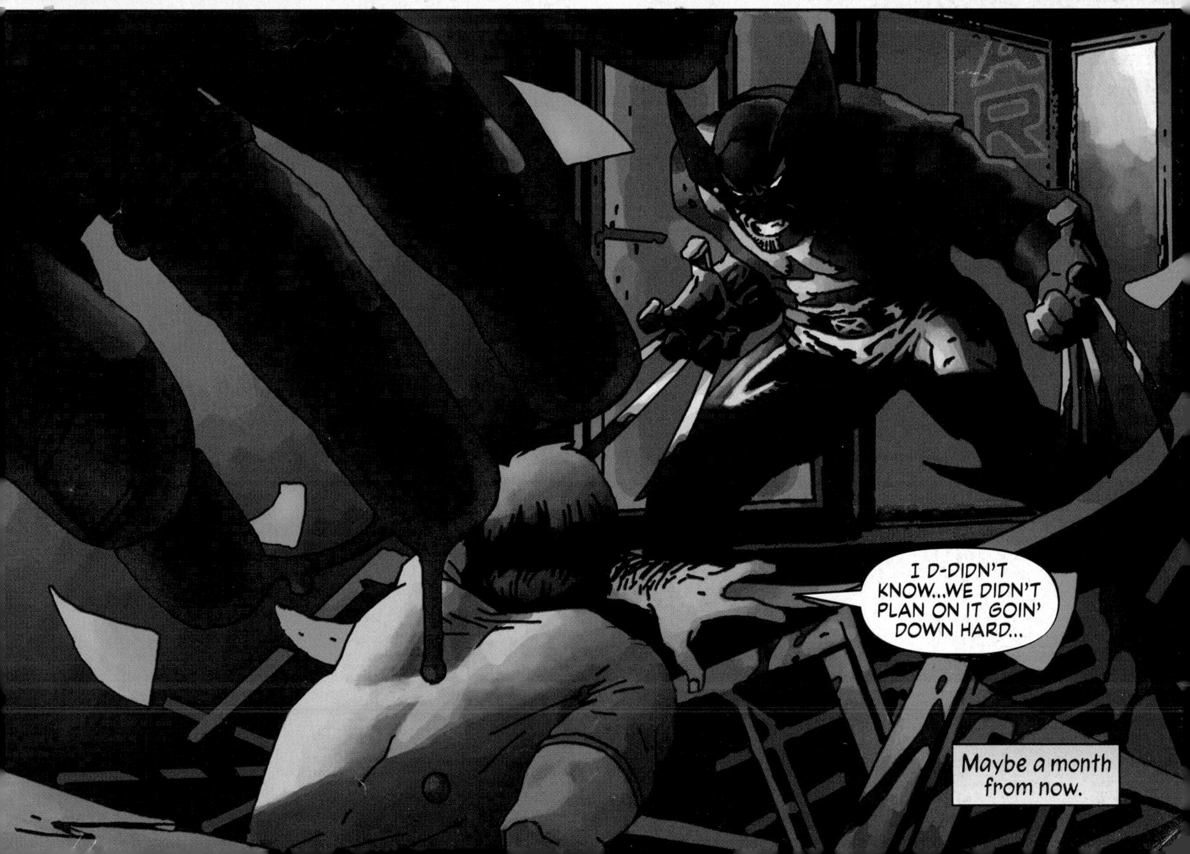
I D-DIDN'T KNOW...WE DIDN'T PLAN ON IT GOIN' DOWN HARD...
Maybe a month from now.

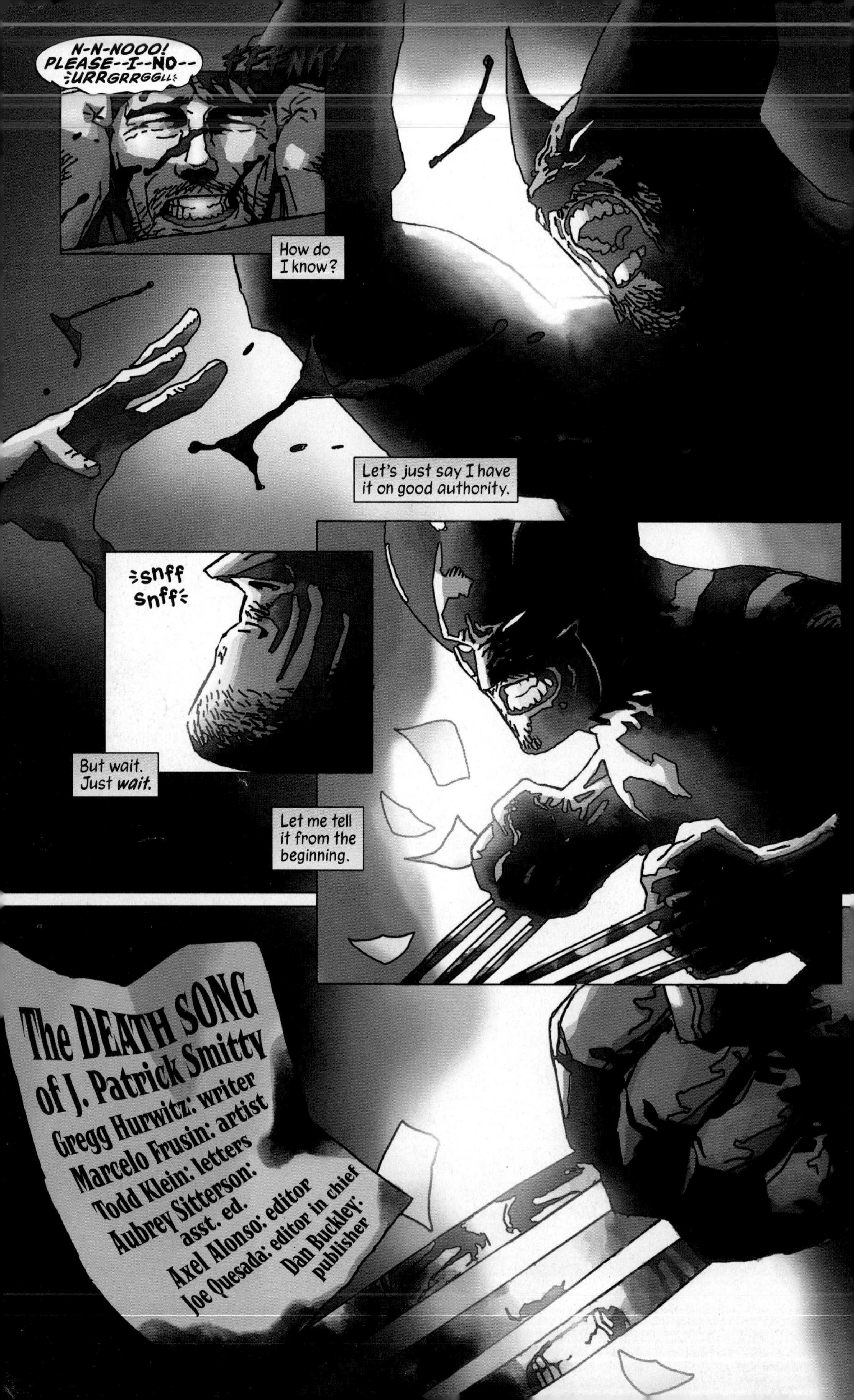

N-N-NOOO! PLEASE--I--NO-- URRGRRGGLL
FFFNK!
How do I know?
Let's just say I have it on good authority.
snff snff
But wait. Just *wait.*
Let me tell it from the beginning.
The DEATH SONG of J. Patrick Smitty
Gregg Hurwitz: writer
Marcelo Frusin: artist
Todd Klein: letters
Aubrey Sitterson: asst. ed.
Axel Alonso: editor
Joe Quesada: editor in chief
Dan Buckley: publisher

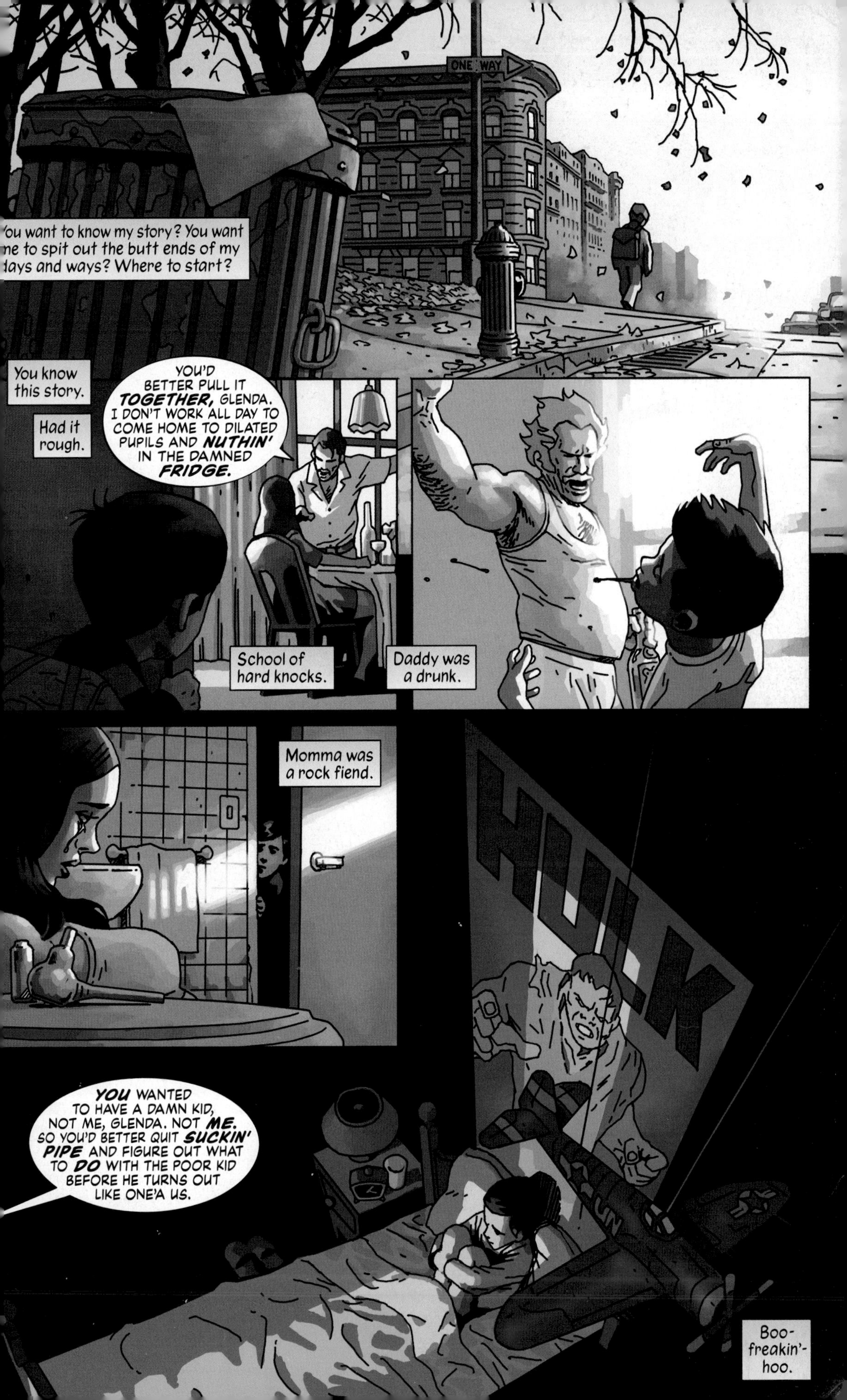

ONE WAY
You want to know my story? You want me to spit out the butt ends of my days and ways? Where to start?
You know this story.
Had it rough.
YOU'D BETTER PULL IT **TOGETHER,** GLENDA. I DON'T WORK ALL DAY TO COME HOME TO DILATED PUPILS AND **NUTHIN'** IN THE DAMNED **FRIDGE.**
School of hard knocks.
Daddy was a drunk.
Momma was a rock fiend.
YOU WANTED TO HAVE A DAMN KID, NOT ME, GLENDA. NOT **ME.** SO YOU'D BETTER QUIT **SUCKIN' PIPE** AND FIGURE OUT WHAT TO **DO** WITH THE POOR KID BEFORE HE TURNS OUT LIKE ONE'A US.
HULK
Boo-freakin'-hoo.

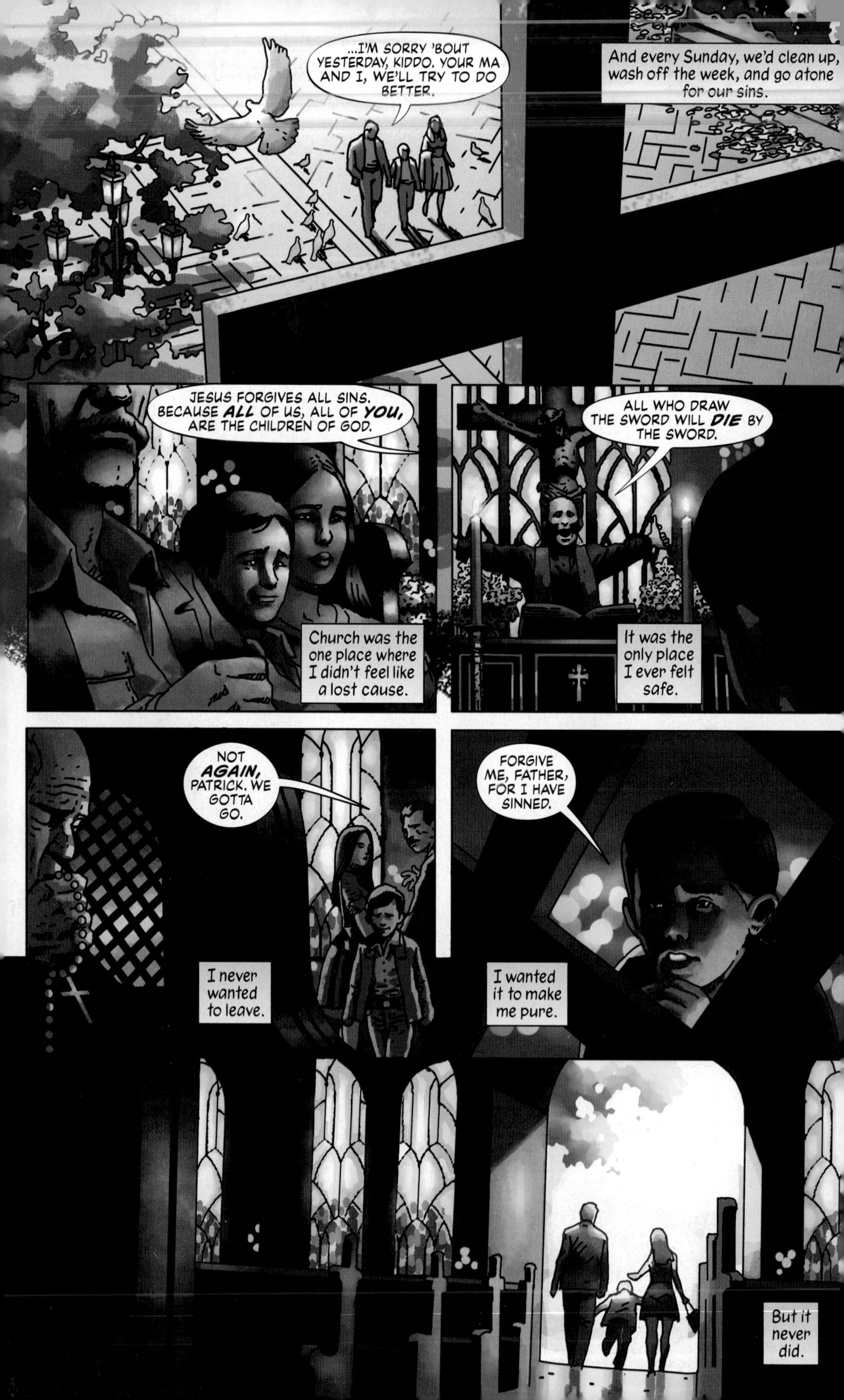
...I'M SORRY 'BOUT YESTERDAY, KIDDO. YOUR MA AND I, WE'LL TRY TO DO BETTER.
And every Sunday, we'd clean up, wash off the week, and go atone for our sins.
JESUS FORGIVES ALL SINS. BECAUSE ALL OF US, ALL OF YOU, ARE THE CHILDREN OF GOD.
Church was the one place where I didn't feel like a lost cause.
ALL WHO DRAW THE SWORD WILL DIE BY THE SWORD.
It was the only place I ever felt safe.
NOT AGAIN, PATRICK. WE GOTTA GO.
I never wanted to leave.
FORGIVE ME, FATHER, FOR I HAVE SINNED.
I wanted it to make me pure.
But it never did.

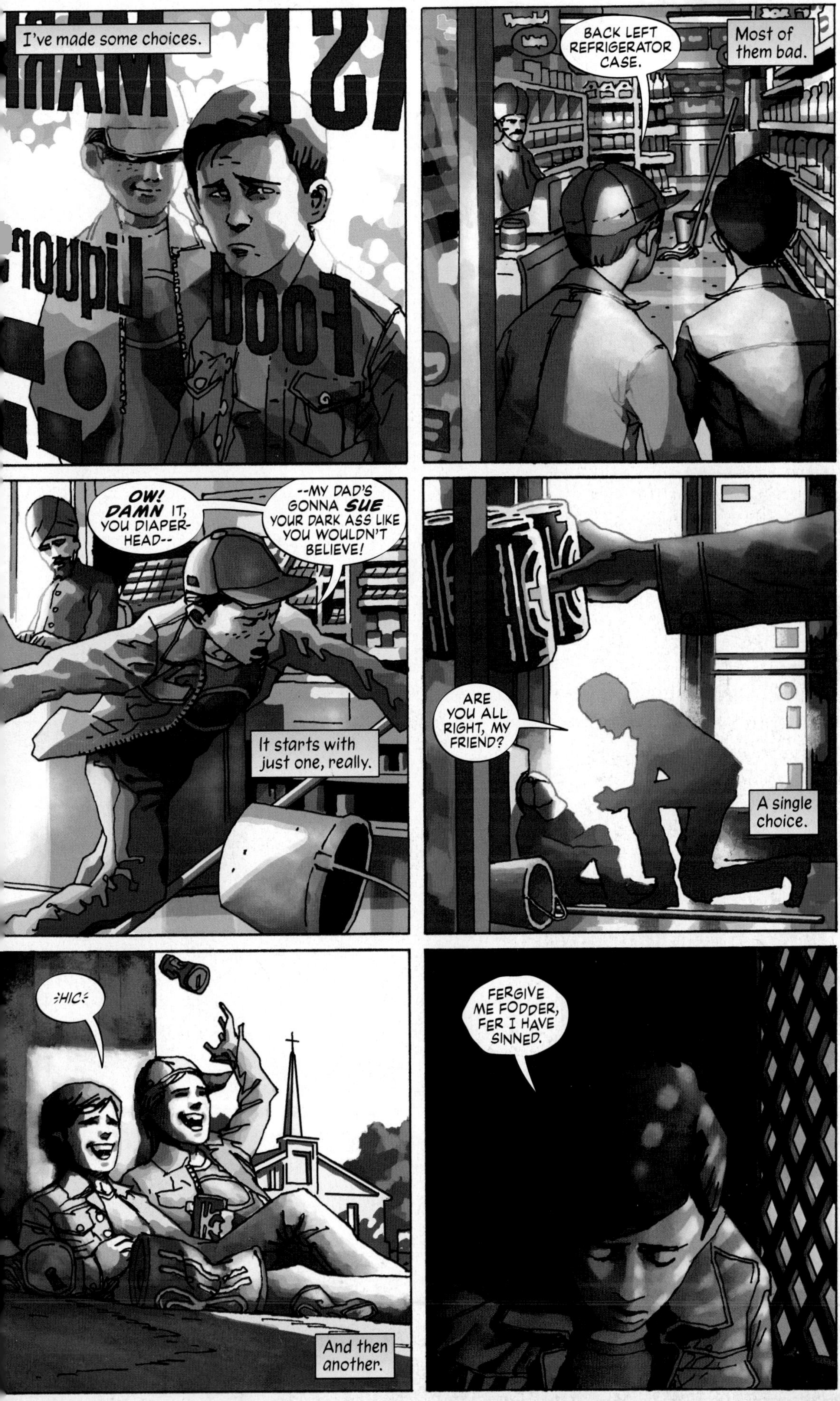

I've made some choices.
BACK LEFT REFRIGERATOR CASE.
Most of them bad.
OW! DAMN IT, YOU DIAPER-HEAD--
--MY DAD'S GONNA SUE YOUR DARK ASS LIKE YOU WOULDN'T BELIEVE!
It starts with just one, really.
ARE YOU ALL RIGHT, MY FRIEND?
A single choice.
HIC
And then another.
FERGIVE ME FODDER, FER I HAVE SINNED.

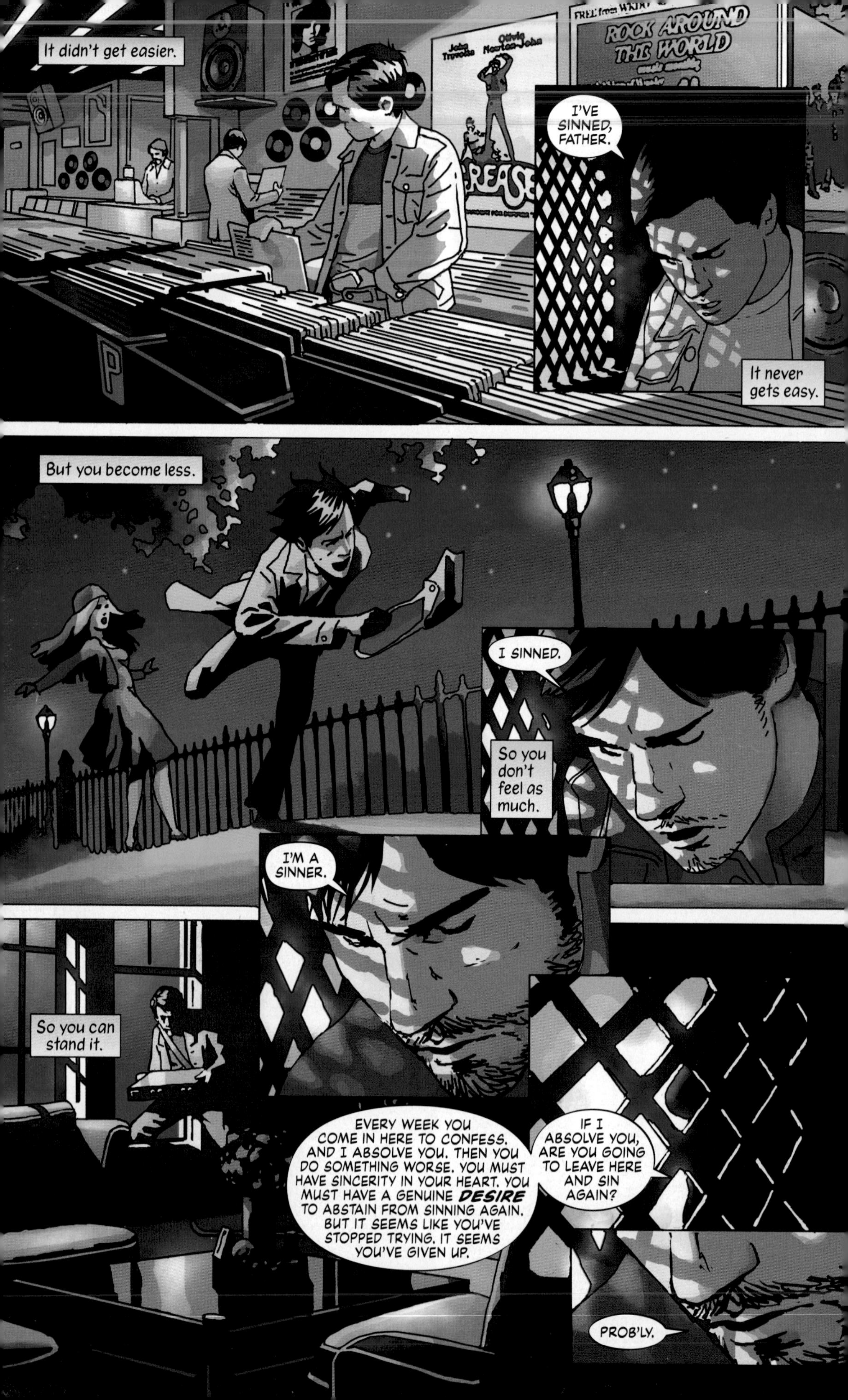
It didn't get easier.
ROCK AROUND THE WORLD
John Travolta
Olivia Newton-John
I'VE SINNED, FATHER.
It never gets easy.
But you become less.
I SINNED.
So you don't feel as much.
I'M A SINNER.
So you can stand it.
EVERY WEEK YOU COME IN HERE TO CONFESS, AND I ABSOLVE YOU. THEN YOU DO SOMETHING WORSE. YOU MUST HAVE SINCERITY IN YOUR HEART. YOU MUST HAVE A GENUINE ***DESIRE*** TO ABSTAIN FROM SINNING AGAIN. BUT IT SEEMS LIKE YOU'VE STOPPED TRYING. IT SEEMS YOU'VE GIVEN UP.
IF I ABSOLVE YOU, ARE YOU GOING TO LEAVE HERE AND SIN AGAIN?
PROB'LY.

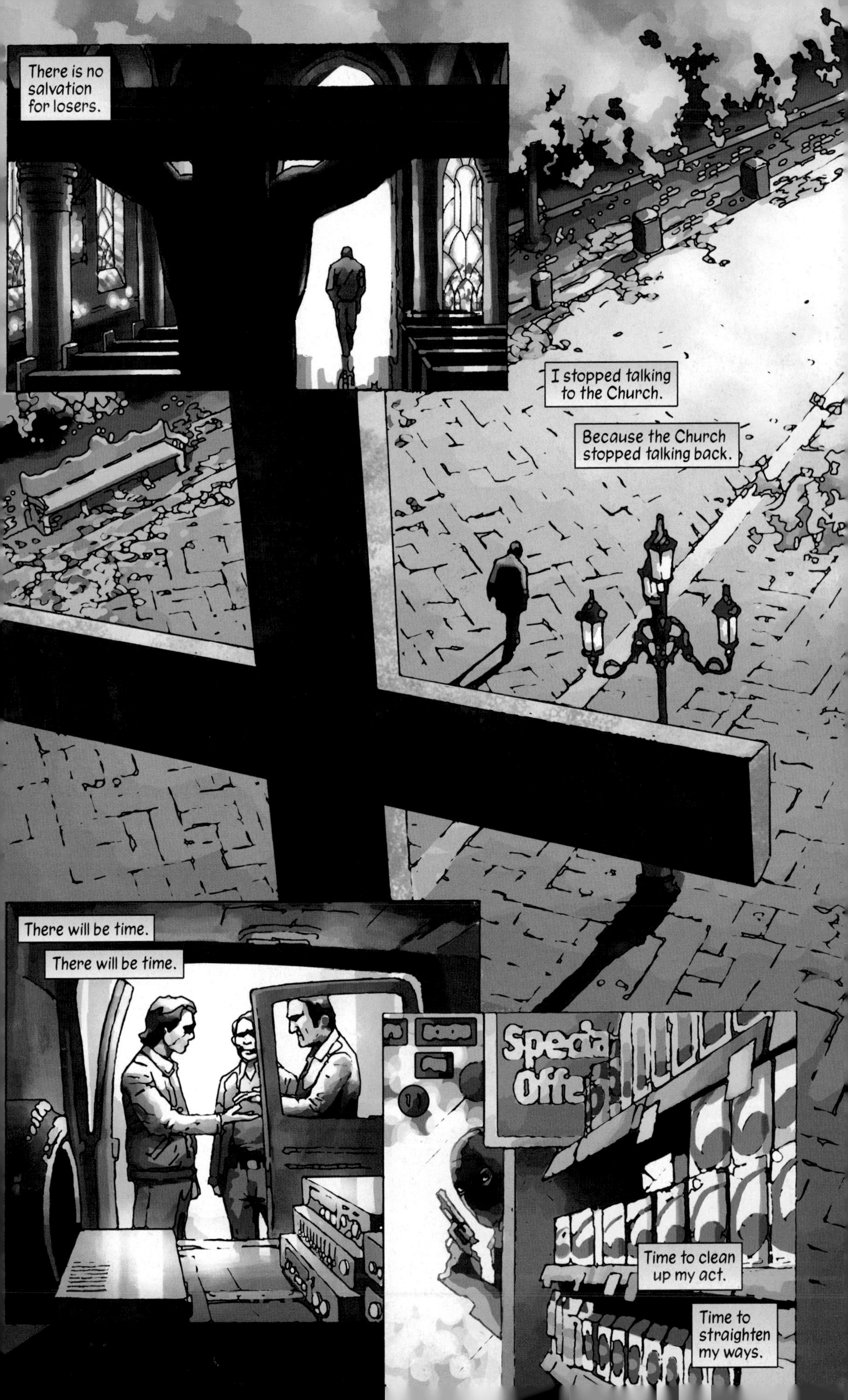
There is no salvation for losers.
I stopped talking to the Church.
Because the Church stopped talking back.
There will be time.
There will be time.
Special Offer
Time to clean up my act.
Time to straighten my ways.

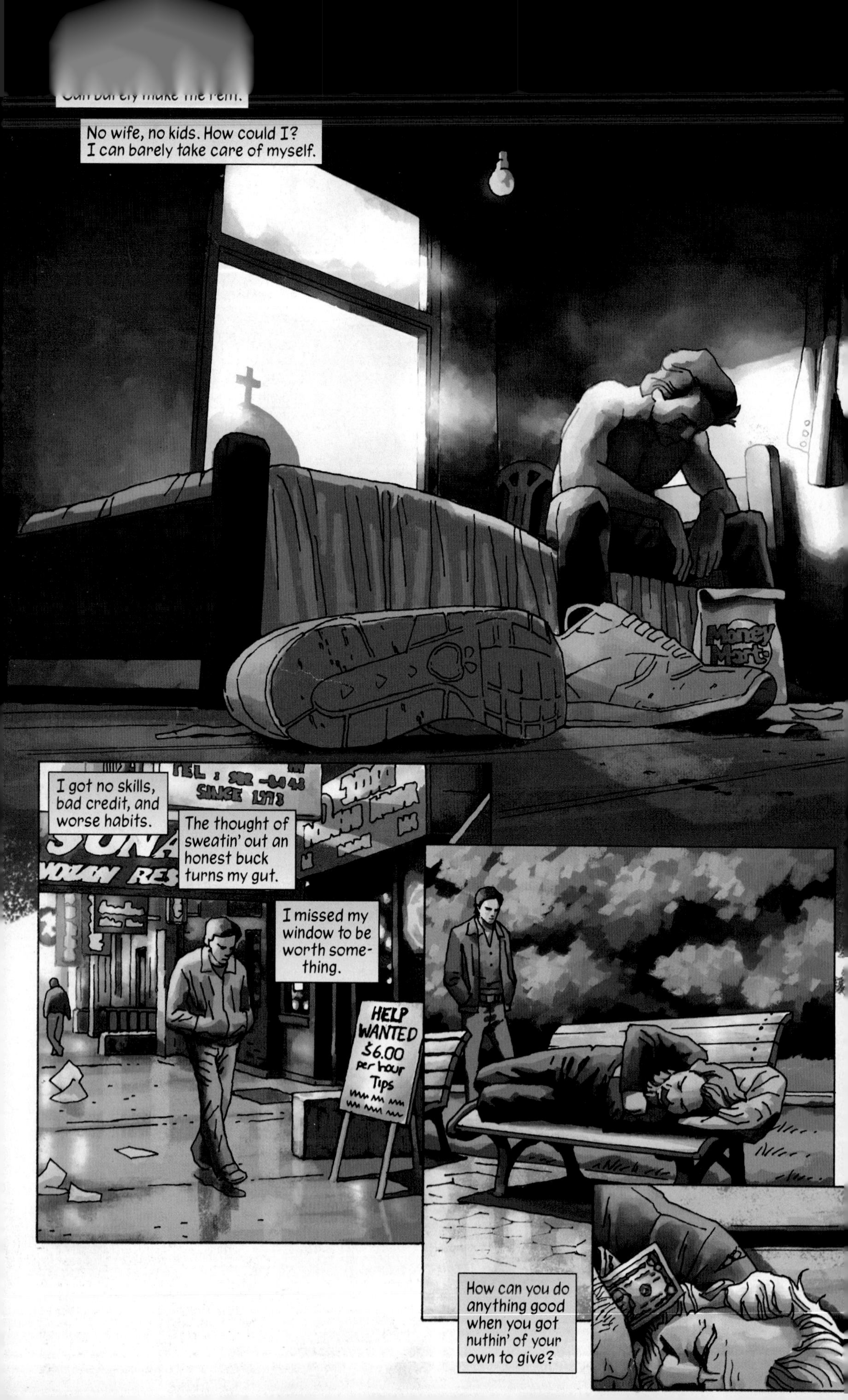

No wife, no kids. How could I? I can barely take care of myself.
Money Mart
I got no skills, bad credit, and worse habits.
The thought of sweatin' out an honest buck turns my gut.
I missed my window to be worth some-thing.
HELP WANTED $6.00 per hour Tips
How can you do anything good when you got nuthin' of your own to give?

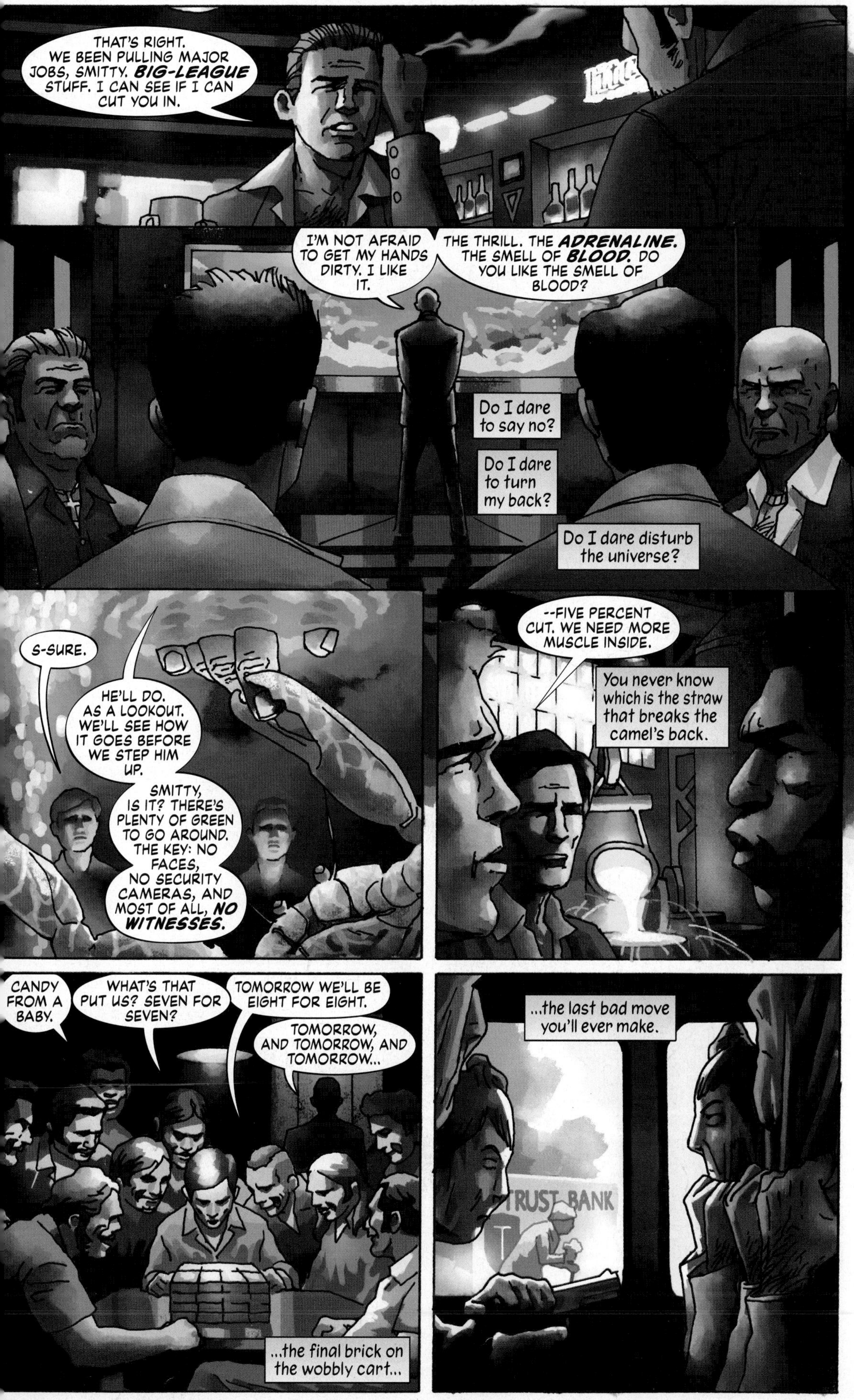
THAT'S RIGHT. WE BEEN PULLING MAJOR JOBS, SMITTY. BIG-LEAGUE STUFF. I CAN SEE IF I CAN CUT YOU IN.
I'M NOT AFRAID TO GET MY HANDS DIRTY. I LIKE IT.
THE THRILL. THE ADRENALINE. THE SMELL OF BLOOD. DO YOU LIKE THE SMELL OF BLOOD?
Do I dare to say no?
Do I dare to turn my back?
Do I dare disturb the universe?
S-SURE.
HE'LL DO. AS A LOOKOUT. WE'LL SEE HOW IT GOES BEFORE WE STEP HIM UP.
SMITTY, IS IT? THERE'S PLENTY OF GREEN TO GO AROUND. THE KEY: NO FACES, NO SECURITY CAMERAS, AND MOST OF ALL, NO WITNESSES.
--FIVE PERCENT CUT. WE NEED MORE MUSCLE INSIDE.
You never know which is the straw that breaks the camel's back.
CANDY FROM A BABY.
WHAT'S THAT PUT US? SEVEN FOR SEVEN?
TOMORROW WE'LL BE EIGHT FOR EIGHT.
TOMORROW, AND TOMORROW, AND TOMORROW...
...the final brick on the wobbly cart...
...the last bad move you'll ever make.
TRUST BANK

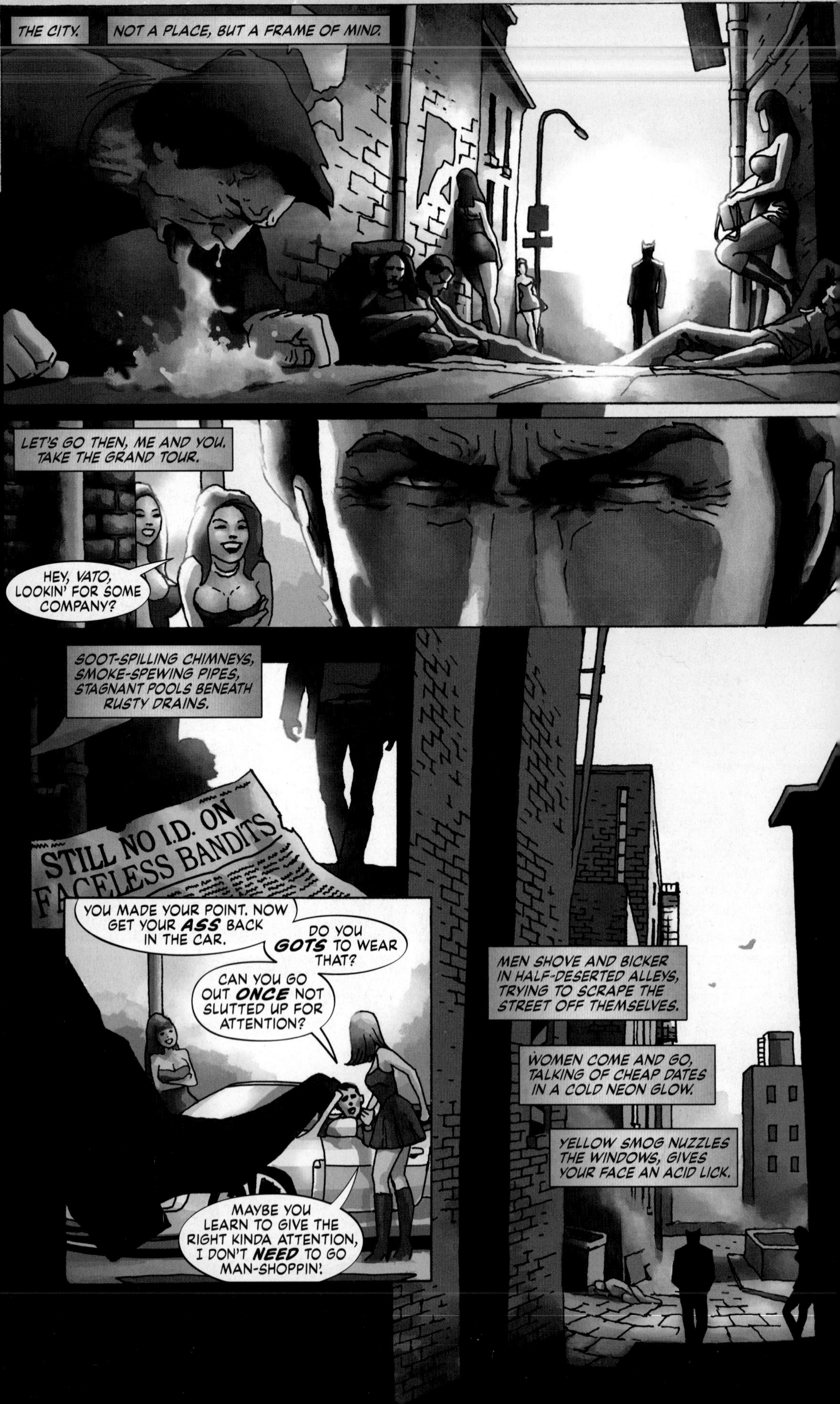
THE CITY.
NOT A PLACE, BUT A FRAME OF MIND.
LET'S GO THEN, ME AND YOU. TAKE THE GRAND TOUR.
HEY, VATO, LOOKIN' FOR SOME COMPANY?
SOOT-SPILLING CHIMNEYS, SMOKE-SPEWING PIPES, STAGNANT POOLS BENEATH RUSTY DRAINS.
STILL NO I.D. ON FACELESS BANDITS
YOU MADE YOUR POINT. NOW GET YOUR ASS BACK IN THE CAR.
DO YOU GOTS TO WEAR THAT?
CAN YOU GO OUT ONCE NOT SLUTTED UP FOR ATTENTION?
MAYBE YOU LEARN TO GIVE THE RIGHT KINDA ATTENTION, I DON'T NEED TO GO MAN-SHOPPIN'.
MEN SHOVE AND BICKER IN HALF-DESERTED ALLEYS, TRYING TO SCRAPE THE STREET OFF THEMSELVES.
WOMEN COME AND GO, TALKING OF CHEAP DATES IN A COLD NEON GLOW.
YELLOW SMOG NUZZLES THE WINDOWS, GIVES YOUR FACE AN ACID LICK.

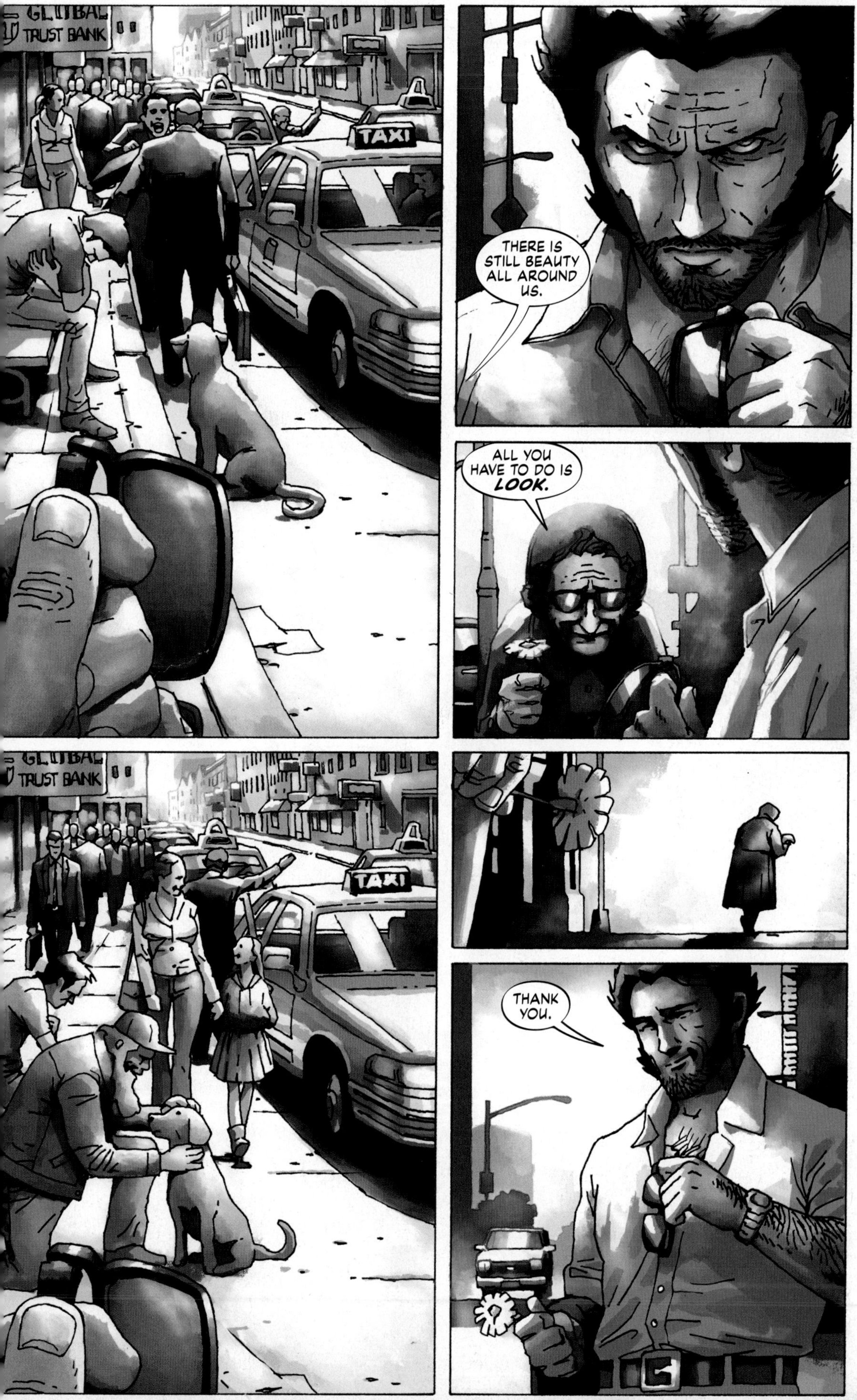
GLOBAL
TRUST BANK
TAXI
THERE IS STILL BEAUTY ALL AROUND US.
ALL YOU HAVE TO DO IS *LOOK.*
GLOBAL
TRUST BANK
TAXI
THANK YOU.

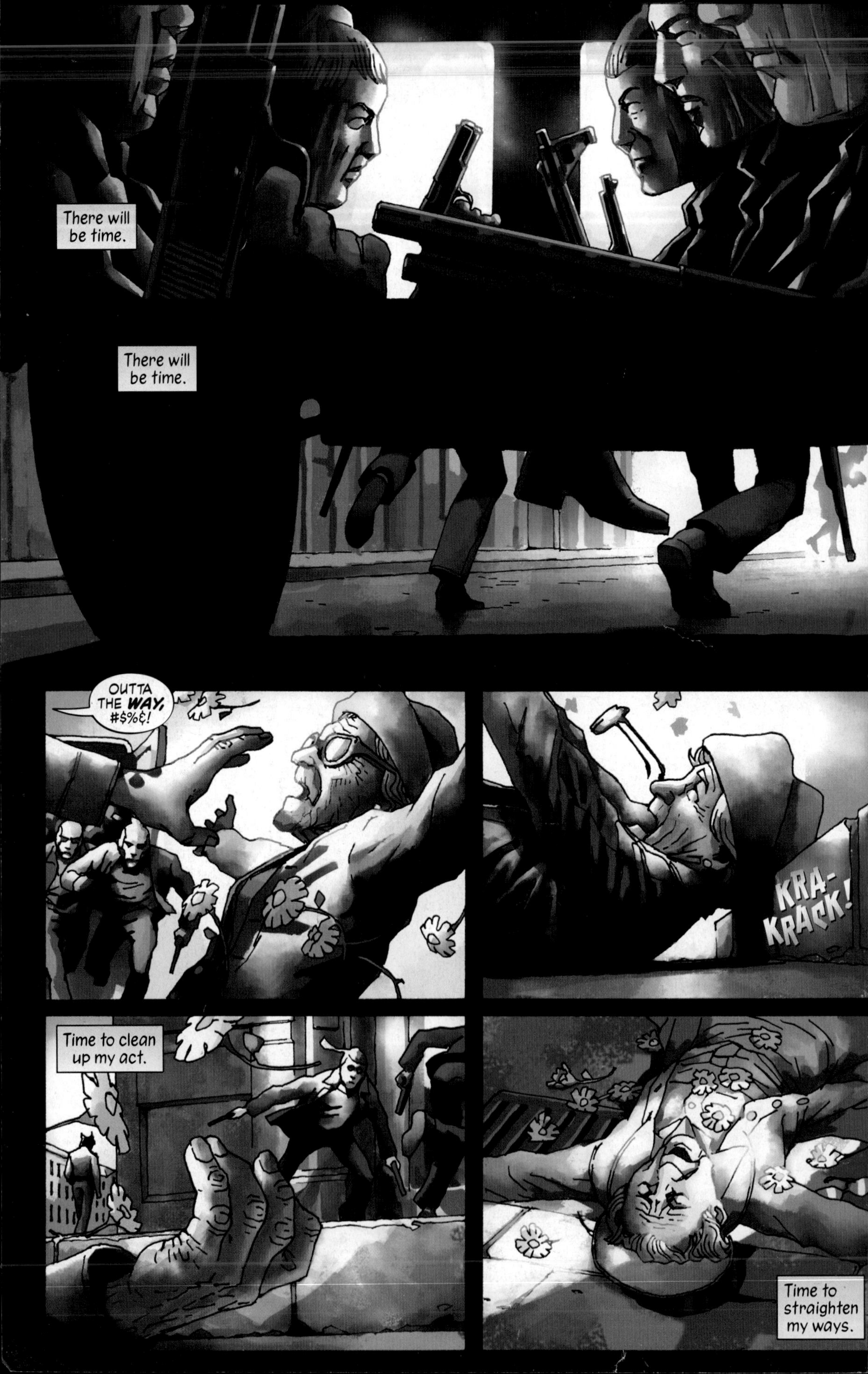
There will be time.
There will be time.
OUTTA THE WAY, #$%&!
KRA-KRACK!
Time to clean up my act.
Time to straighten my ways.

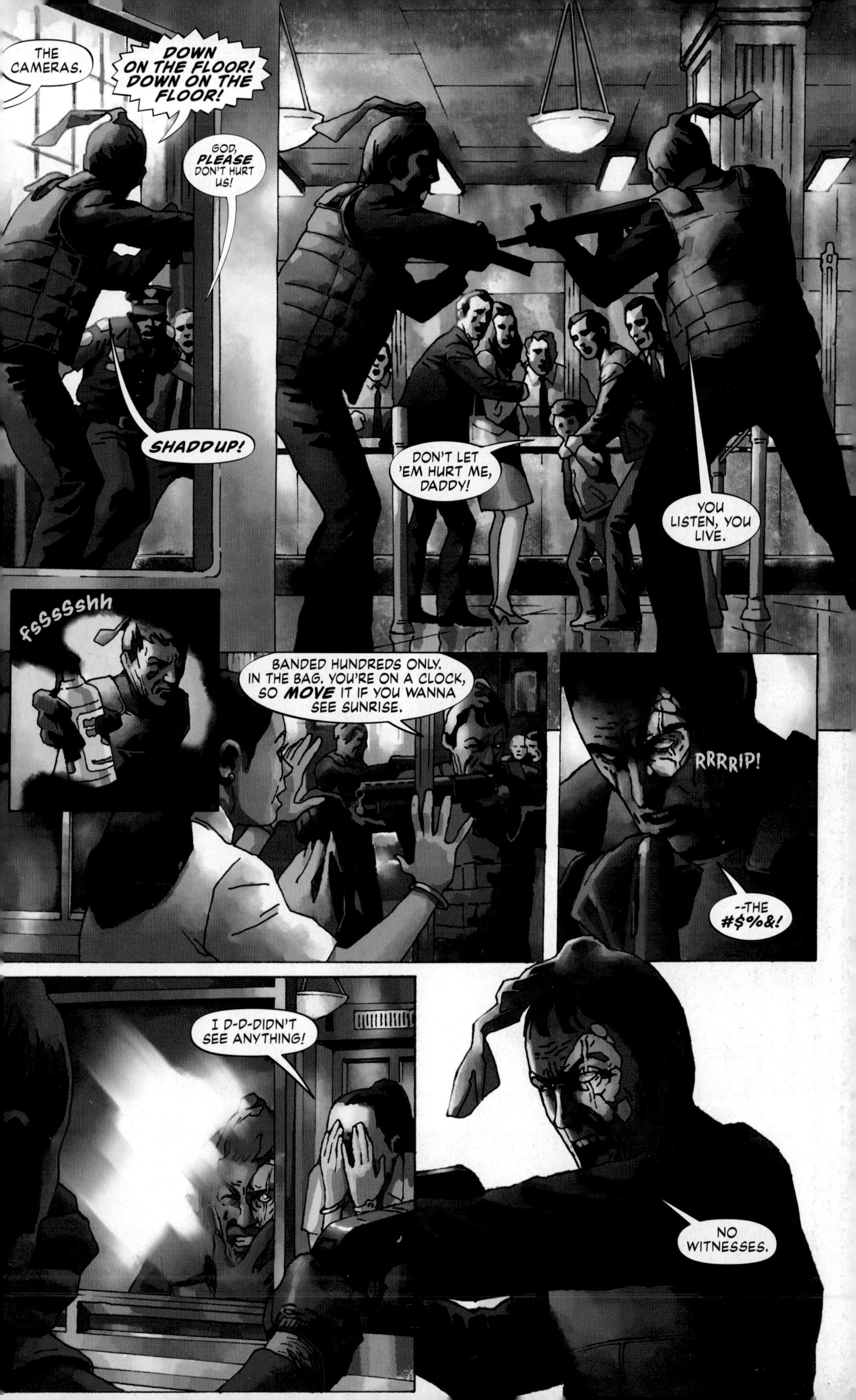
THE CAMERAS.
DOWN ON THE FLOOR! DOWN ON THE FLOOR!
GOD, PLEASE DON'T HURT US!
SHADDUP!
DON'T LET 'EM HURT ME, DADDY!
YOU LISTEN, YOU LIVE.
fsSsSshh
BANDED HUNDREDS ONLY. IN THE BAG. YOU'RE ON A CLOCK, SO MOVE IT IF YOU WANNA SEE SUNRISE.
RRRRIP!
--THE #$%&!
I D-D-DIDN'T SEE ANYTHING!
NO WITNESSES.

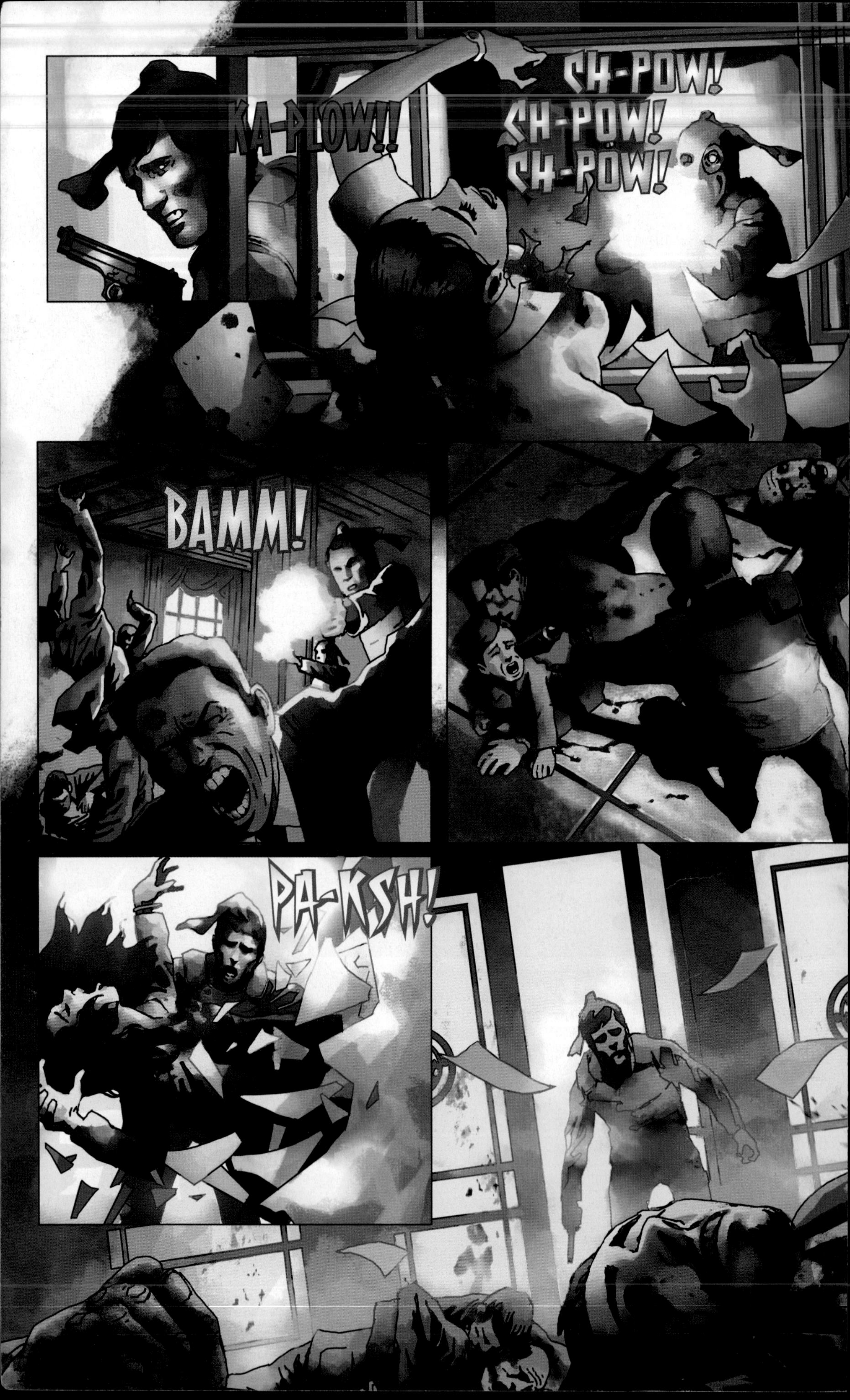
KA-PLOW!!
CH-POW!
CH-POW!
CH-POW!
BAMM!
PA-KSH!

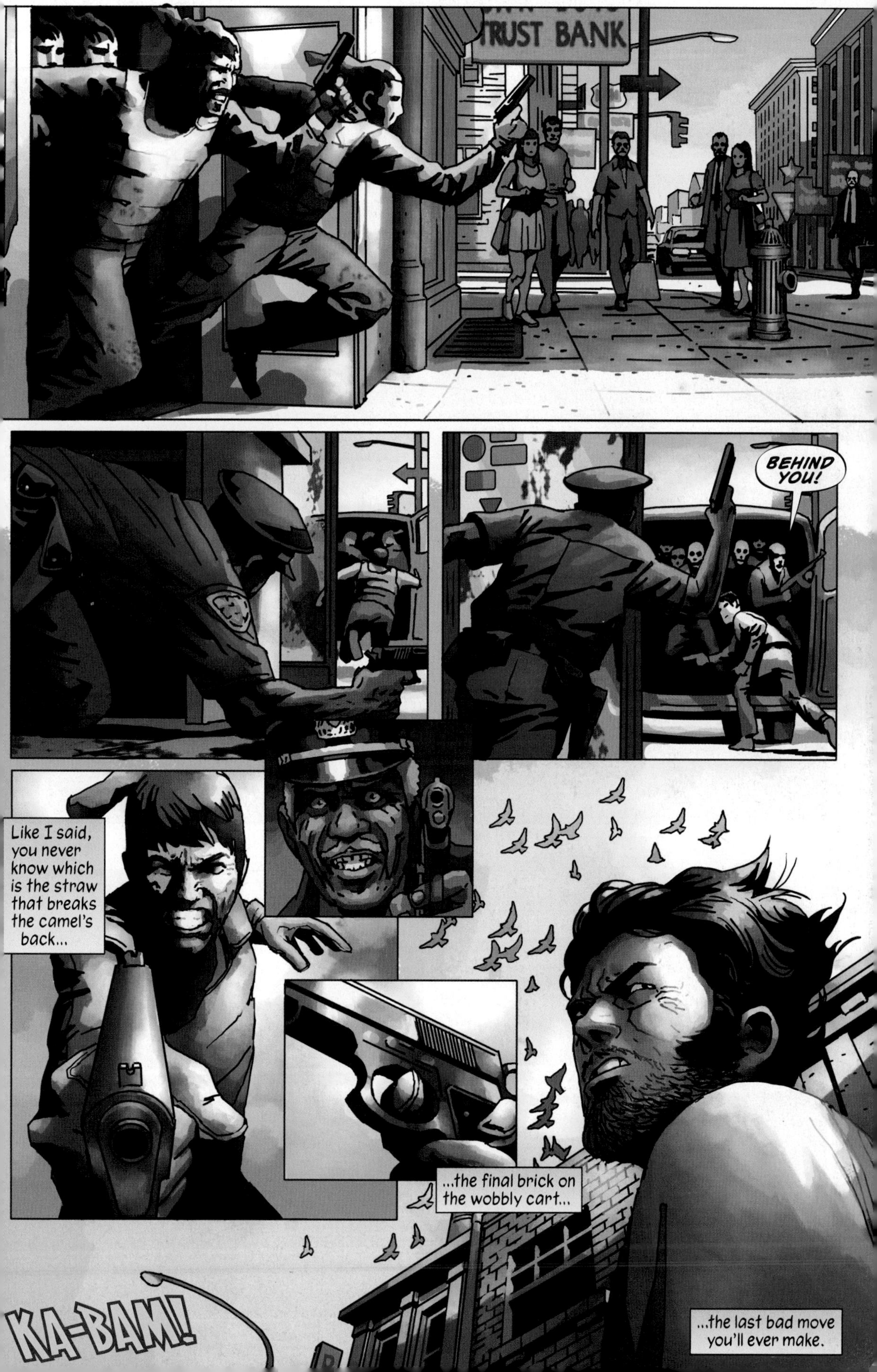
TRUST BANK
BEHIND YOU!
Like I said, you never know which is the straw that breaks the camel's back...
...the final brick on the wobbly cart...
KA-BAM!
...the last bad move you'll ever make.

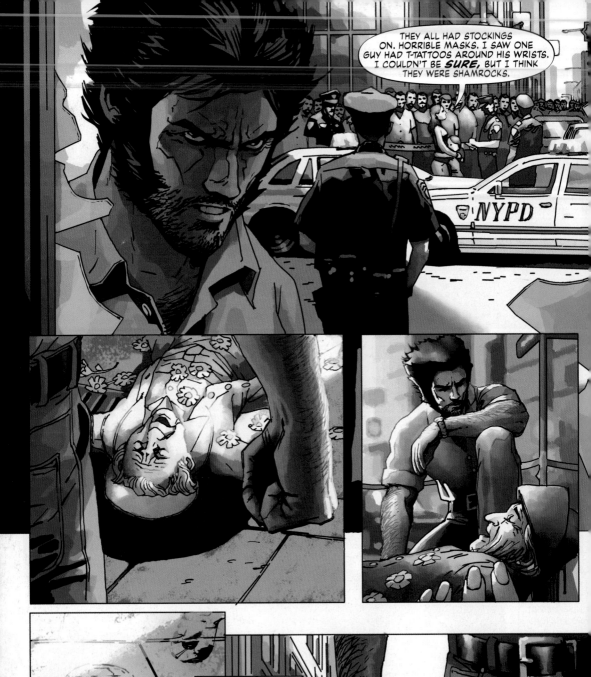

THEY ALL HAD STOCKINGS ON. HORRIBLE MASKS. I SAW ONE GUY HAD T-TATTOOS AROUND HIS WRISTS. I COULDN'T BE **SURE,** BUT I THINK THEY WERE SHAMROCKS.

‹snff snff›

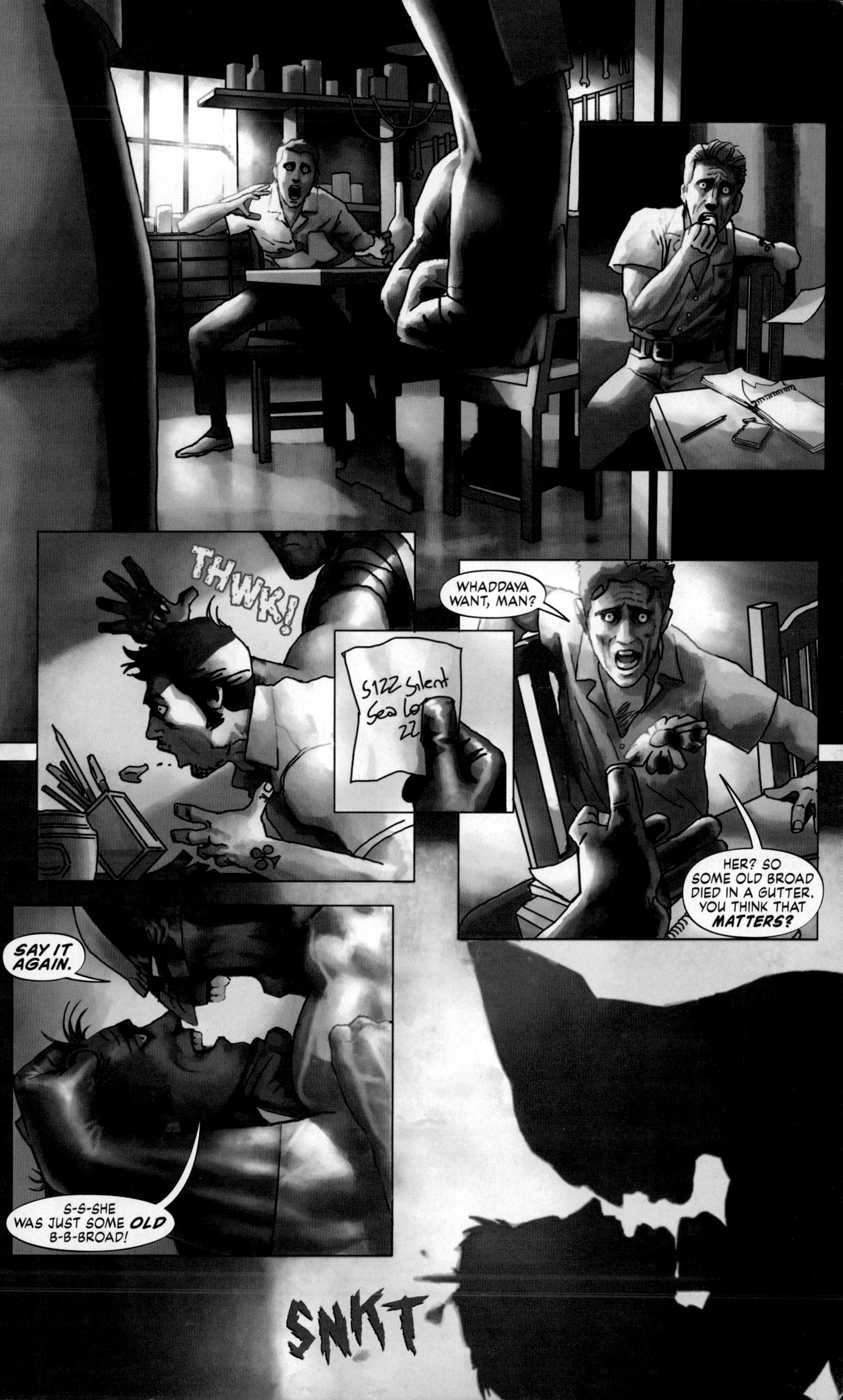
THWK!
5122 Silent
Sea Lo
22
WHADDAYA WANT, MAN?
HER? SO SOME OLD BROAD DIED IN A GUTTER. YOU THINK THAT MATTERS?
SAY IT AGAIN.
S-S-SHE WAS JUST SOME OLD B-B-BROAD!
SNKT

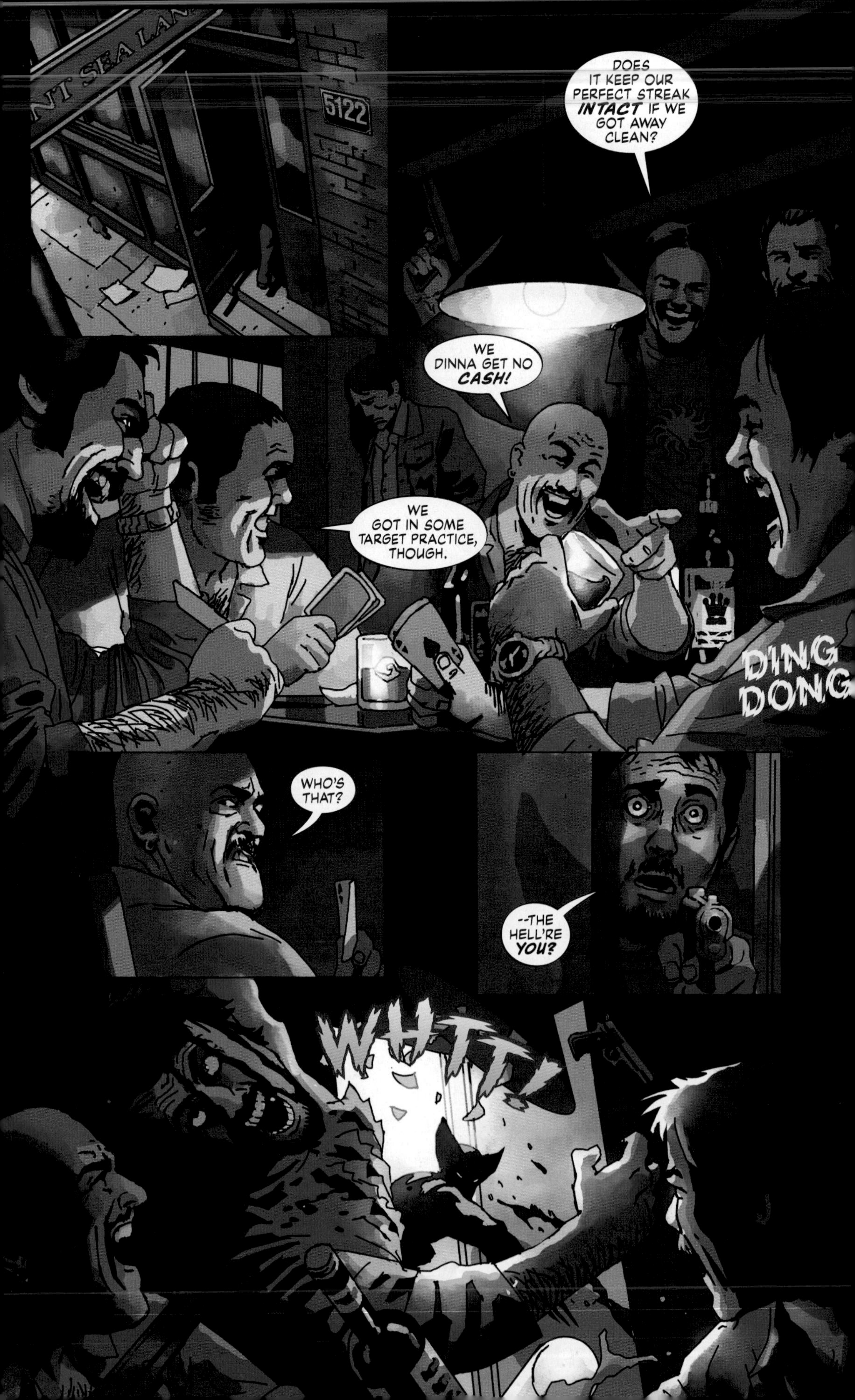
NT SEA LAN
5122
DOES IT KEEP OUR PERFECT STREAK INTACT IF WE GOT AWAY CLEAN?
WE DINNA GET NO CASH!
WE GOT IN SOME TARGET PRACTICE, THOUGH.
DING DONG
WHO'S THAT?
--THE HELL'RE YOU?
WHTT!

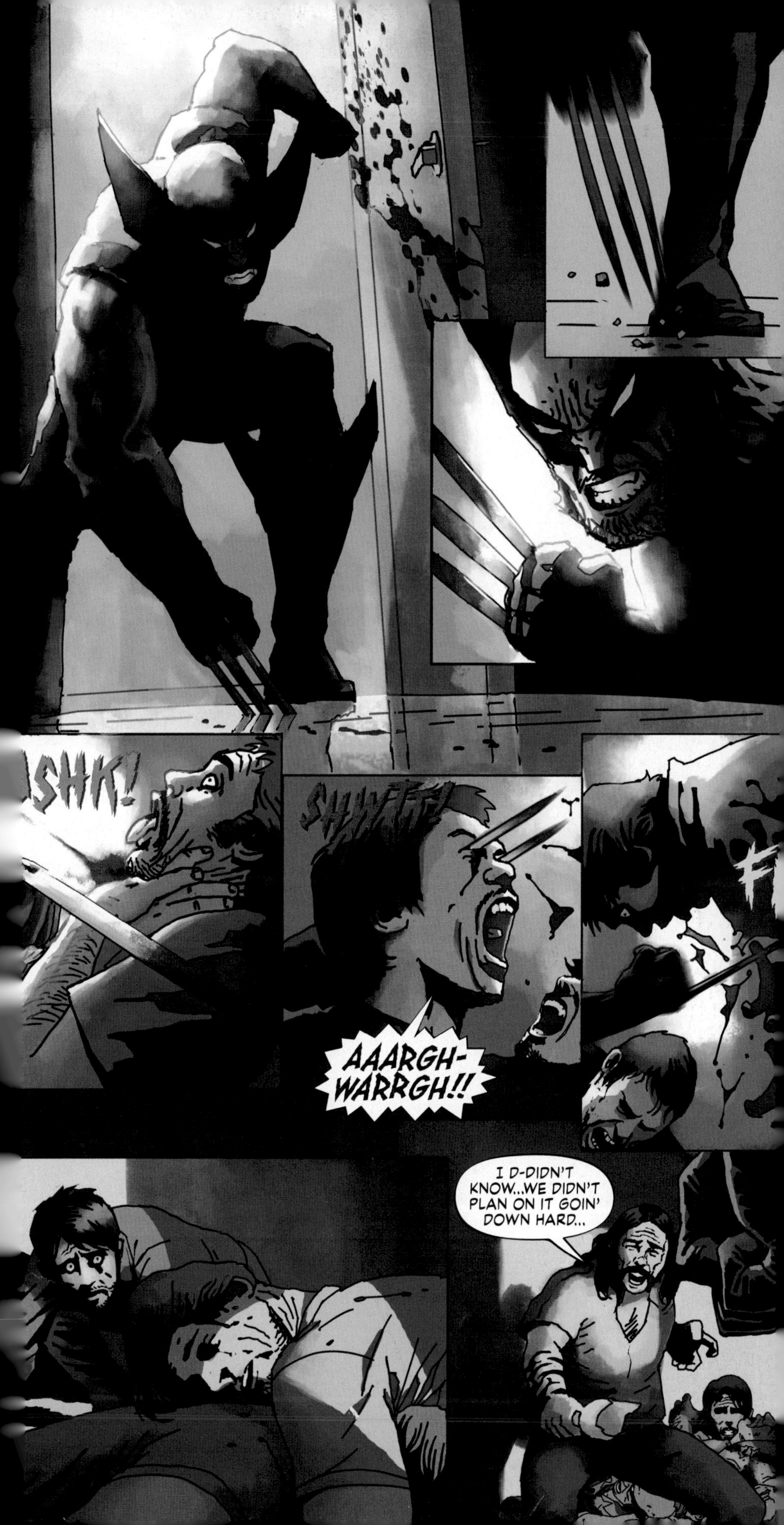
SHK!
AAARGH-WARRGH!!
I D-DIDN'T KNOW...WE DIDN'T PLAN ON IT GOIN' DOWN HARD...

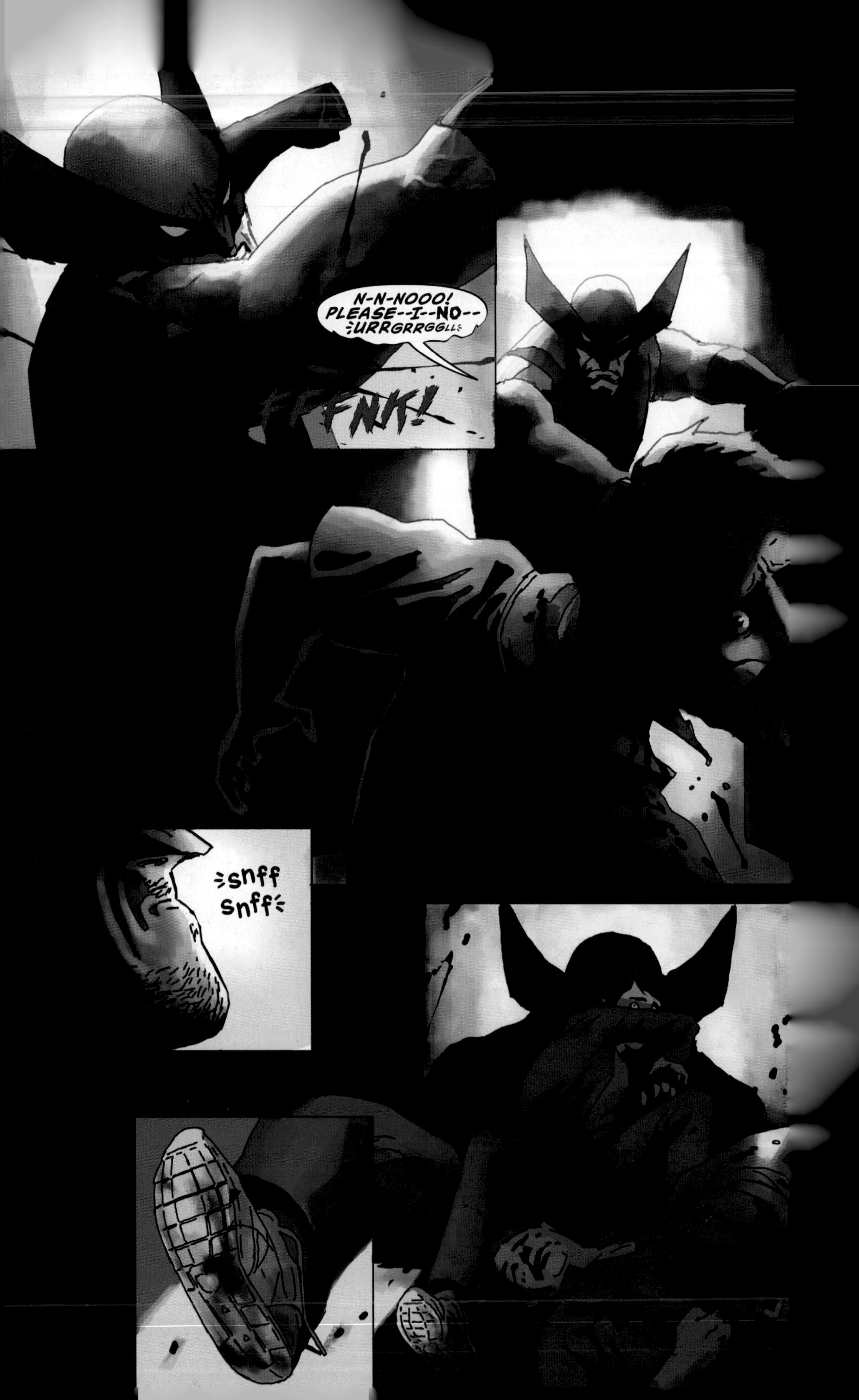
N-N-NOOO! PLEASE--I--NO-- URRGRRGGLL
FFFNK!
snff snff

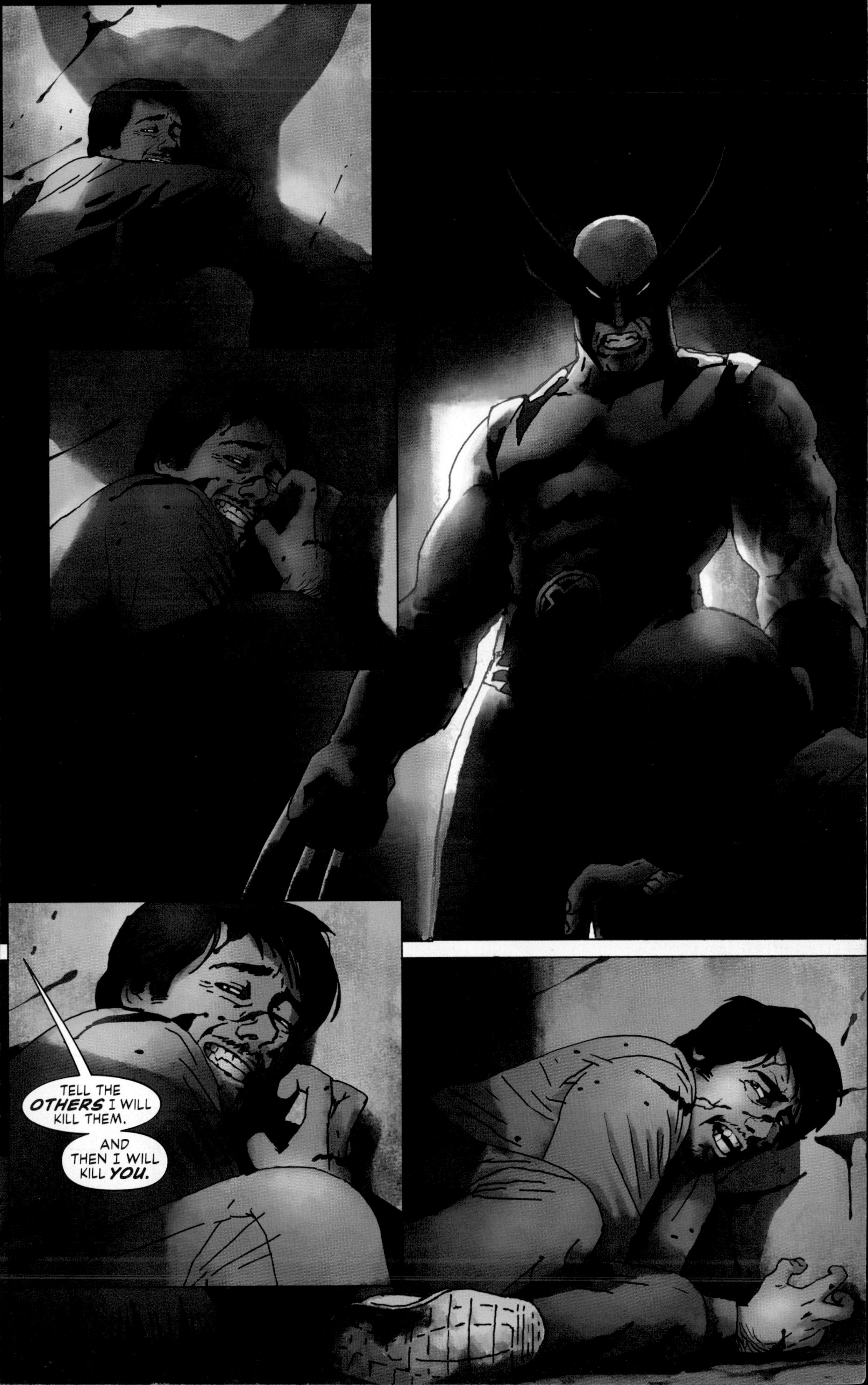
TELL THE OTHERS I WILL KILL THEM.
AND THEN I WILL KILL YOU.

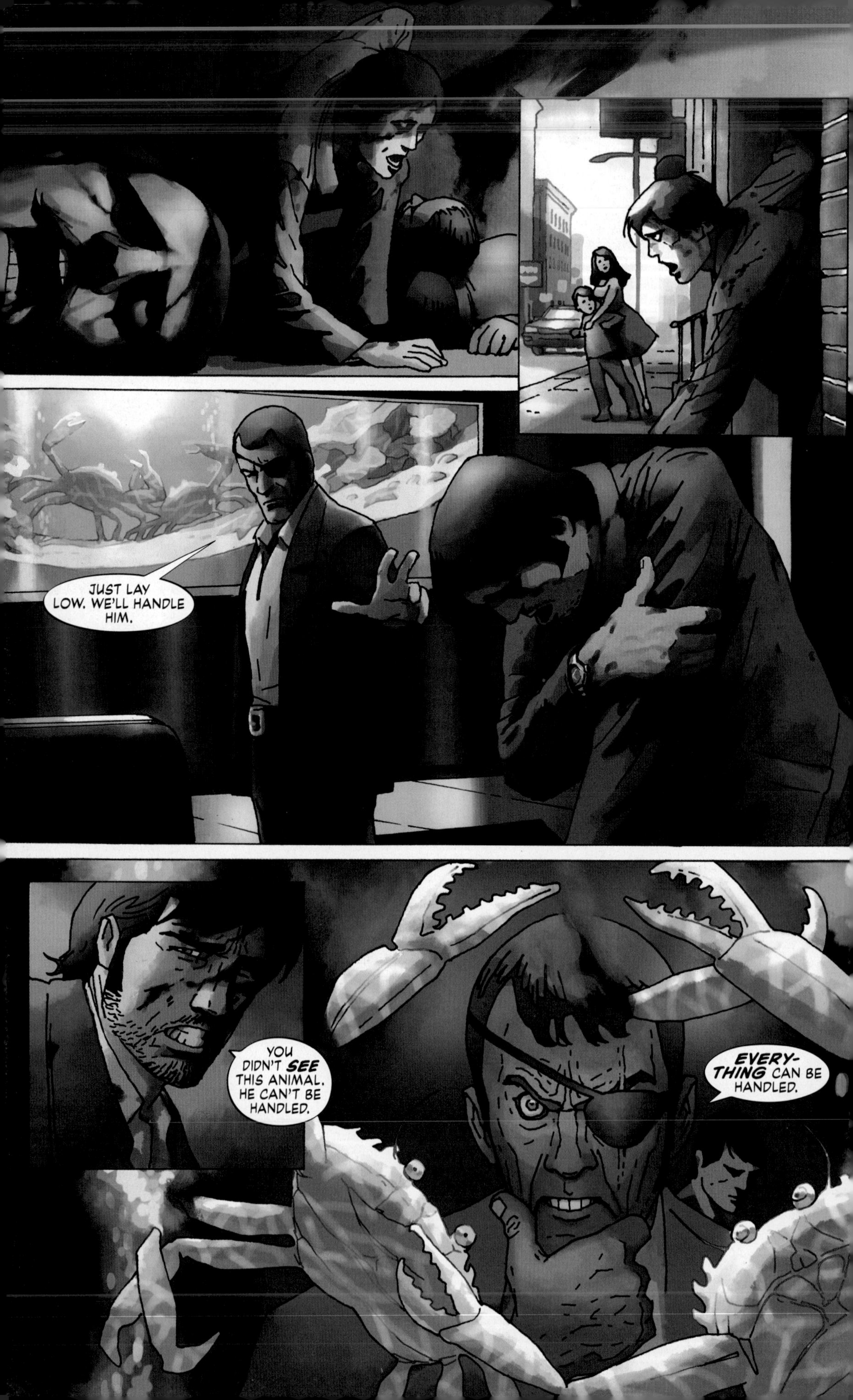
JUST LAY LOW. WE'LL HANDLE HIM.
YOU DIDN'T **SEE** THIS ANIMAL. HE CAN'T BE HANDLED.
EVERY-THING CAN BE HANDLED.

THEATRE
I will die.
CLOP CLOP CLOP
Maybe a month from now.
Maybe in two minutes.
Maybe right now.
What w
it be like
Will those claws pin me wriggling to the wall, a cockroach on a thumbtack?

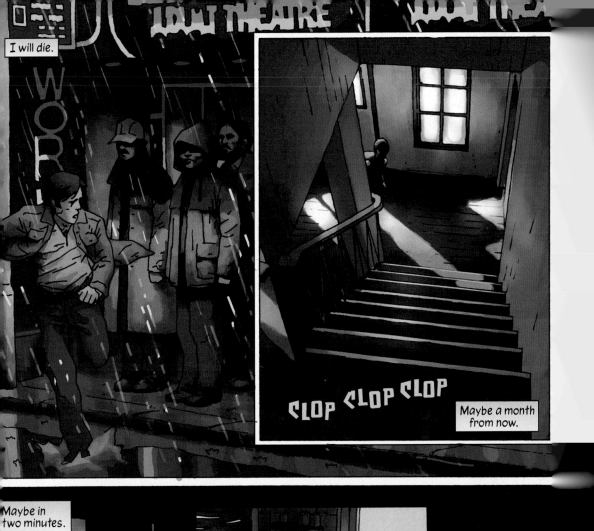

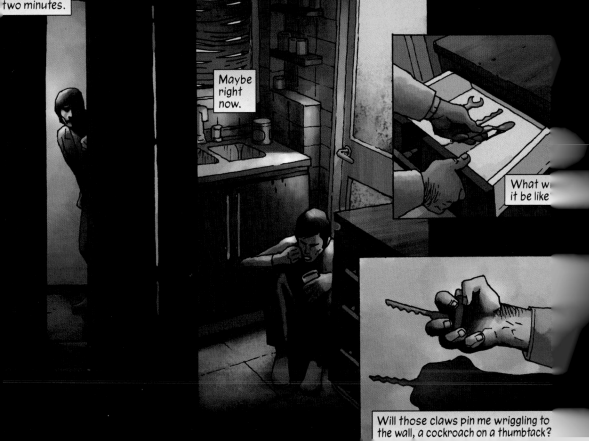

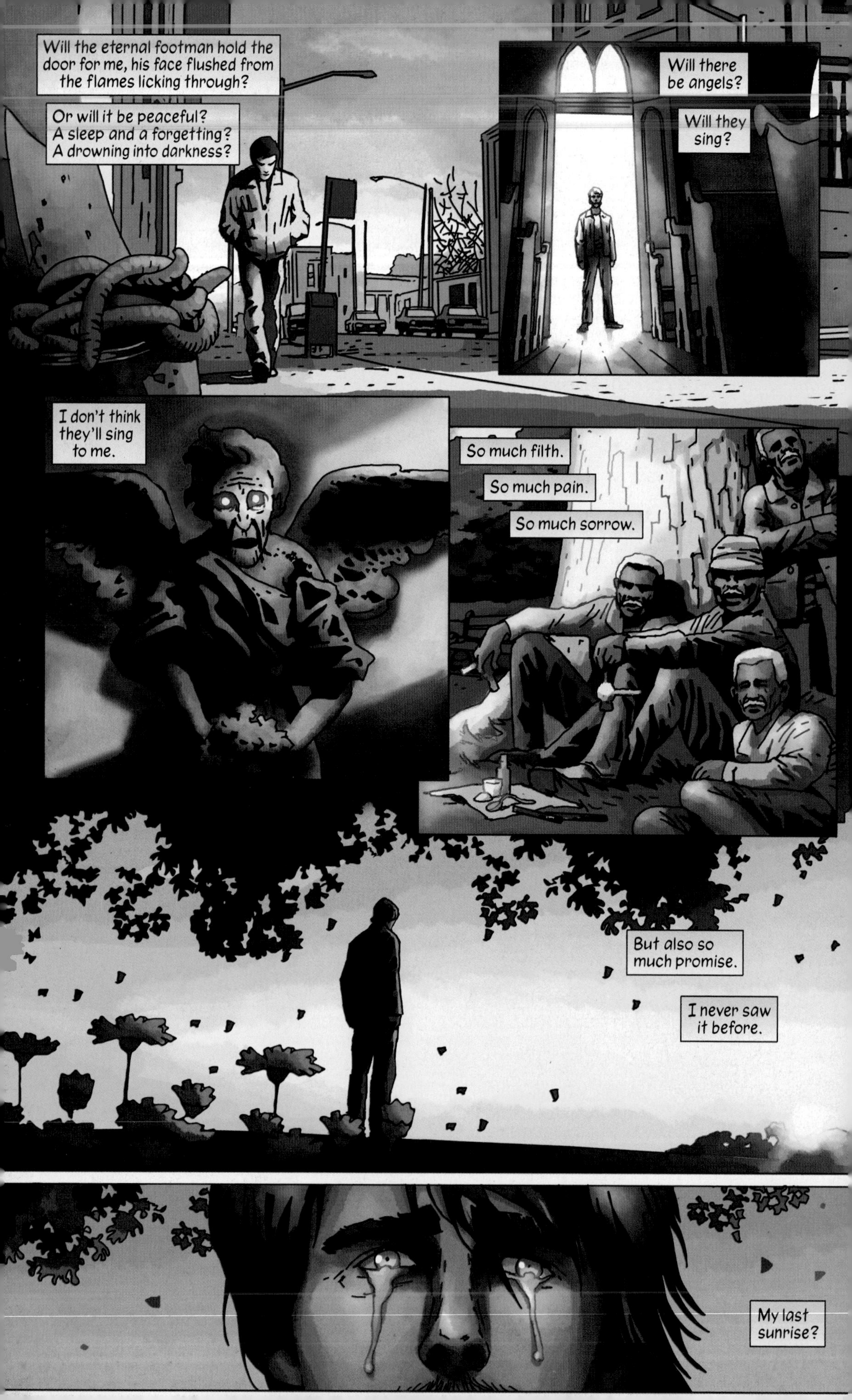
Will the eternal footman hold the door for me, his face flushed from the flames licking through?
Or will it be peaceful? A sleep and a forgetting? A drowning into darkness?
Will there be angels?
Will they sing?
I don't think they'll sing to me.
So much filth.
So much pain.
So much sorrow.
But also so much promise.
I never saw it before.
My last sunrise?

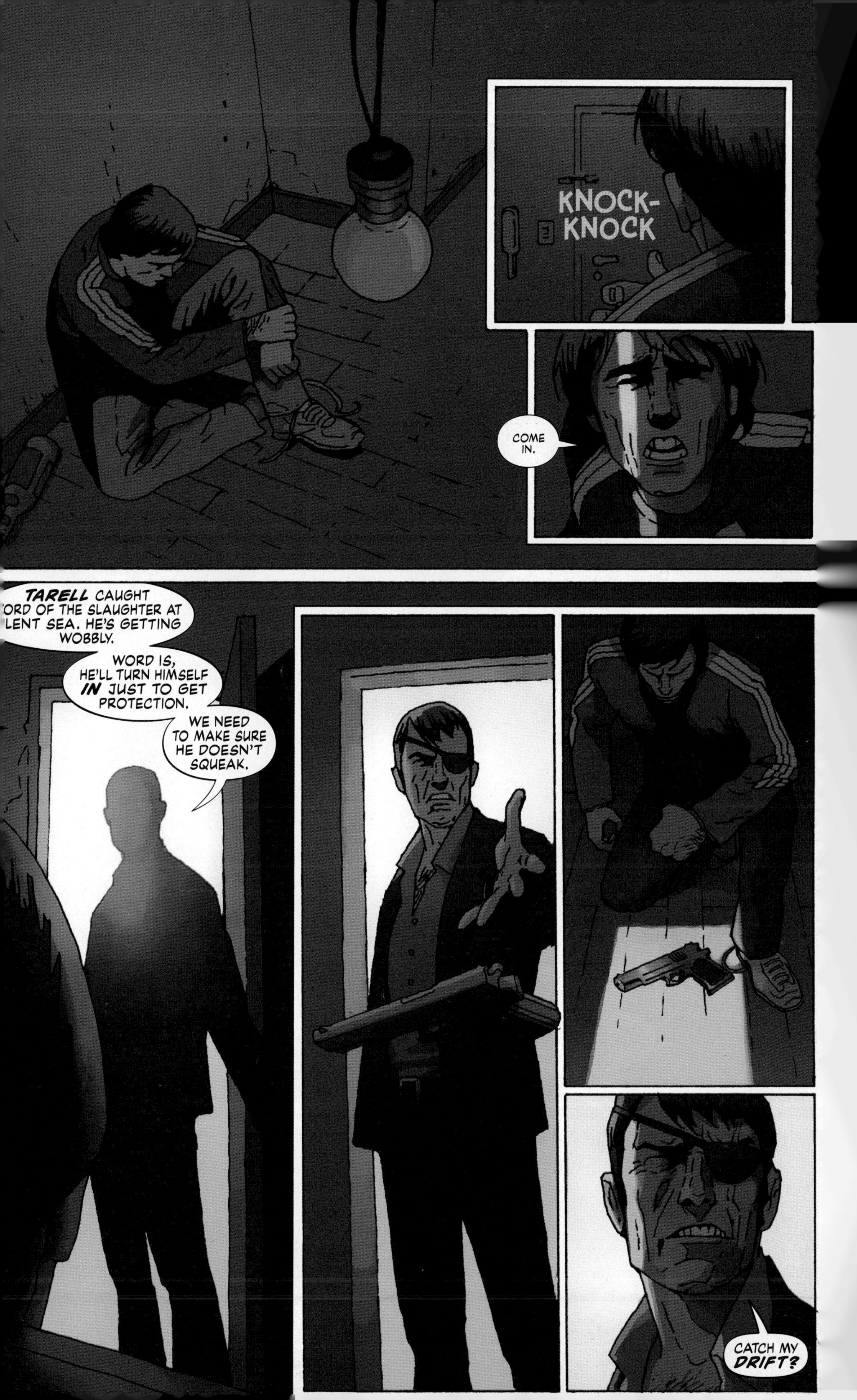
KNOCK-KNOCK
COME IN.
TARELL CAUGHT
ORD OF THE SLAUGHTER AT
LENT SEA. HE'S GETTING WOBBLY.
WORD IS, HE'LL TURN HIMSELF IN JUST TO GET PROTECTION.
WE NEED TO MAKE SURE HE DOESN'T SQUEAK.
CATCH MY DRIFT?

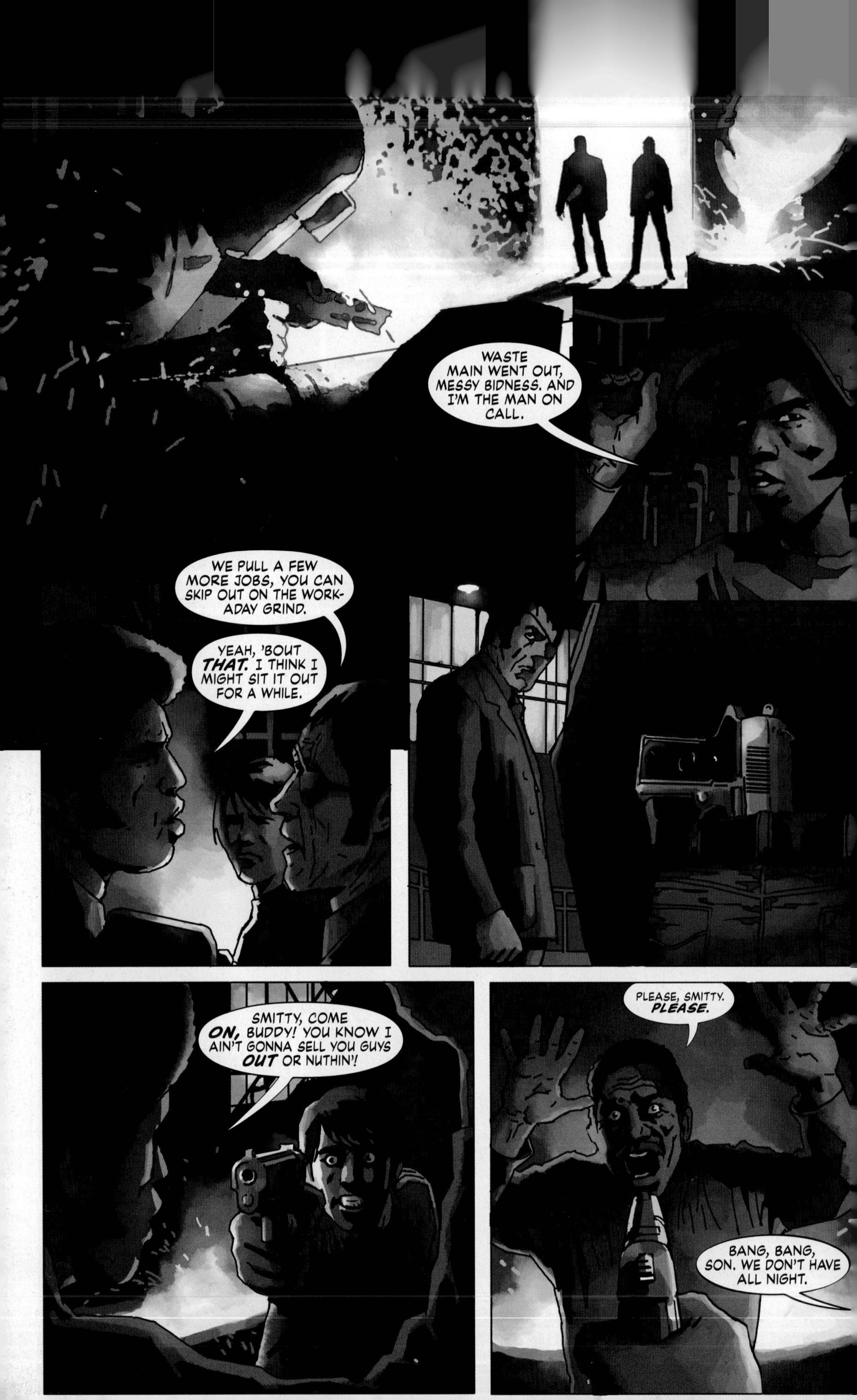
WASTE MAIN WENT OUT, MESSY BIDNESS. AND I'M THE MAN ON CALL.
WE PULL A FEW MORE JOBS, YOU CAN SKIP OUT ON THE WORK-ADAY GRIND.
YEAH, 'BOUT **THAT.** I THINK I MIGHT SIT IT OUT FOR A WHILE.
SMITTY, COME **ON,** BUDDY! YOU KNOW I AIN'T GONNA SELL YOU GUYS **OUT** OR NUTHIN'!
PLEASE, SMITTY. **PLEASE.**
BANG, BANG, SON. WE DON'T HAVE ALL NIGHT.

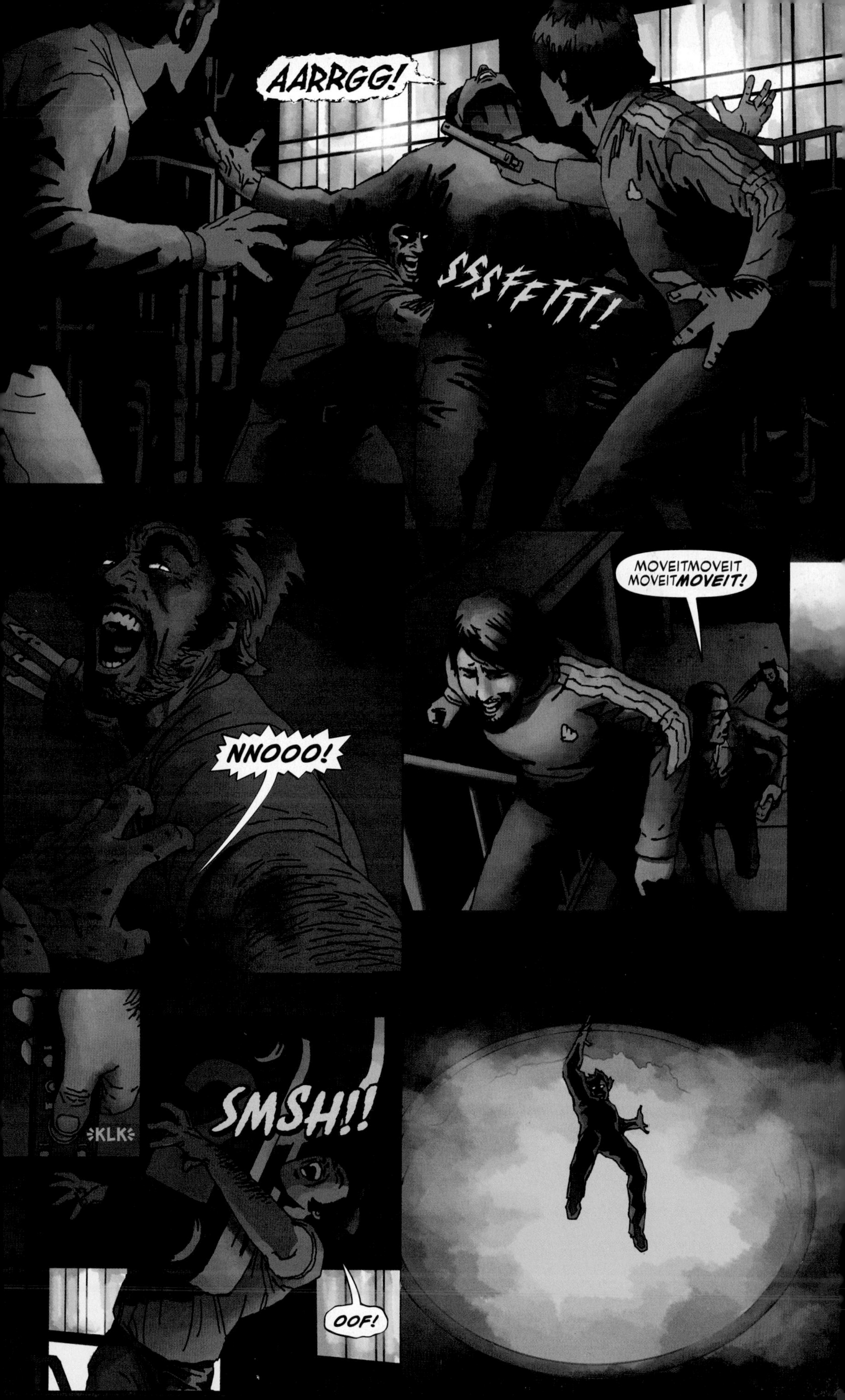
AARRGG!
SSFFTTT!
NNOOO!
MOVEITMOVEIT MOVEITMOVEIT!
KLK
SMSH!!
OOF!

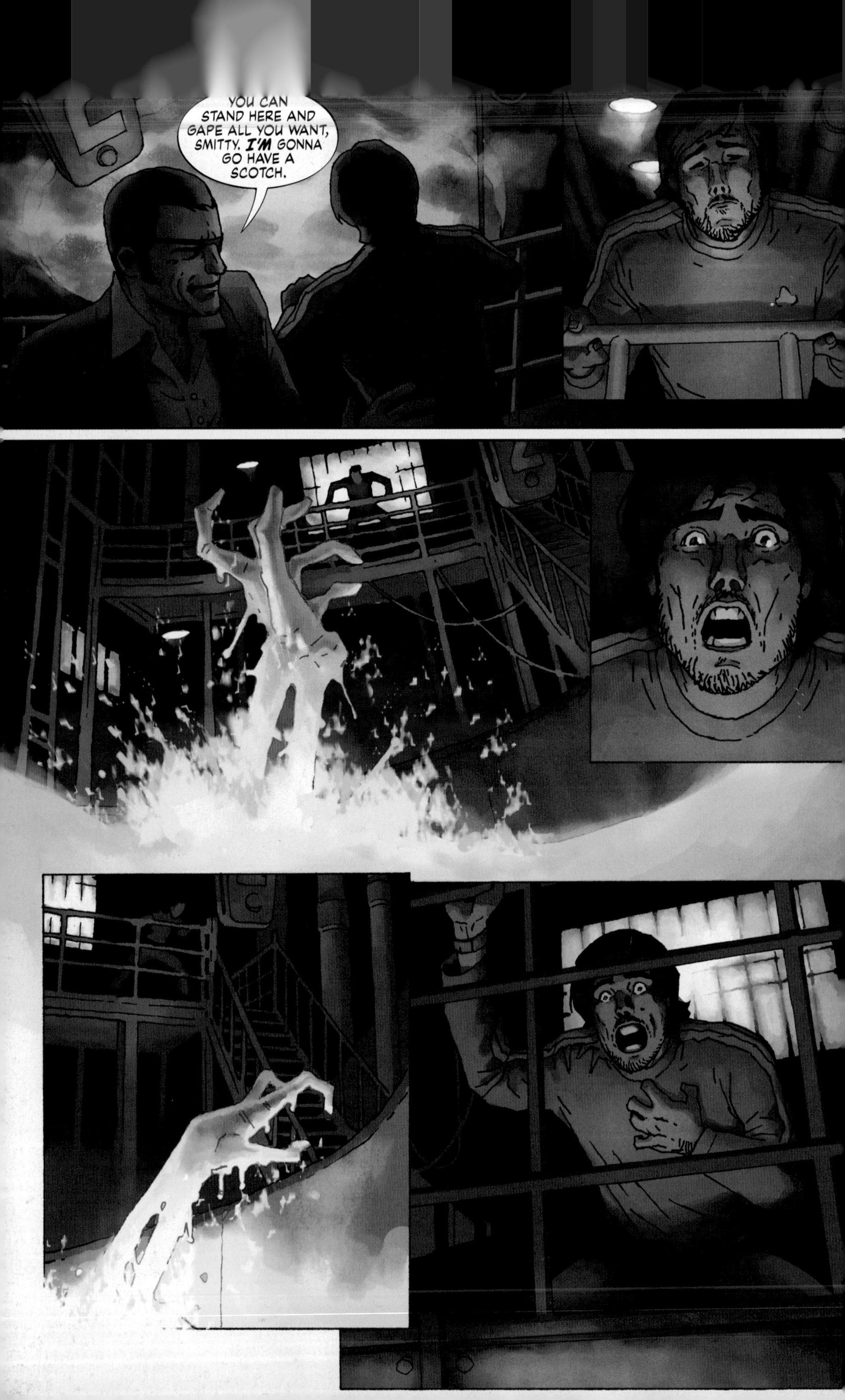
YOU CAN STAND HERE AND GAPE ALL YOU WANT, SMITTY. ***I'M*** GONNA GO HAVE A SCOTCH.

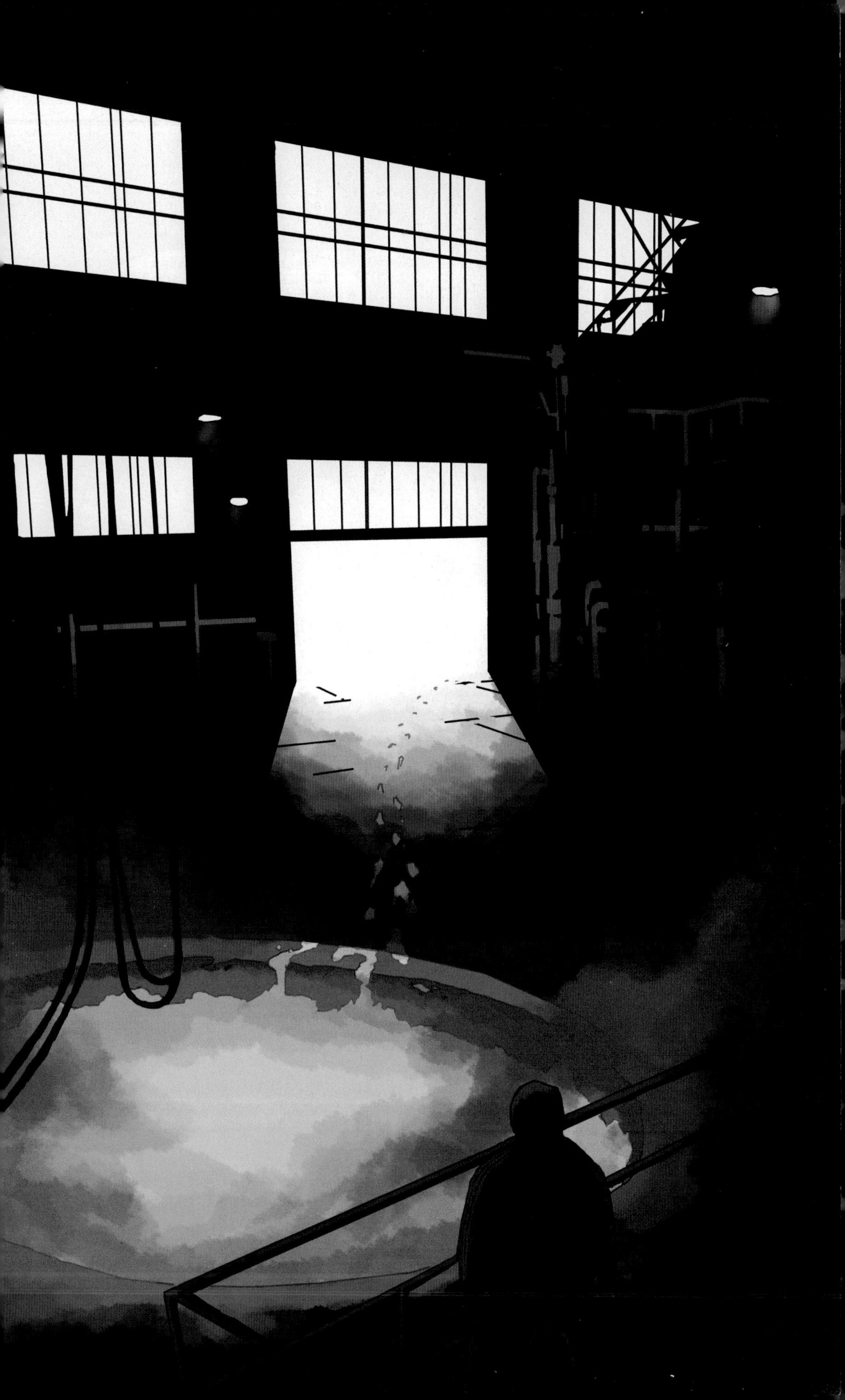

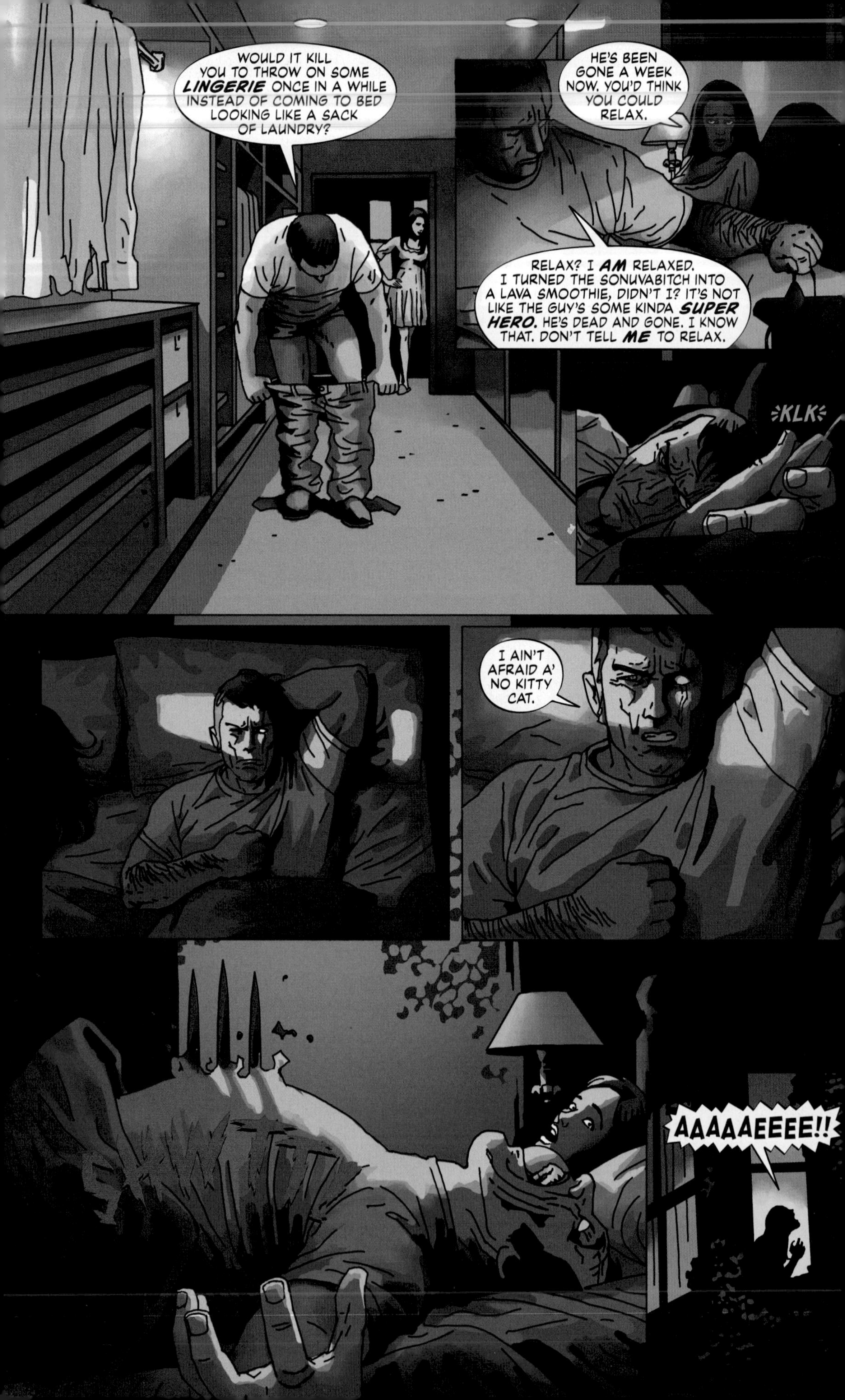
WOULD IT KILL YOU TO THROW ON SOME LINGERIE ONCE IN A WHILE INSTEAD OF COMING TO BED LOOKING LIKE A SACK OF LAUNDRY?
HE'S BEEN GONE A WEEK NOW. YOU'D THINK YOU COULD RELAX.
RELAX? I AM RELAXED. I TURNED THE SONUVABITCH INTO A LAVA SMOOTHIE, DIDN'T I? IT'S NOT LIKE THE GUY'S SOME KINDA SUPER HERO. HE'S DEAD AND GONE. I KNOW THAT. DON'T TELL ME TO RELAX.
KLK
I AIN'T AFRAID A' NO KITTY CAT.
AAAAAEEEE!!

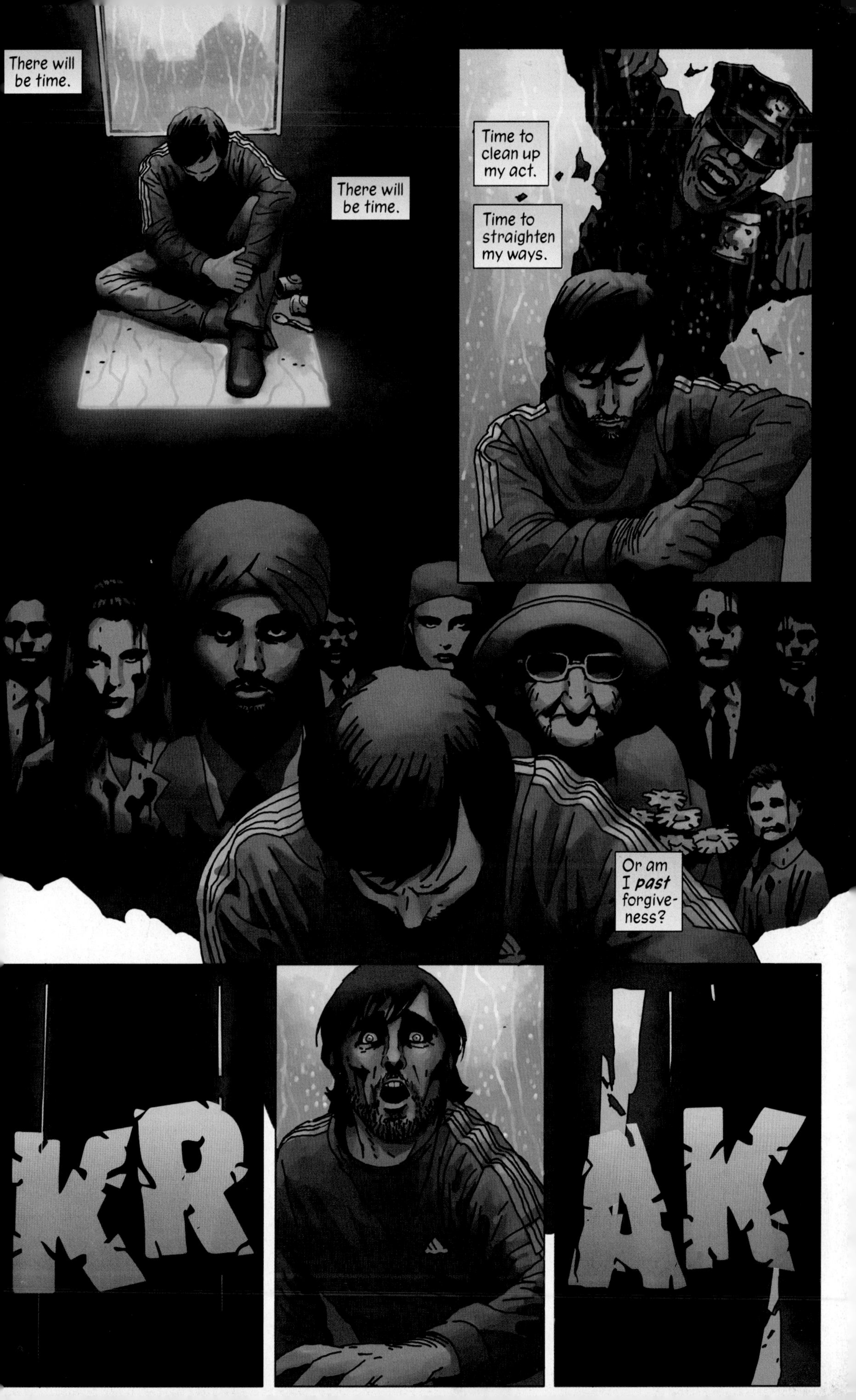
There will be time.
There will be time.
Time to clean up my act.
Time to straighten my ways.
Or am I *past* forgive-ness?
KRAK

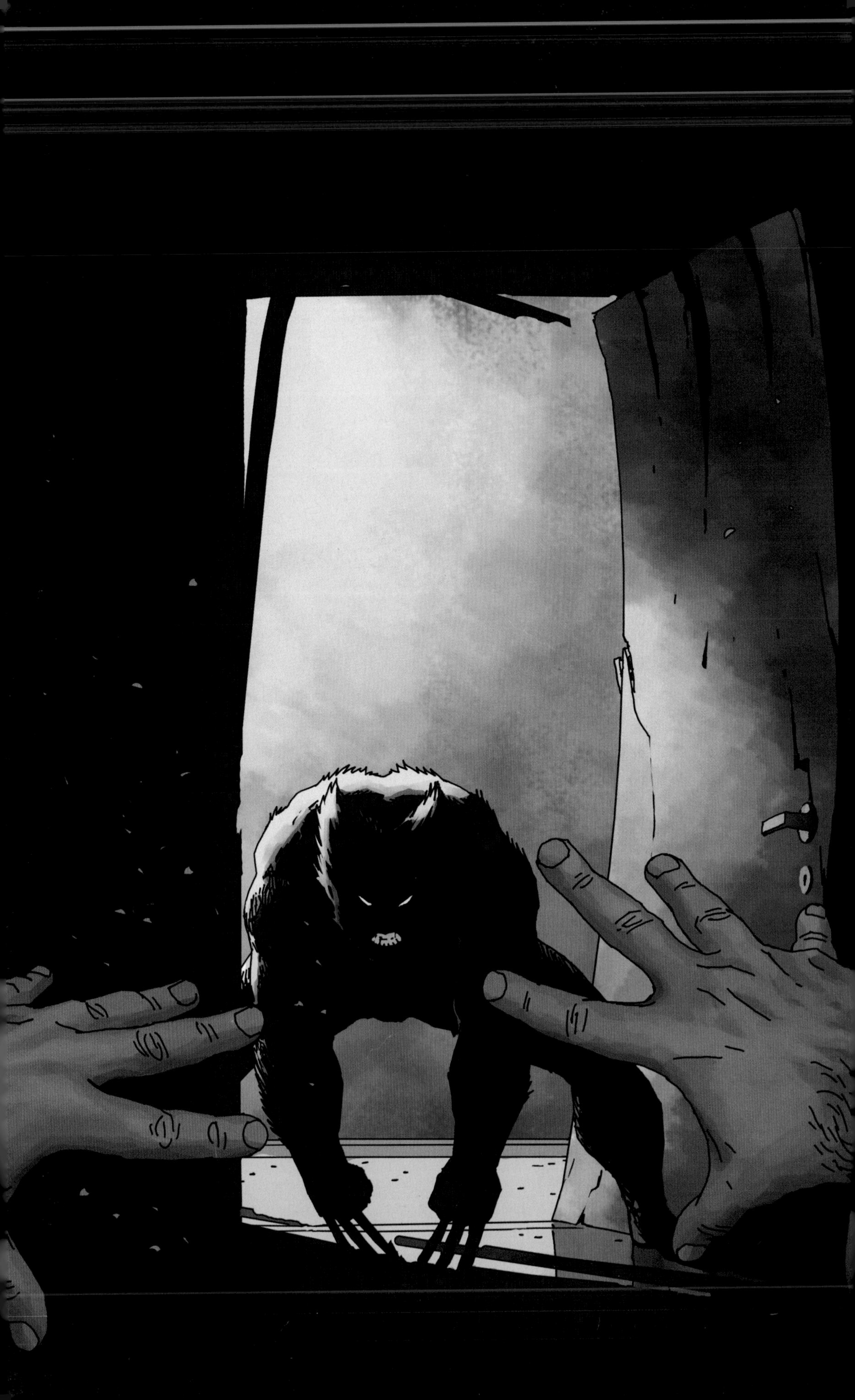

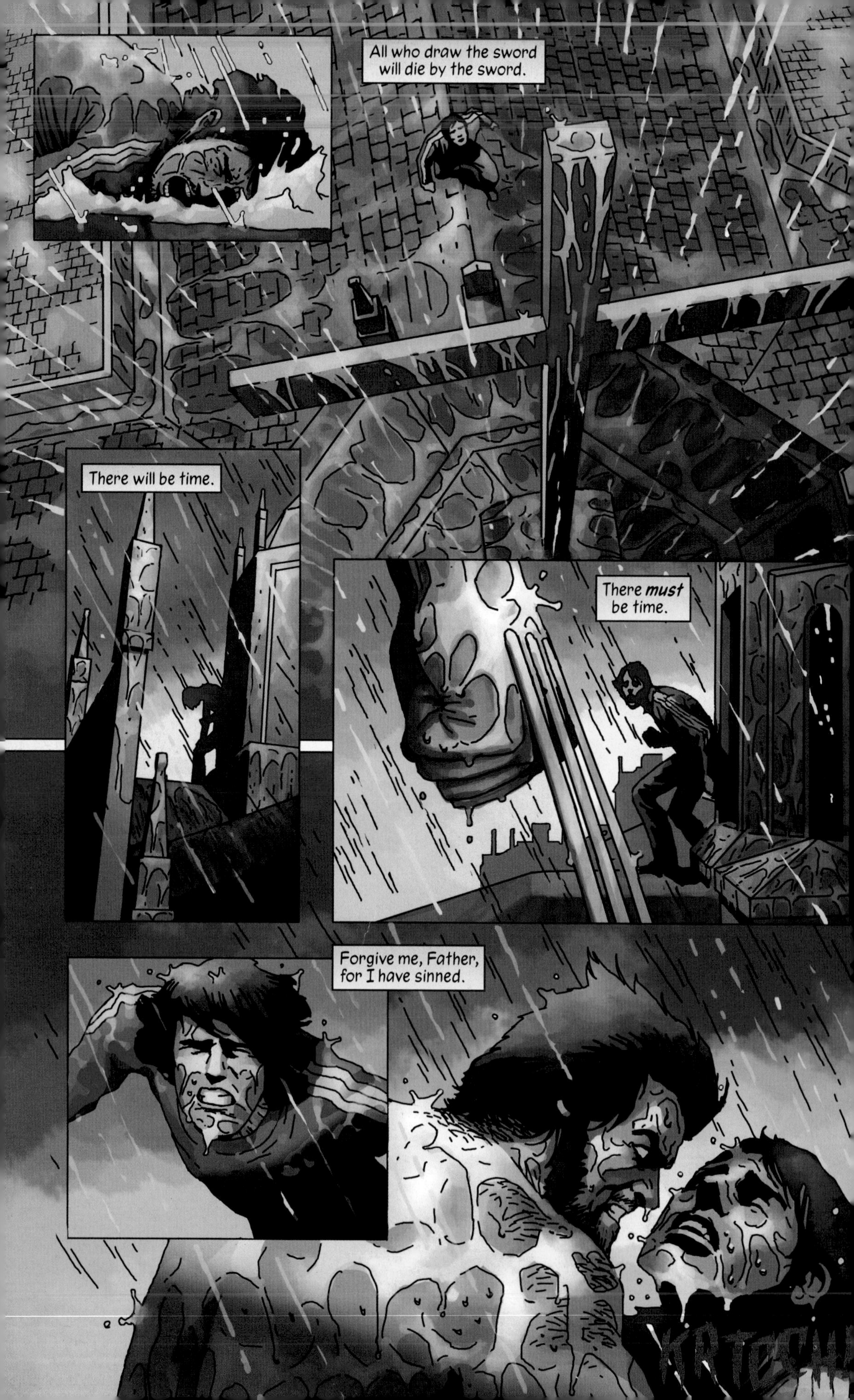
All who draw the sword will die by the sword.
There will be time.
There *must* be time.
Forgive me, Father, for I have sinned.

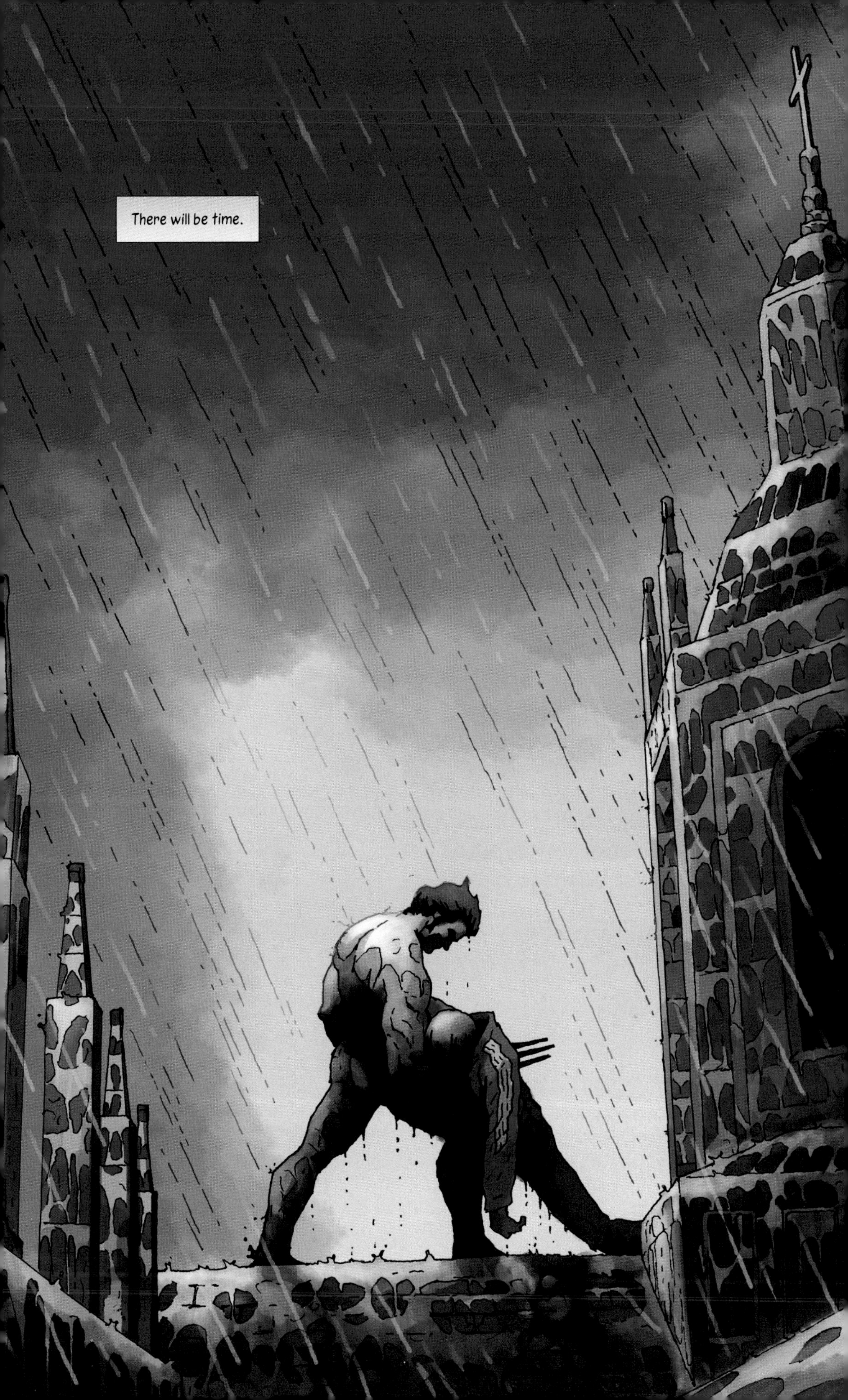
There will be time.

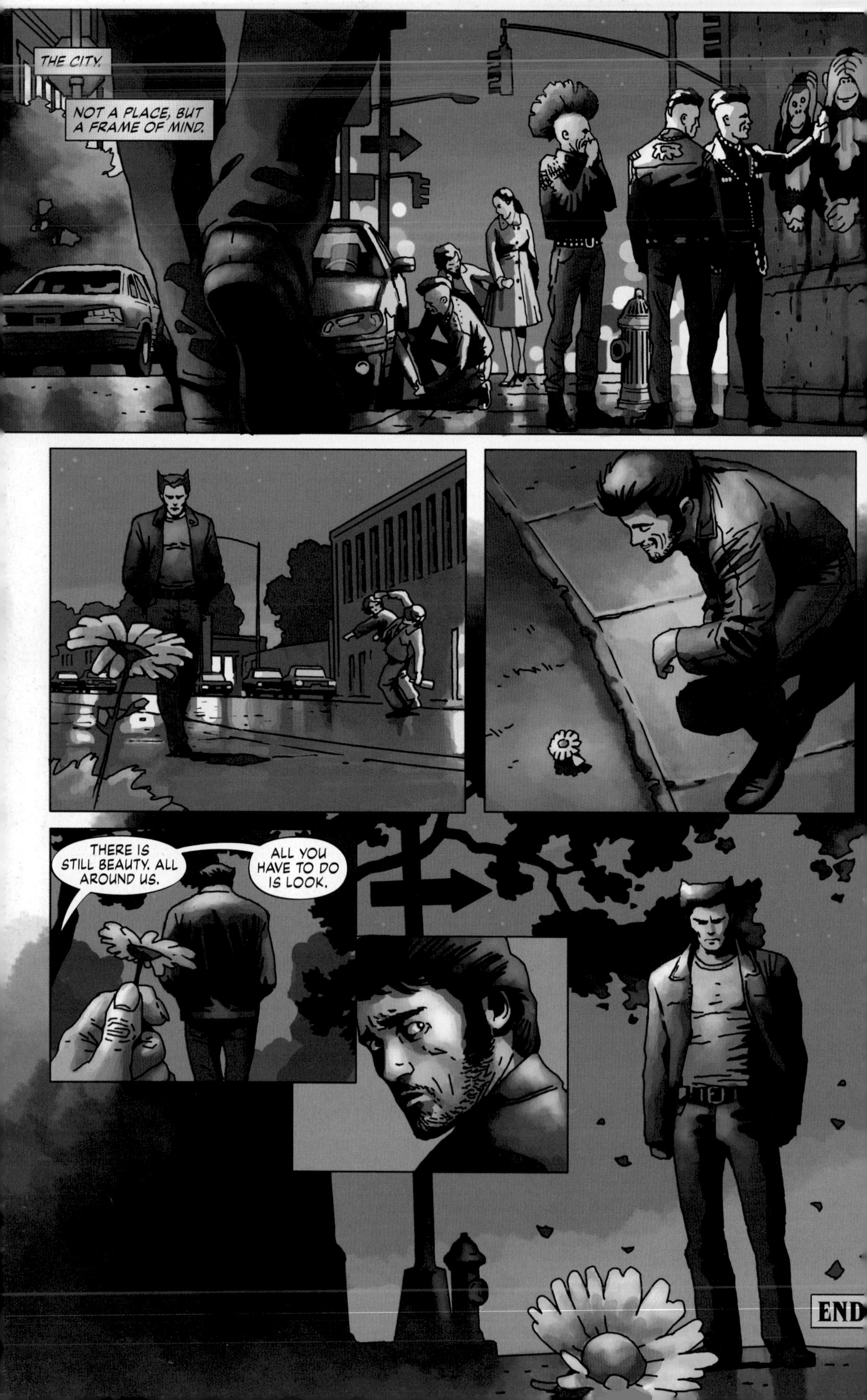
THE CITY.
NOT A PLACE, BUT A FRAME OF MIND.
THERE IS STILL BEAUTY. ALL AROUND US.
ALL YOU HAVE TO DO IS LOOK.
END

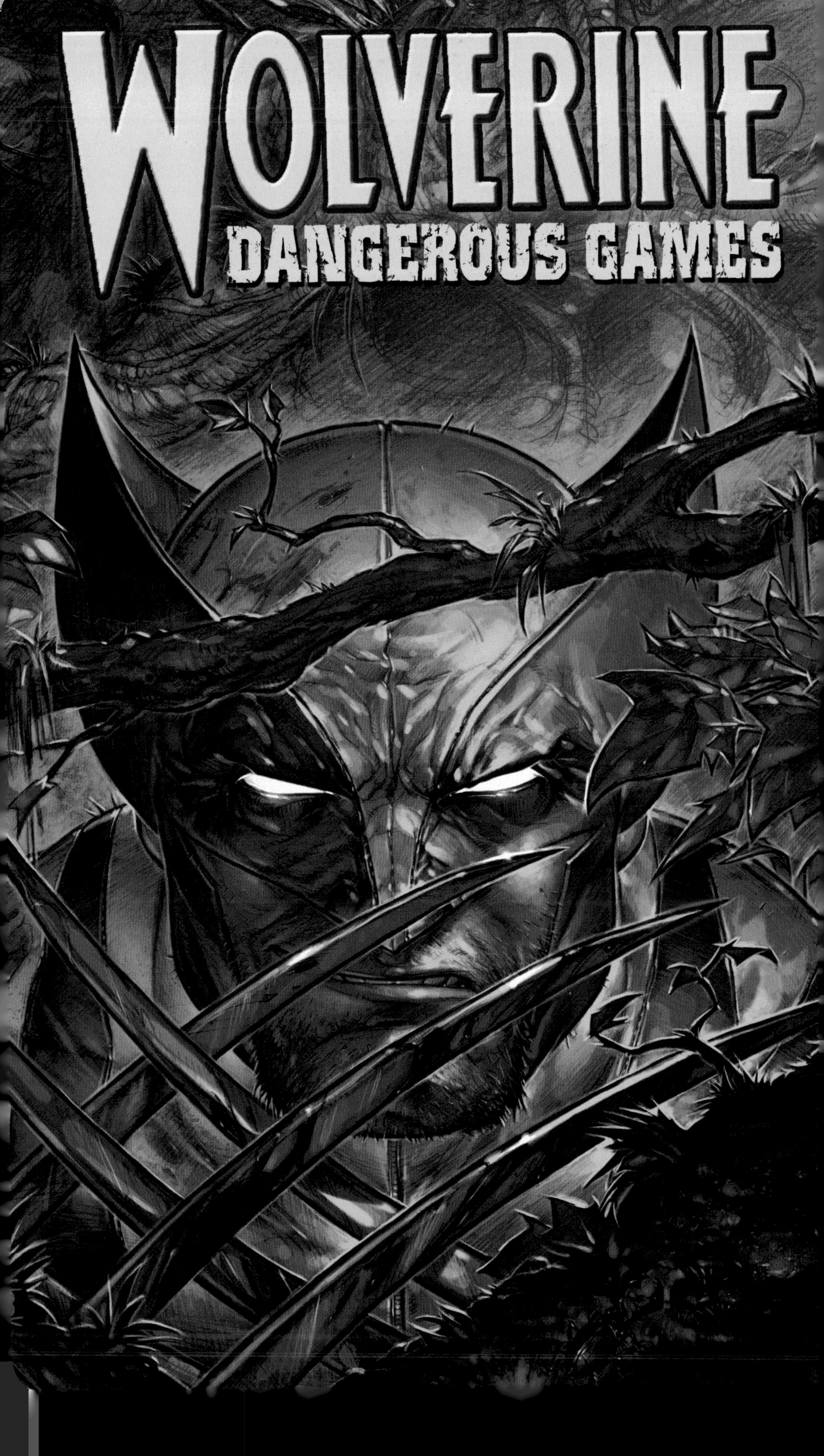
WOLVERINE
DANGEROUS GAMES

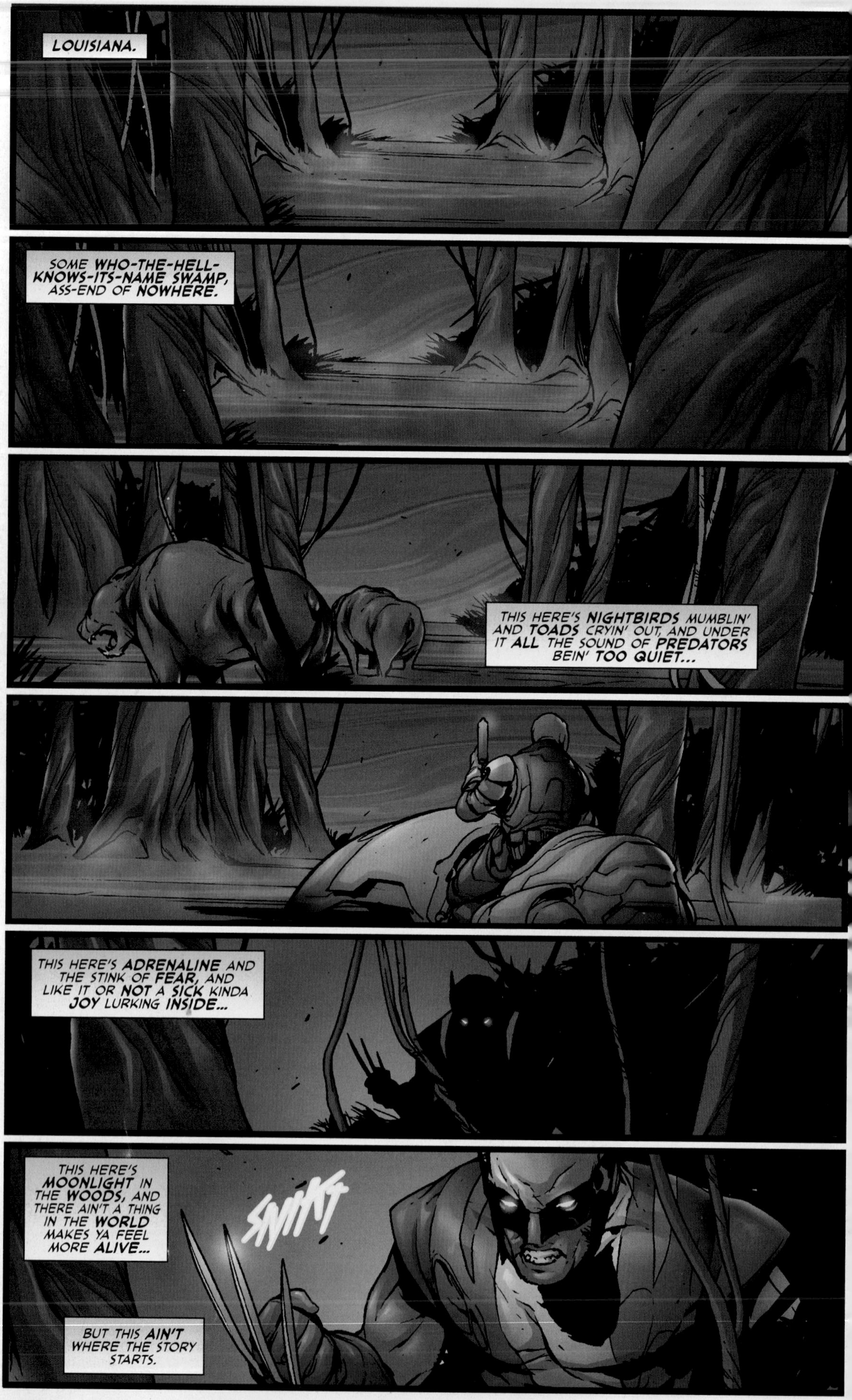
LOUISIANA.
SOME WHO-THE-HELL-KNOWS-ITS-NAME SWAMP, ASS-END OF NOWHERE.
THIS HERE'S NIGHTBIRDS MUMBLIN' AND TOADS CRYIN' OUT, AND UNDER IT ALL THE SOUND OF PREDATORS BEIN' TOO QUIET...
THIS HERE'S ADRENALINE AND THE STINK OF FEAR, AND LIKE IT OR NOT A SICK KINDA JOY LURKING INSIDE...
THIS HERE'S MOONLIGHT IN THE WOODS, AND THERE AIN'T A THING IN THE WORLD MAKES YA FEEL MORE ALIVE...
SNIKT
BUT THIS AIN'T WHERE THE STORY STARTS.

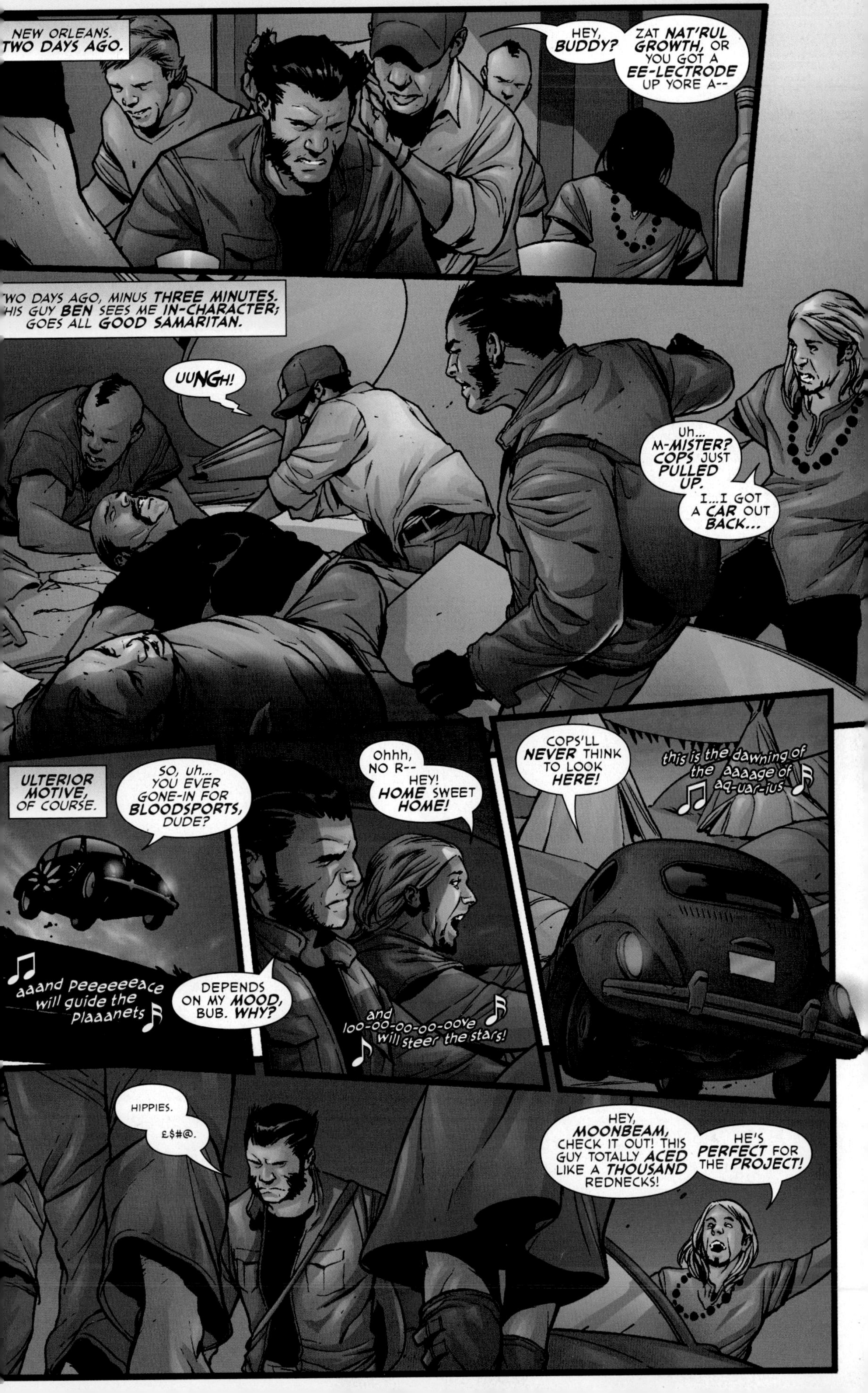
NEW ORLEANS. TWO DAYS AGO.
HEY, BUDDY?
ZAT NAT'RUL GROWTH, OR YOU GOT A EE-LECTRODE UP YORE A--
TWO DAYS AGO, MINUS THREE MINUTES. THIS GUY BEN SEES ME IN-CHARACTER; GOES ALL GOOD SAMARITAN.
UUNGH!
Uh... M-MISTER? COPS JUST PULLED UP.
I...I GOT A CAR OUT BACK...
ULTERIOR MOTIVE, OF COURSE.
SO, uh... YOU EVER GONE-IN FOR BLOODSPORTS, DUDE?
aaand peeeeeeace will guide the plaaanets
DEPENDS ON MY MOOD, BUB. WHY?
Ohhh, NO R--
HEY! HOME SWEET HOME!
and loo-oo-oo-oo-oove will steer the stars!
COPS'LL NEVER THINK TO LOOK HERE!
this is the dawning of the aaaage of aq-uar-ius
HIPPIES.
£$#@.
HEY, MOONBEAM, CHECK IT OUT! THIS GUY TOTALLY ACED LIKE A THOUSAND REDNECKS!
HE'S PERFECT FOR THE PROJECT!

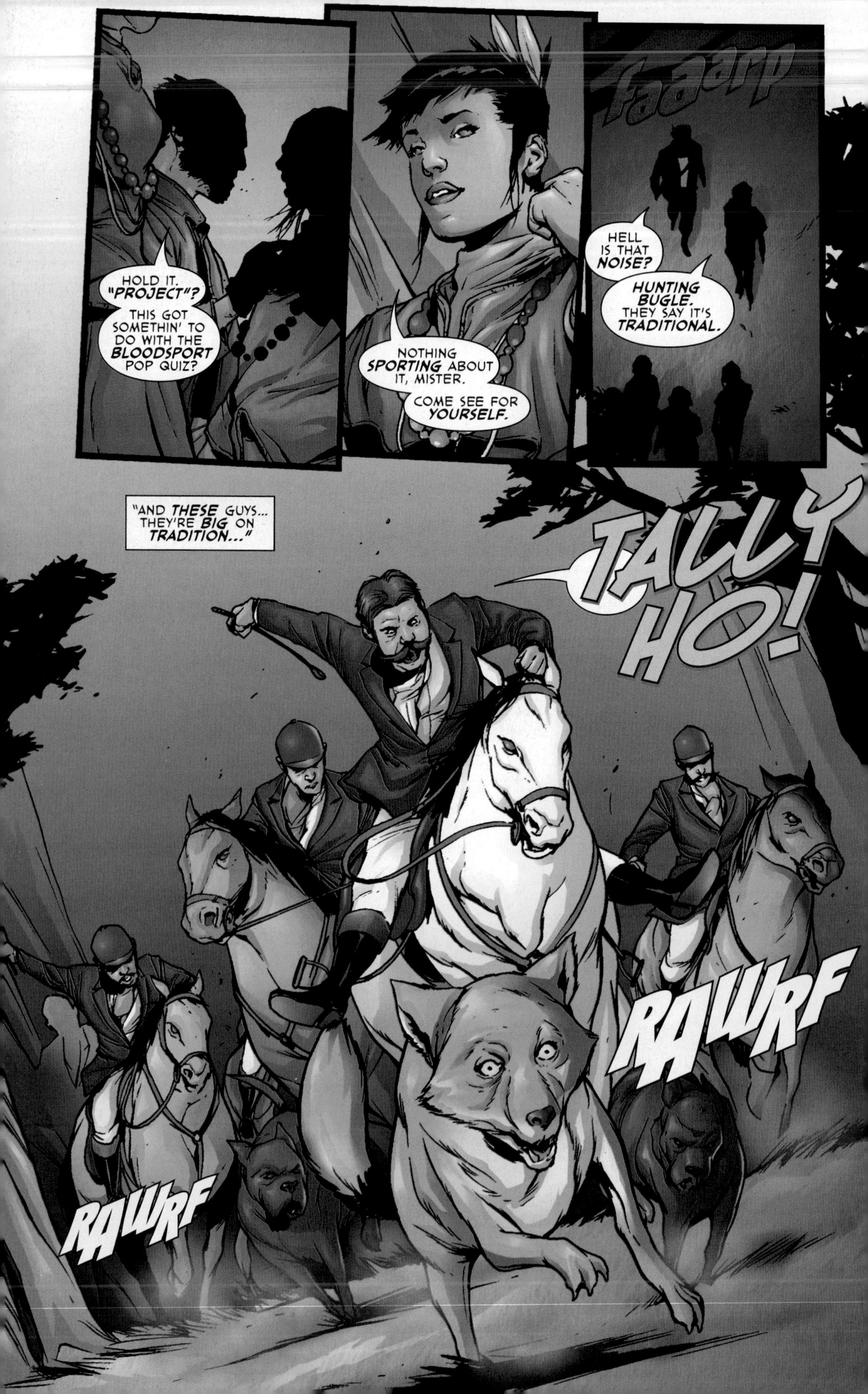
HOLD IT. "PROJECT"?
THIS GOT SOMETHIN' TO DO WITH THE BLOODSPORT POP QUIZ?
NOTHING SPORTING ABOUT IT, MISTER.
COME SEE FOR YOURSELF.
FAAARP
HELL IS THAT NOISE?
HUNTING BUGLE. THEY SAY IT'S TRADITIONAL.
"AND THESE GUYS... THEY'RE BIG ON TRADITION..."
TALLY HO!
RAWRF
RAWRF

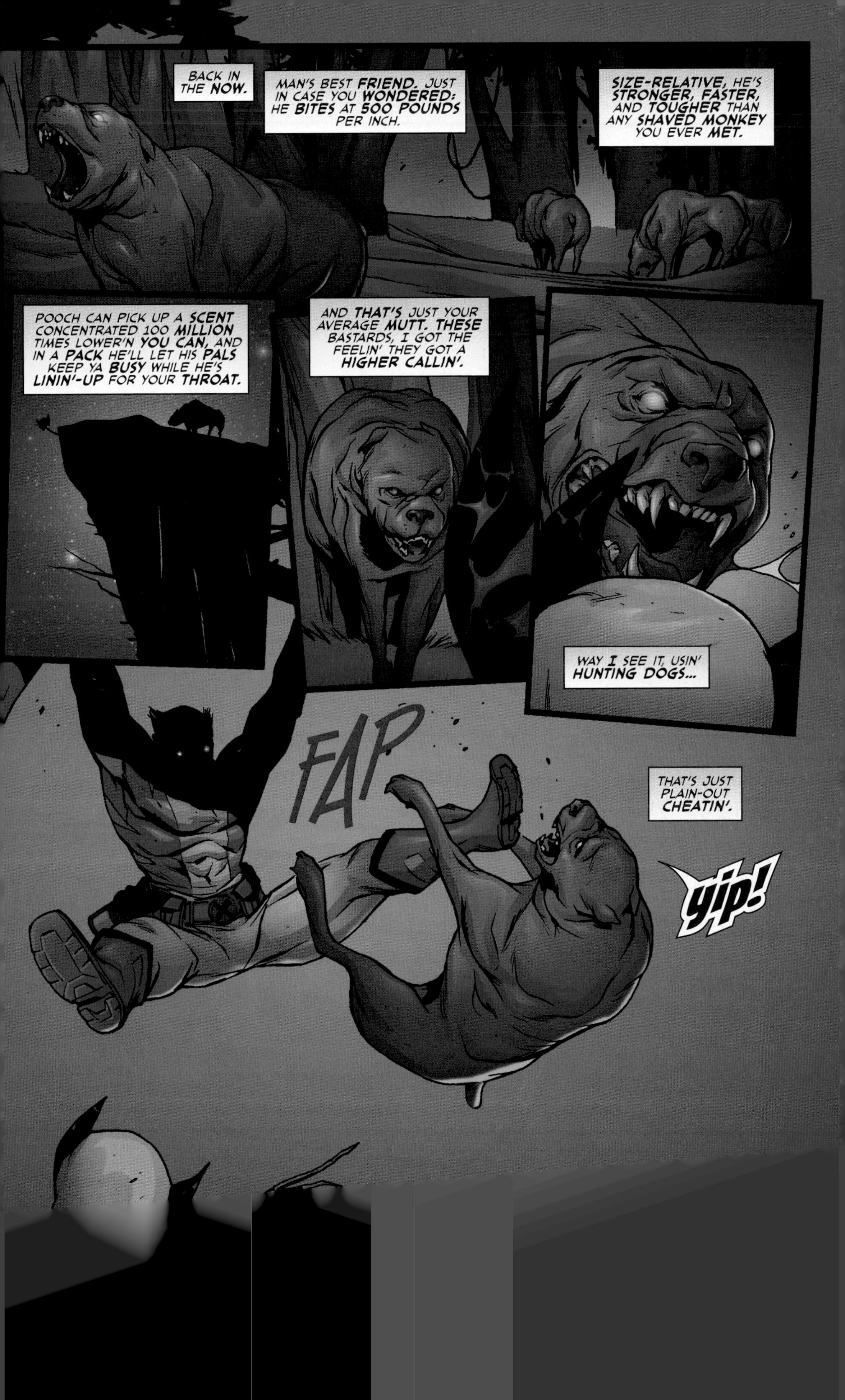
BACK IN THE NOW.
MAN'S BEST FRIEND. JUST IN CASE YOU WONDERED: HE BITES AT 500 POUNDS PER INCH.
SIZE-RELATIVE, HE'S STRONGER, FASTER, AND TOUGHER THAN ANY SHAVED MONKEY YOU EVER MET.
POOCH CAN PICK UP A SCENT CONCENTRATED 100 MILLION TIMES LOWER'N YOU CAN, AND IN A PACK HE'LL LET HIS PALS KEEP YA BUSY WHILE HE'S LININ'-UP FOR YOUR THROAT.
AND THAT'S JUST YOUR AVERAGE MUTT. THESE BASTARDS, I GOT THE FEELIN' THEY GOT A HIGHER CALLIN'.
WAY I SEE IT, USIN' HUNTING DOGS...
FAP
THAT'S JUST PLAIN-OUT CHEATIN'.
yip!

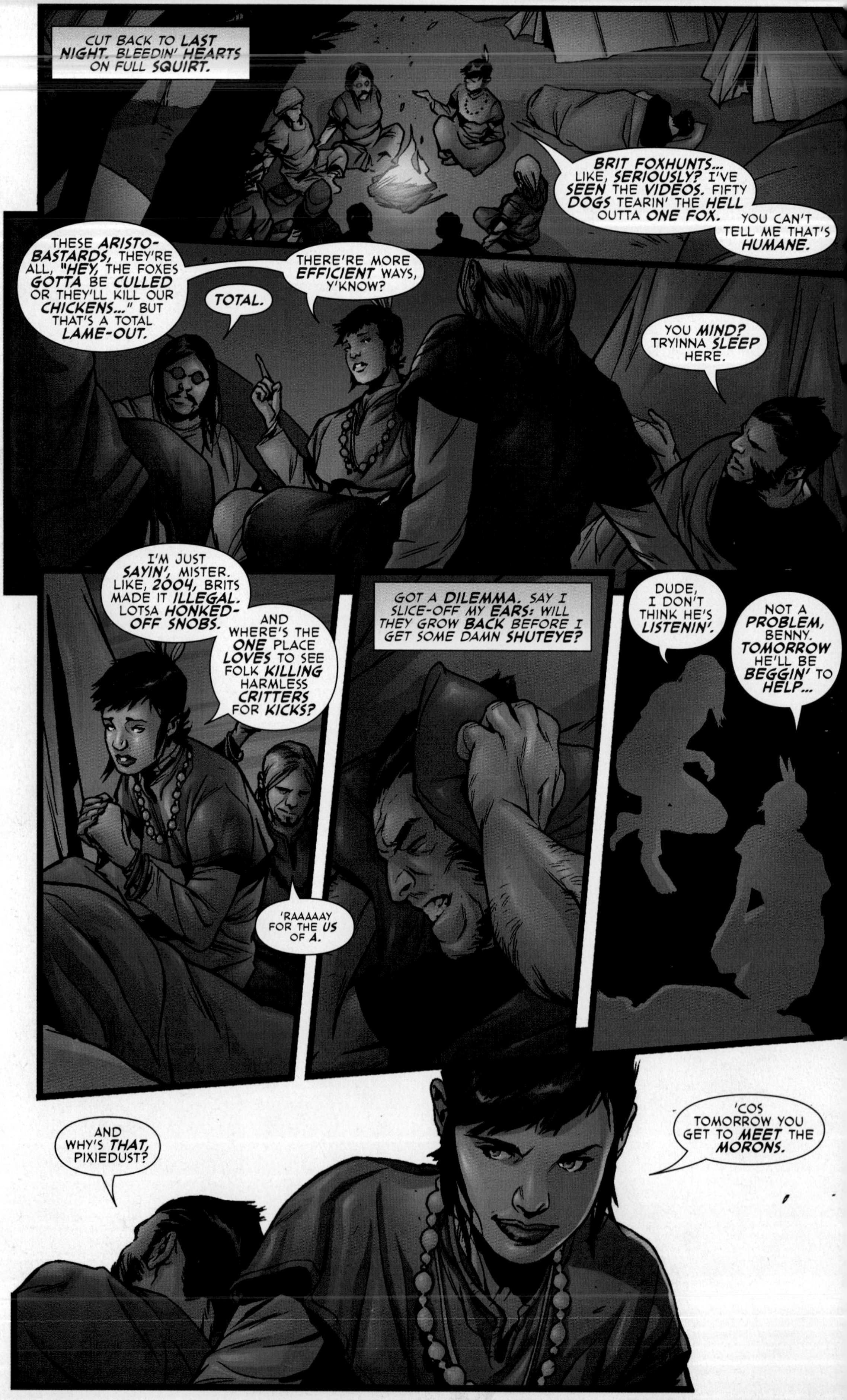
CUT BACK TO LAST NIGHT. BLEEDIN' HEARTS ON FULL SQUIRT.
BRIT FOXHUNTS... LIKE, SERIOUSLY? I'VE SEEN THE VIDEOS. FIFTY DOGS TEARIN' THE HELL OUTTA ONE FOX.
YOU CAN'T TELL ME THAT'S HUMANE.
THESE ARISTO-BASTARDS, THEY'RE ALL, "HEY, THE FOXES GOTTA BE CULLED OR THEY'LL KILL OUR CHICKENS..." BUT THAT'S A TOTAL LAME-OUT.
TOTAL.
THERE'RE MORE EFFICIENT WAYS, Y'KNOW?
YOU MIND? TRYINNA SLEEP HERE.
I'M JUST SAYIN', MISTER. LIKE, 2004, BRITS MADE IT ILLEGAL. LOTSA HONKED-OFF SNOBS.
AND WHERE'S THE ONE PLACE LOVES TO SEE FOLK KILLING HARMLESS CRITTERS FOR KICKS?
'RAAAAAY FOR THE US OF A.
GOT A DILEMMA. SAY I SLICE-OFF MY EARS: WILL THEY GROW BACK BEFORE I GET SOME DAMN SHUTEYE?
DUDE, I DON'T THINK HE'S LISTENIN'.
NOT A PROBLEM, BENNY. TOMORROW HE'LL BE BEGGIN' TO HELP...
AND WHY'S THAT, PIXIEDUST?
'COS TOMORROW YOU GET TO MEET THE MORONS.

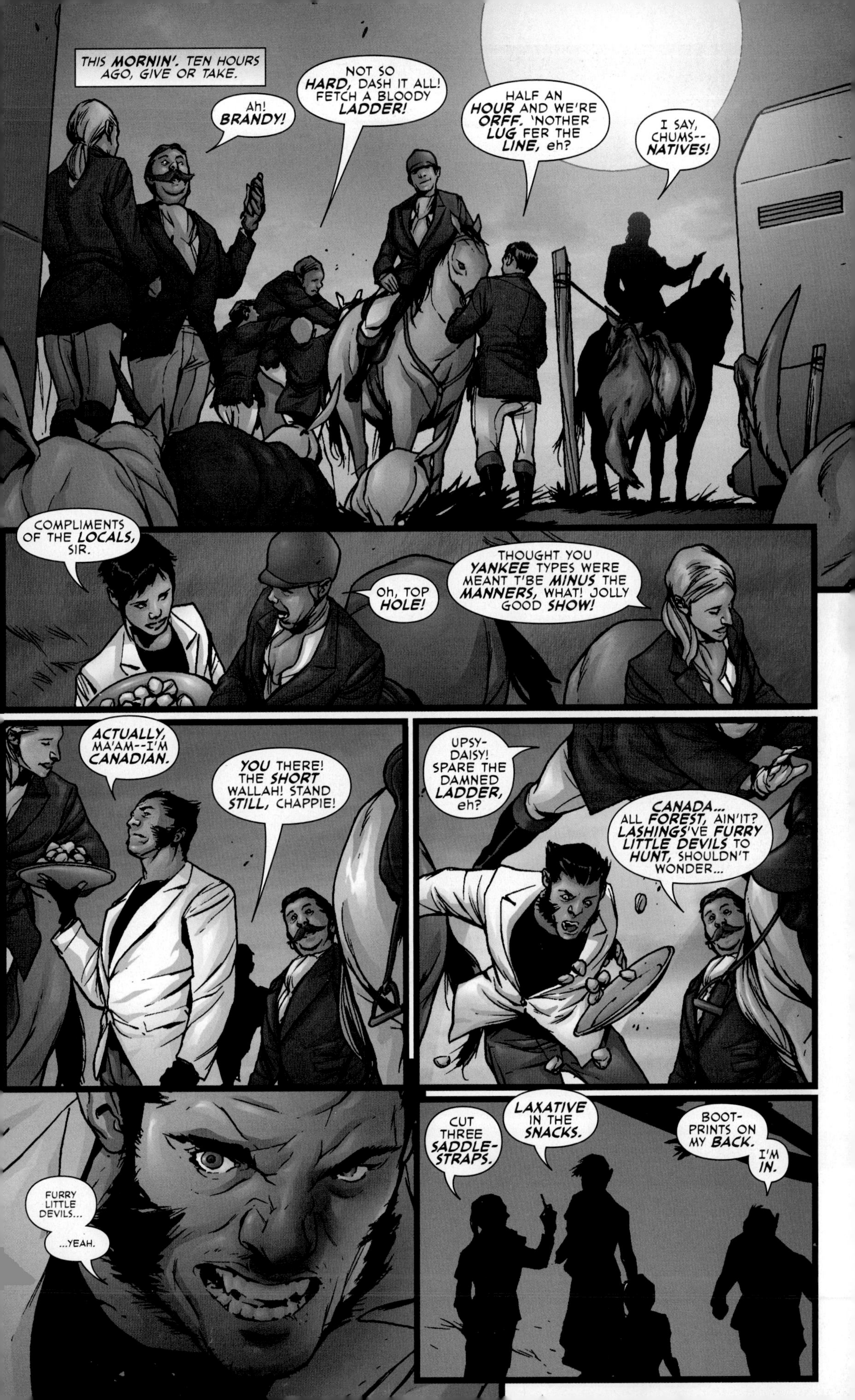
THIS MORNIN'. TEN HOURS AGO, GIVE OR TAKE.
Ah! BRANDY!
NOT SO HARD, DASH IT ALL! FETCH A BLOODY LADDER!
HALF AN HOUR AND WE'RE ORFF. 'NOTHER LUG FER THE LINE, eh?
I SAY, CHUMS-- NATIVES!
COMPLIMENTS OF THE LOCALS, SIR.
Oh, TOP HOLE!
THOUGHT YOU YANKEE TYPES WERE MEANT T'BE MINUS THE MANNERS, WHAT! JOLLY GOOD SHOW!
ACTUALLY, MA'AM--I'M CANADIAN.
YOU THERE! THE SHORT WALLAH! STAND STILL, CHAPPIE!
UPSY-DAISY! SPARE THE DAMNED LADDER, eh?
CANADA... ALL FOREST, AIN'T IT? LASHINGS'VE FURRY LITTLE DEVILS TO HUNT, SHOULDN'T WONDER...
FURRY LITTLE DEVILS...
...YEAH.
CUT THREE SADDLE-STRAPS.
LAXATIVE IN THE SNACKS.
BOOT-PRINTS ON MY BACK.
I'M IN.

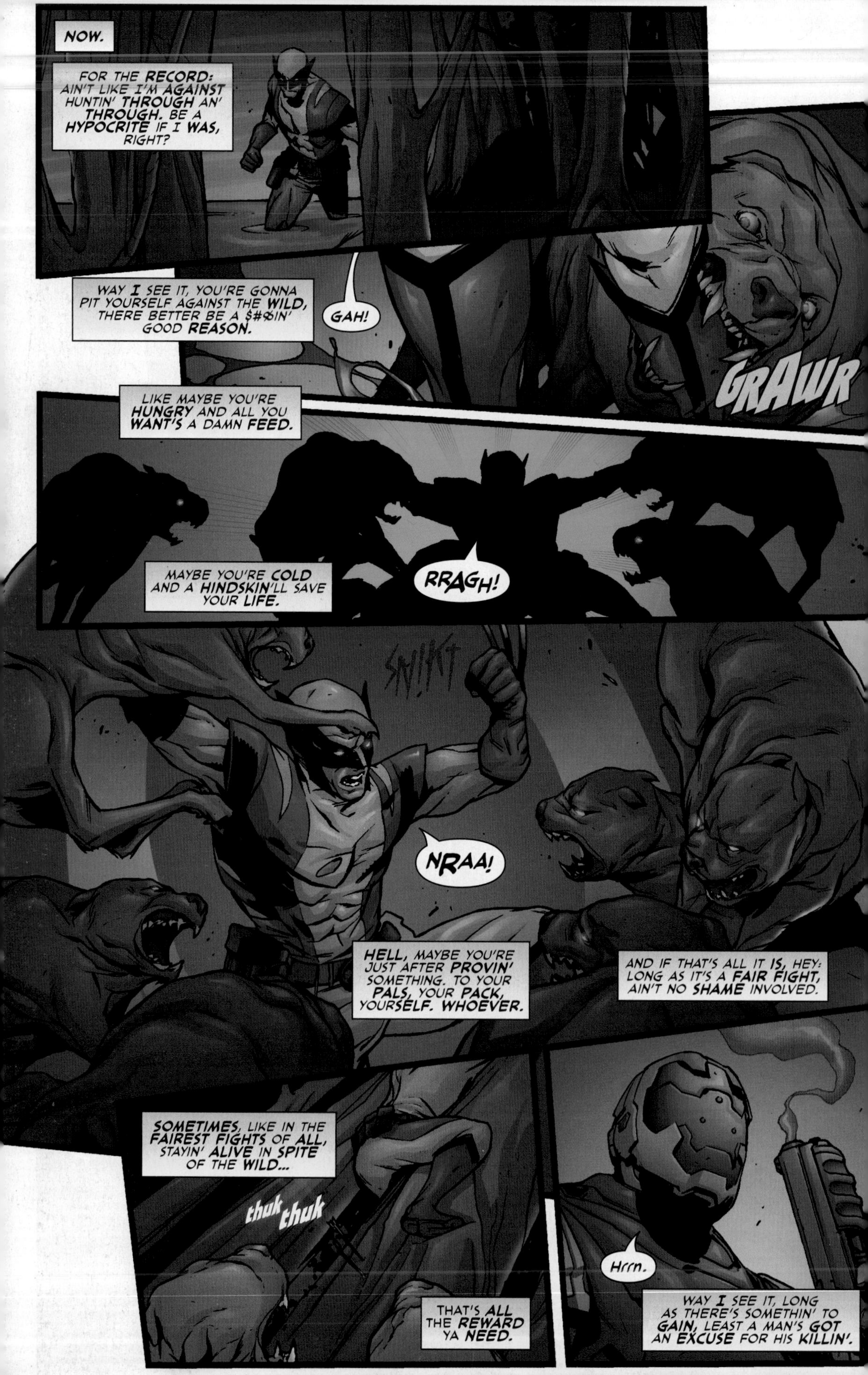
NOW.
FOR THE RECORD: AIN'T LIKE I'M AGAINST HUNTIN' THROUGH AN' THROUGH. BE A HYPOCRITE IF I WAS, RIGHT?
WAY I SEE IT, YOU'RE GONNA PIT YOURSELF AGAINST THE WILD, THERE BETTER BE A $#%IN' GOOD REASON.
GAH!
GRAWR
LIKE MAYBE YOU'RE HUNGRY AND ALL YOU WANT'S A DAMN FEED.
MAYBE YOU'RE COLD AND A HINDSKIN'LL SAVE YOUR LIFE.
RRAGH!
SNIKT
NRAA!
HELL, MAYBE YOU'RE JUST AFTER PROVIN' SOMETHING. TO YOUR PALS, YOUR PACK, YOURSELF. WHOEVER.
AND IF THAT'S ALL IT IS, HEY: LONG AS IT'S A FAIR FIGHT, AIN'T NO SHAME INVOLVED.
SOMETIMES, LIKE IN THE FAIREST FIGHTS OF ALL, STAYIN' ALIVE IN SPITE OF THE WILD...
thuk thuk
THAT'S ALL THE REWARD YA NEED.
Hrrn.
WAY I SEE IT, LONG AS THERE'S SOMETHIN' TO GAIN, LEAST A MAN'S GOT AN EXCUSE FOR HIS KILLIN'.

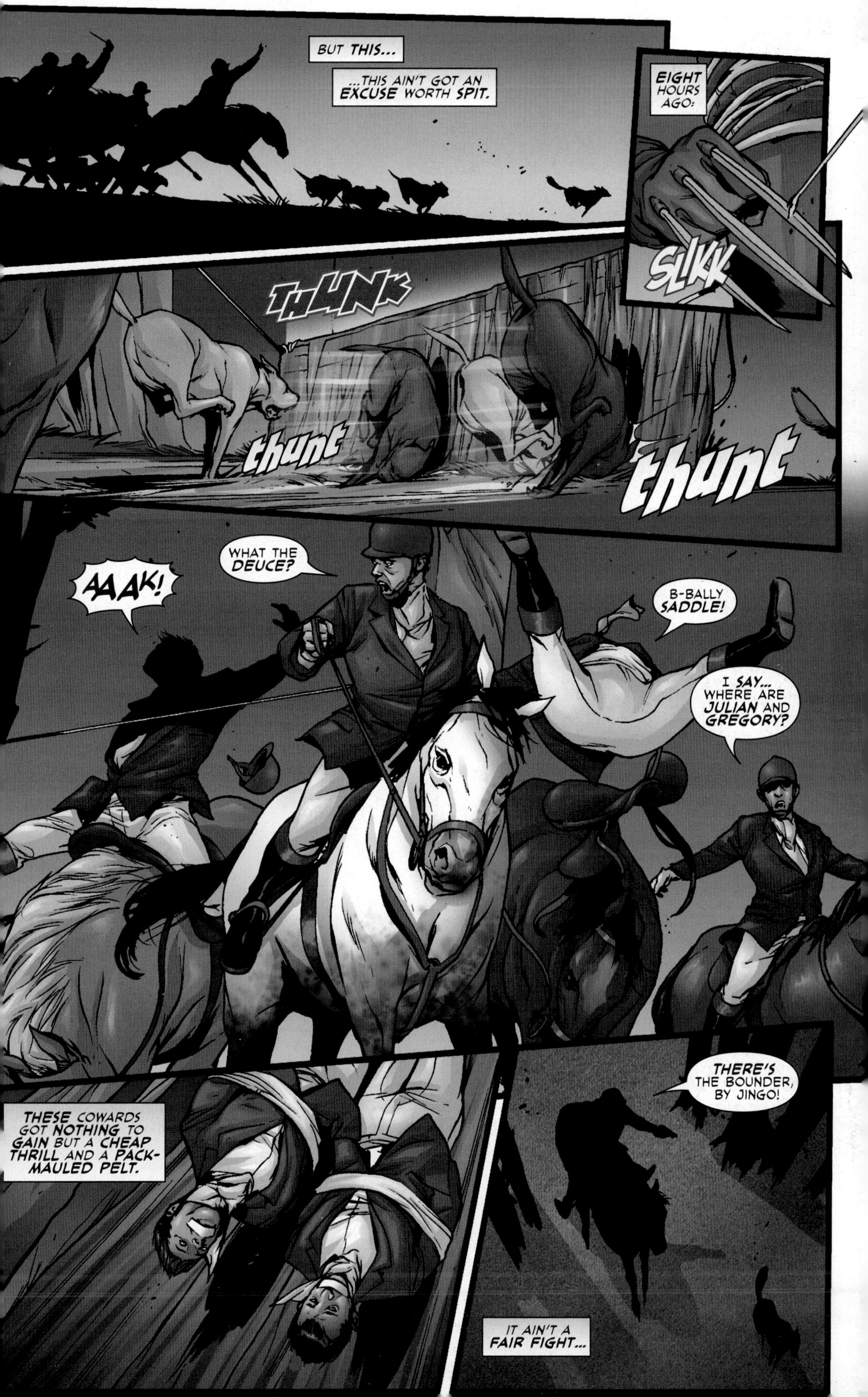

BUT THIS...
...THIS AIN'T GOT AN EXCUSE WORTH SPIT.
EIGHT HOURS AGO:
SLIKK
THUNK
thunt
thunt
AAAK!
WHAT THE DEUCE?
B-BALLY SADDLE!
I SAY... WHERE ARE JULIAN AND GREGORY?
THESE COWARDS GOT NOTHING TO GAIN BUT A CHEAP THRILL AND A PACK-MAULED PELT.
THERE'S THE BOUNDER, BY JINGO!
IT AIN'T A FAIR FIGHT...

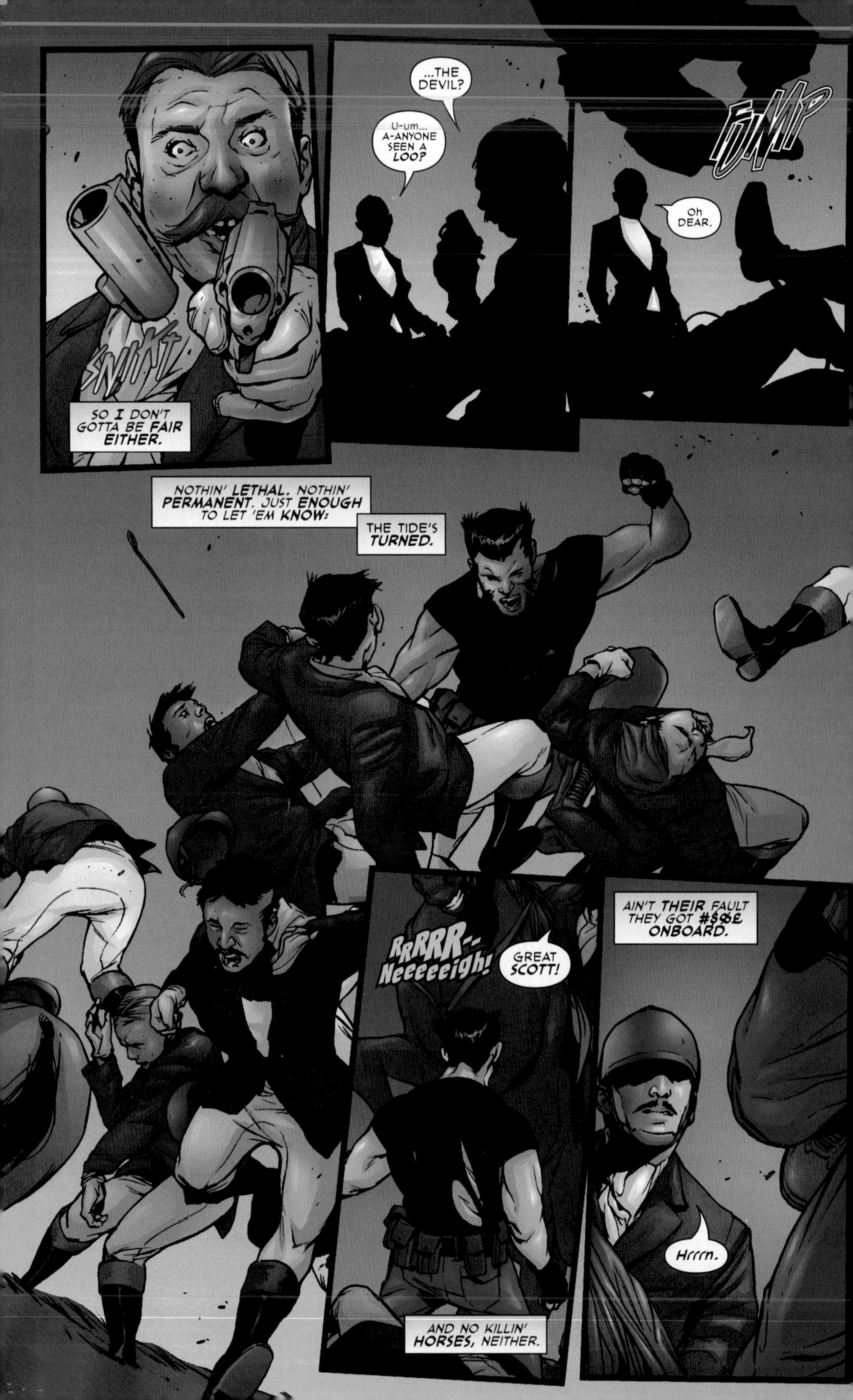

SNIKT
SO I DON'T GOTTA BE FAIR EITHER.
...THE DEVIL?
U-um... A-ANYONE SEEN A LOO?
Oh DEAR.
NOTHIN' LETHAL. NOTHIN' PERMANENT. JUST ENOUGH TO LET 'EM KNOW:
THE TIDE'S TURNED.
RRRRR-- Neeeeeigh!
GREAT SCOTT!
AND NO KILLIN' HORSES, NEITHER.
AIN'T THEIR FAULT THEY GOT #$Ø£ ONBOARD.
Hrrrn.

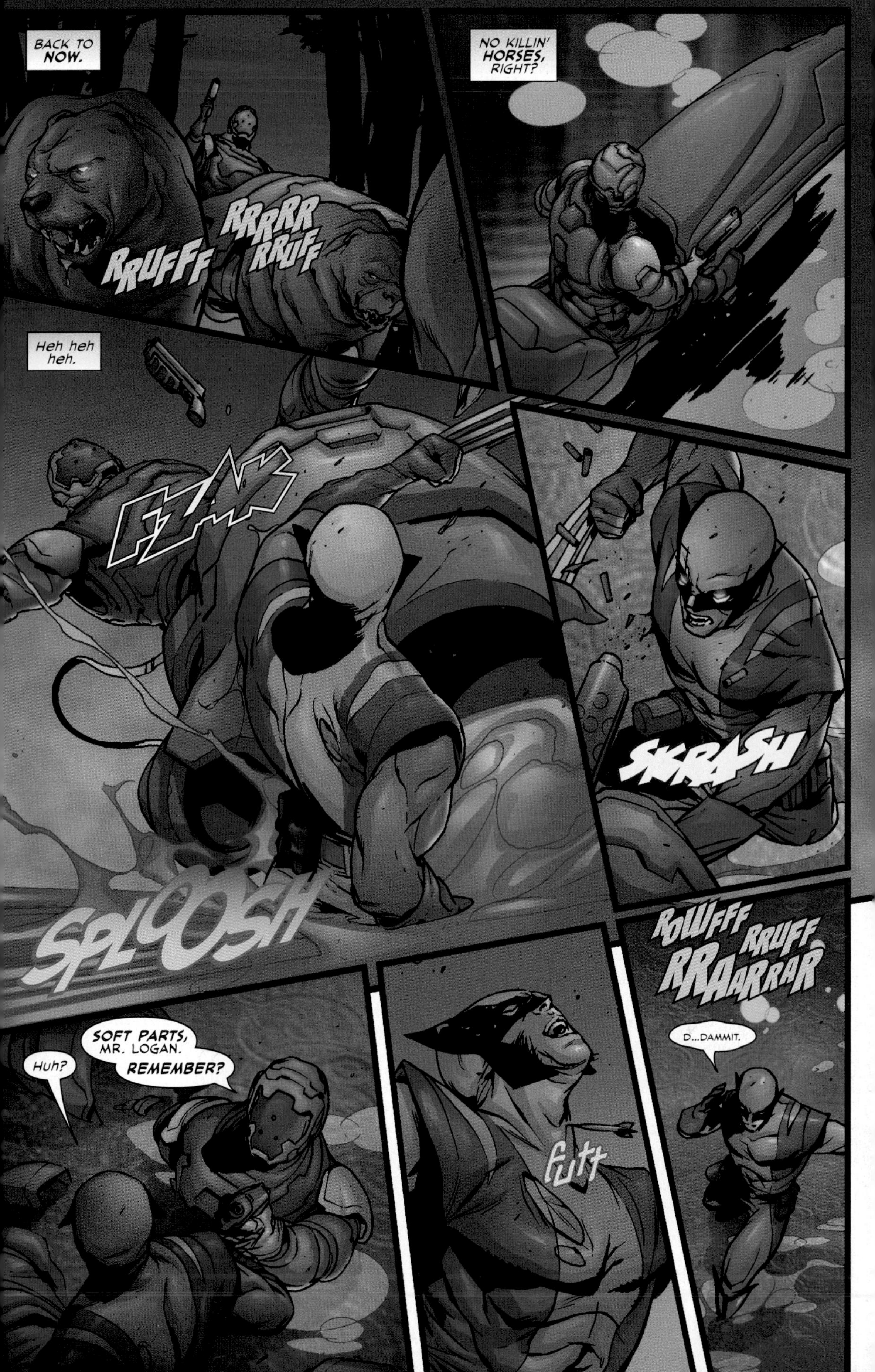
BACK TO NOW.
RRUFFF
RRRRR RRUFF
NO KILLIN' HORSES, RIGHT?
Heh heh heh.
FZAK
SKRASH
SPLOOSH
Huh?
SOFT PARTS, MR. LOGAN. REMEMBER?
FUTT
ROWFFF RRUFF RRAARRAR
D...DAMMIT.

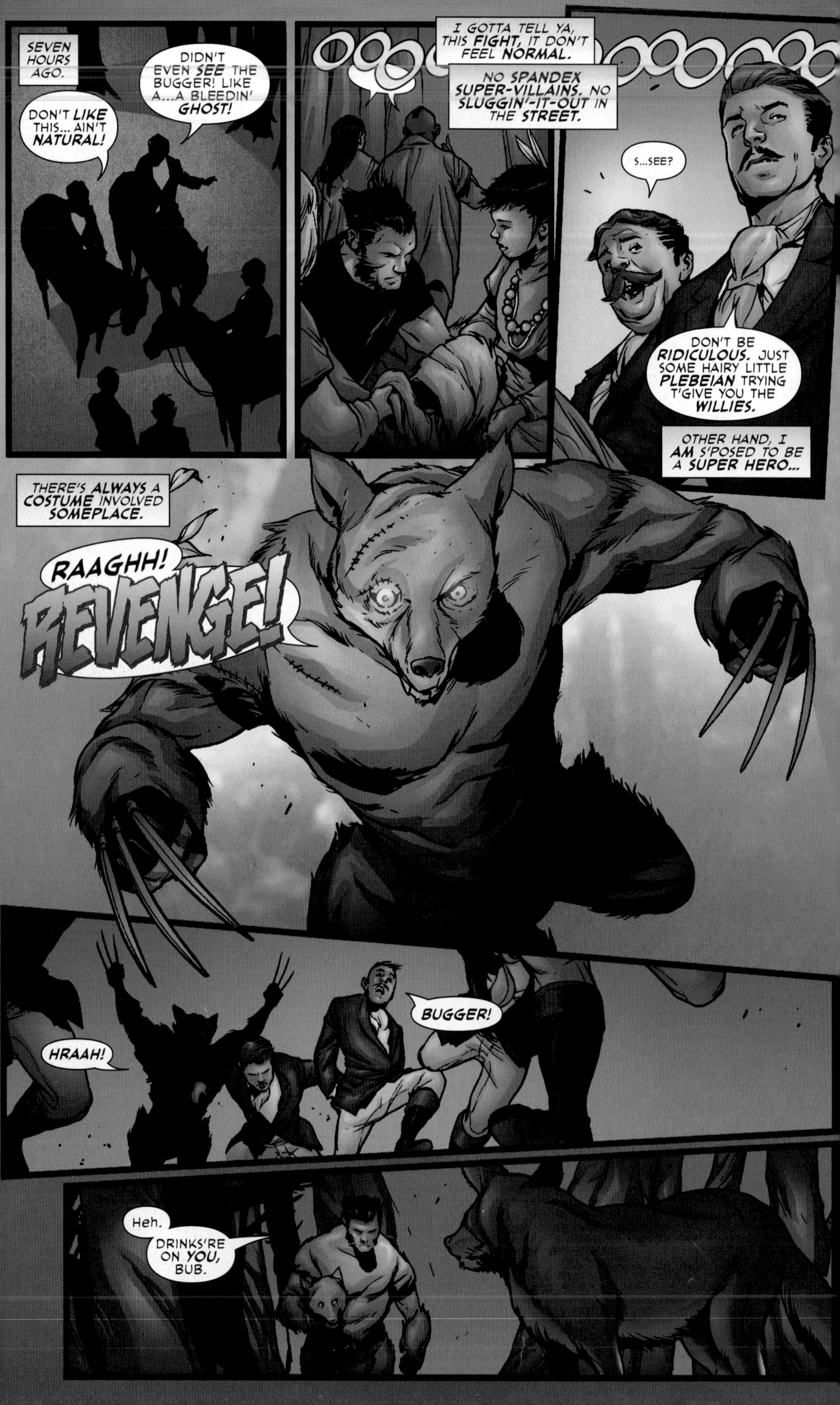
SEVEN HOURS AGO.
DON'T LIKE THIS... AIN'T NATURAL!
DIDN'T EVEN SEE THE BUGGER! LIKE A...A BLEEDIN' GHOST!
I GOTTA TELL YA, THIS FIGHT, IT DON'T FEEL NORMAL.
NO SPANDEX SUPER-VILLAINS. NO SLUGGIN'-IT-OUT IN THE STREET.
S...SEE?
DON'T BE RIDICULOUS. JUST SOME HAIRY LITTLE PLEBEIAN TRYING T'GIVE YOU THE WILLIES.
OTHER HAND, I AM S'POSED TO BE A SUPER HERO...
THERE'S ALWAYS A COSTUME INVOLVED SOMEPLACE.
RAAGHH! REVENGE!
BUGGER!
HRAAH!
Heh.
DRINKS'RE ON YOU, BUB.

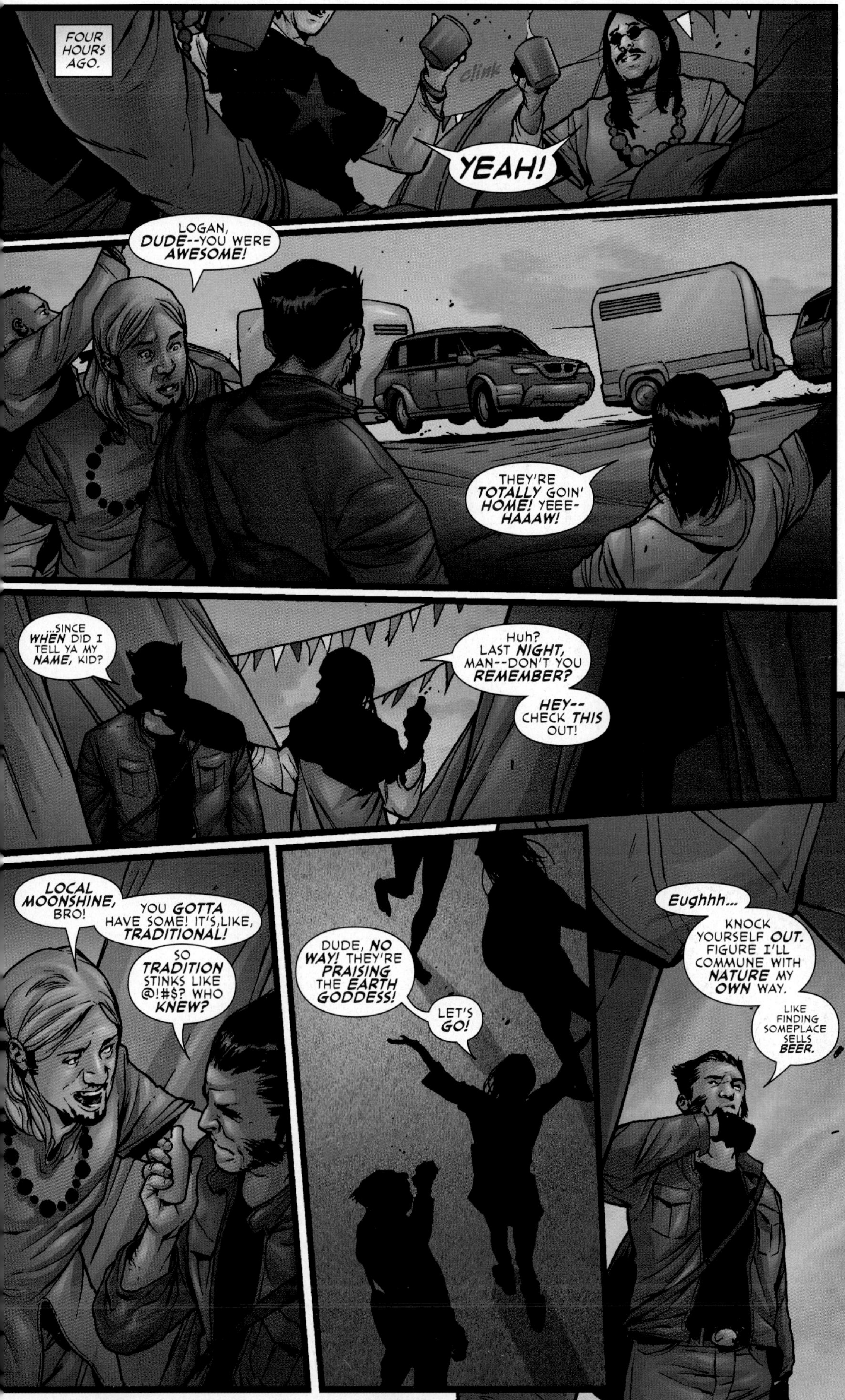
FOUR HOURS AGO.
clink
YEAH!
LOGAN, DUDE--YOU WERE AWESOME!
THEY'RE TOTALLY GOIN' HOME! YEEE-HAAAW!
...SINCE WHEN DID I TELL YA MY NAME, KID?
Huh? LAST NIGHT, MAN--DON'T YOU REMEMBER?
HEY--CHECK THIS OUT!
LOCAL MOONSHINE, BRO!
YOU GOTTA HAVE SOME! IT'S,LIKE, TRADITIONAL!
SO TRADITION STINKS LIKE @!#$? WHO KNEW?
DUDE, NO WAY! THEY'RE PRAISING THE EARTH GODDESS!
LET'S GO!
Eughhh...
KNOCK YOURSELF OUT. FIGURE I'LL COMMUNE WITH NATURE MY OWN WAY.
LIKE FINDING SOMEPLACE SELLS BEER.

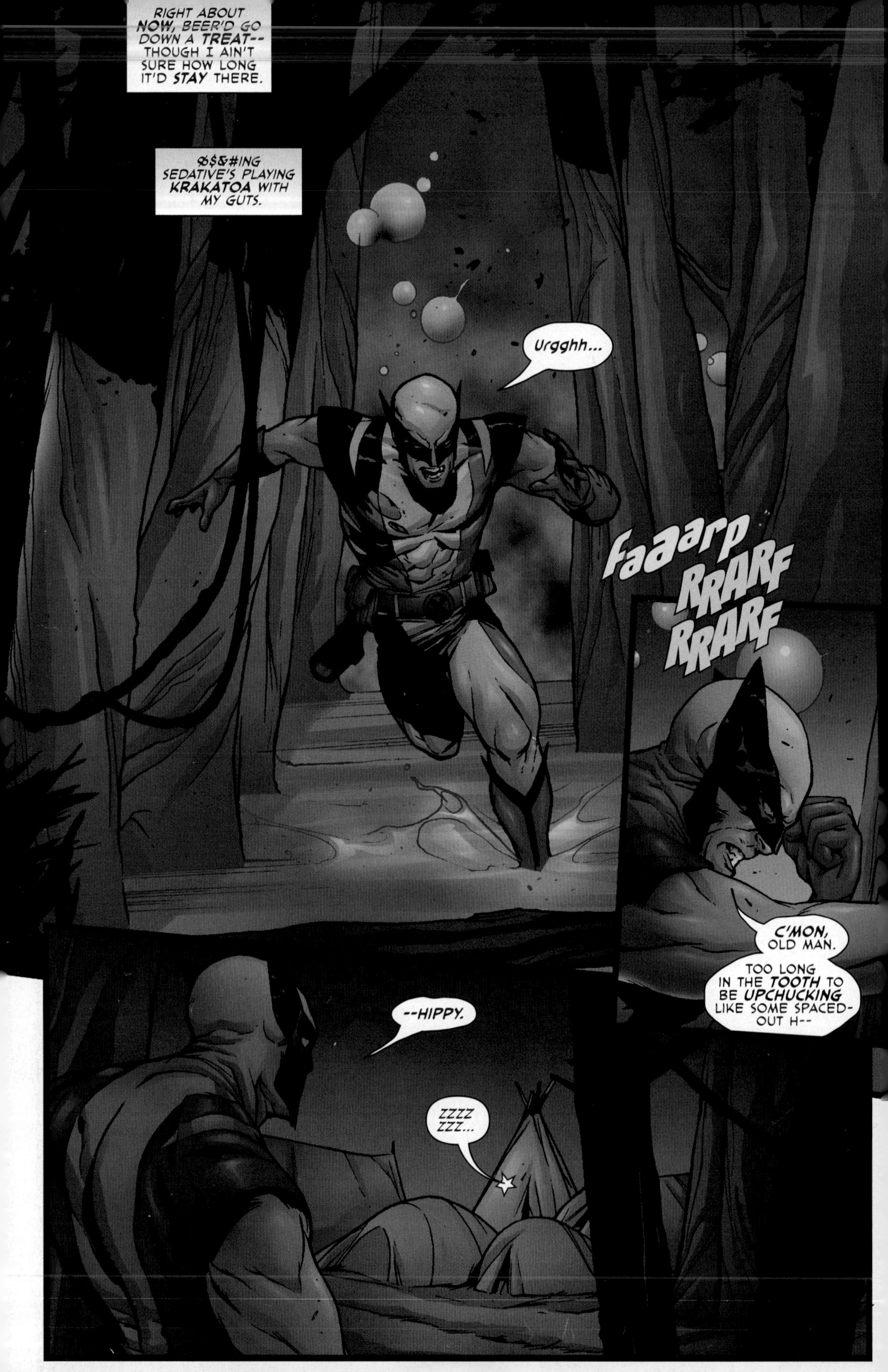
RIGHT ABOUT NOW, BEER'D GO DOWN A TREAT-- THOUGH I AIN'T SURE HOW LONG IT'D STAY THERE.
%$&#ING SEDATIVE'S PLAYING KRAKATOA WITH MY GUTS.
Urgghh...
Faaarp
RRARF
RRARF
C'MON, OLD MAN.
TOO LONG IN THE TOOTH TO BE UPCHUCKING LIKE SOME SPACED-OUT H--
--HIPPY.
ZZZZ ZZZ...

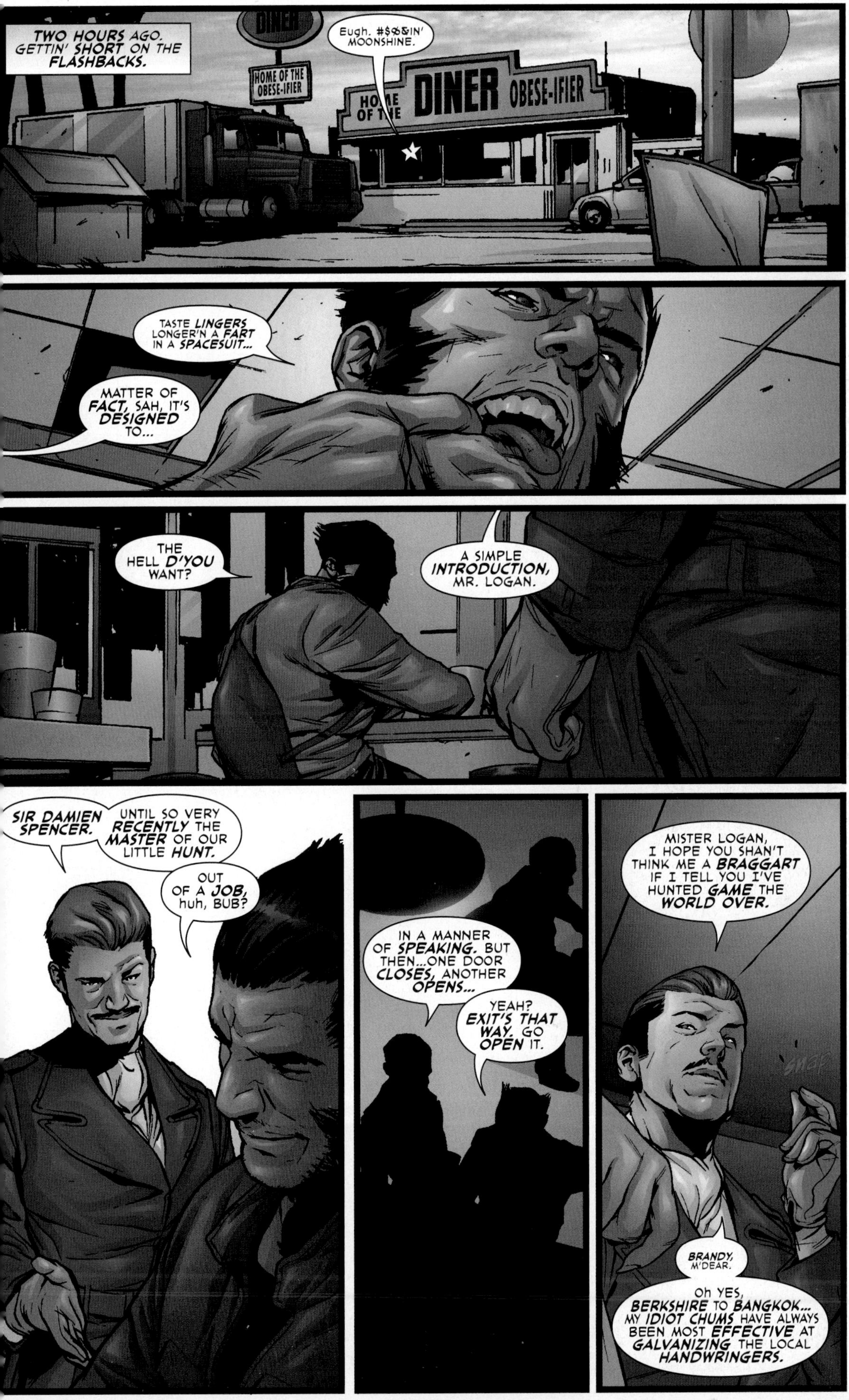
TWO HOURS AGO. GETTIN' SHORT ON THE FLASHBACKS.
DINER
HOME OF THE OBESE-IFIER
Eugh. #$%&IN' MOONSHINE.
HOME OF THE DINER OBESE-IFIER
TASTE LINGERS LONGER'N A FART IN A SPACESUIT...
MATTER OF FACT, SAH, IT'S DESIGNED TO...
THE HELL D'YOU WANT?
A SIMPLE INTRODUCTION, MR. LOGAN.
SIR DAMIEN SPENCER.
UNTIL SO VERY RECENTLY THE MASTER OF OUR LITTLE HUNT.
OUT OF A JOB, huh, BUB?
IN A MANNER OF SPEAKING. BUT THEN...ONE DOOR CLOSES, ANOTHER OPENS...
YEAH? EXIT'S THAT WAY. GO OPEN IT.
MISTER LOGAN, I HOPE YOU SHAN'T THINK ME A BRAGGART IF I TELL YOU I'VE HUNTED GAME THE WORLD OVER.
SNAP
BRANDY, M'DEAR.
Oh YES, BERKSHIRE TO BANGKOK... MY IDIOT CHUMS HAVE ALWAYS BEEN MOST EFFECTIVE AT GALVANIZING THE LOCAL HANDWRINGERS.

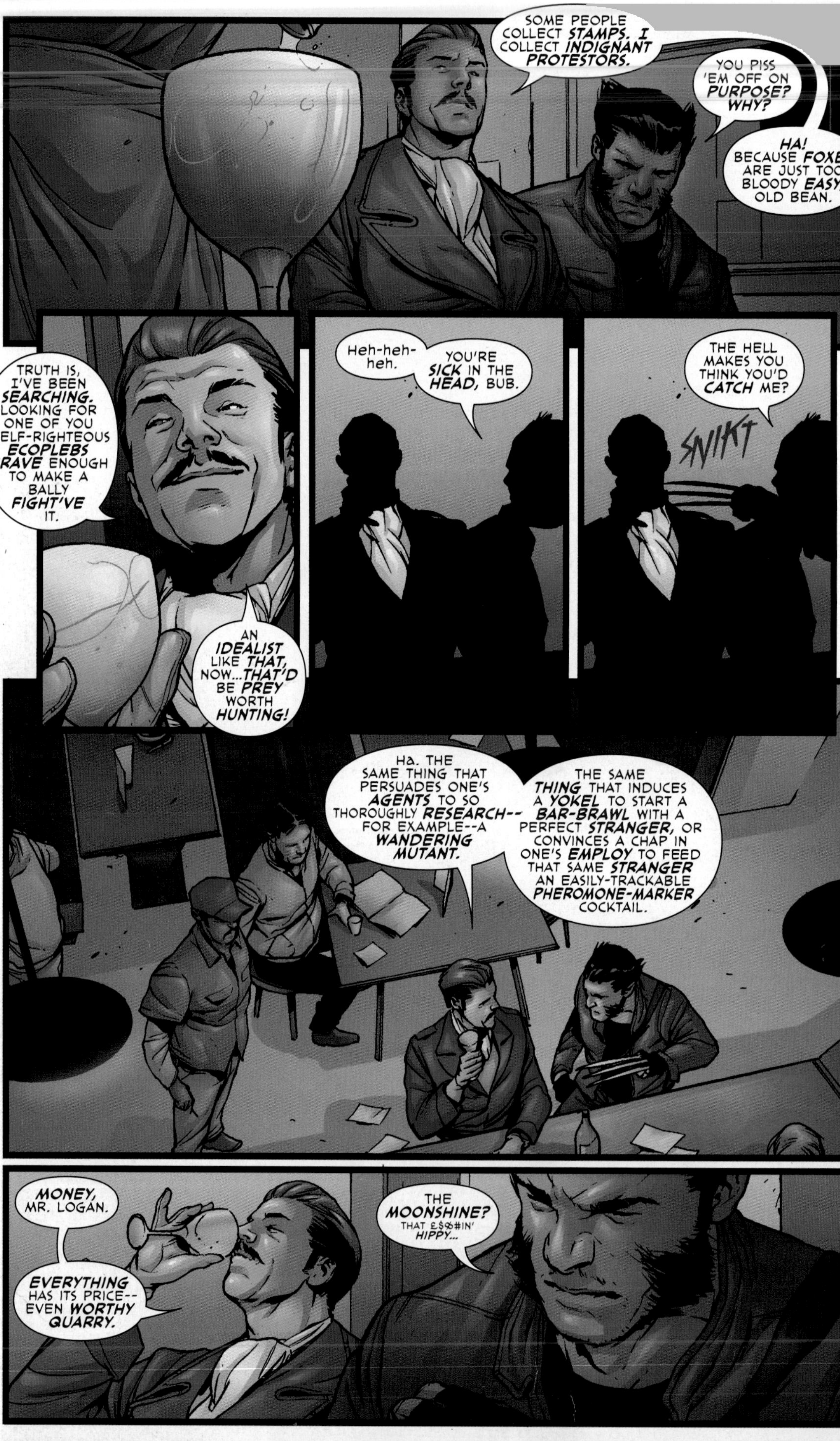
SOME PEOPLE COLLECT STAMPS. I COLLECT INDIGNANT PROTESTORS.
YOU PISS 'EM OFF ON PURPOSE? WHY?
HA! BECAUSE FOXES ARE JUST TOO BLOODY EASY, OLD BEAN.
TRUTH IS, I'VE BEEN SEARCHING. LOOKING FOR ONE OF YOU SELF-RIGHTEOUS ECOPLEBS BRAVE ENOUGH TO MAKE A BALLY FIGHT'VE IT.
AN IDEALIST LIKE THAT, NOW...THAT'D BE PREY WORTH HUNTING!
Heh-heh-heh.
YOU'RE SICK IN THE HEAD, BUB.
THE HELL MAKES YOU THINK YOU'D CATCH ME?
SNIKT
Ha. THE SAME THING THAT PERSUADES ONE'S AGENTS TO SO THOROUGHLY RESEARCH-- FOR EXAMPLE--A WANDERING MUTANT.
THE SAME THING THAT INDUCES A YOKEL TO START A BAR-BRAWL WITH A PERFECT STRANGER, OR CONVINCES A CHAP IN ONE'S EMPLOY TO FEED THAT SAME STRANGER AN EASILY-TRACKABLE PHEROMONE-MARKER COCKTAIL.
MONEY, MR. LOGAN.
EVERYTHING HAS ITS PRICE-- EVEN WORTHY QUARRY.
THE MOONSHINE? THAT £$%#IN' HIPPY...

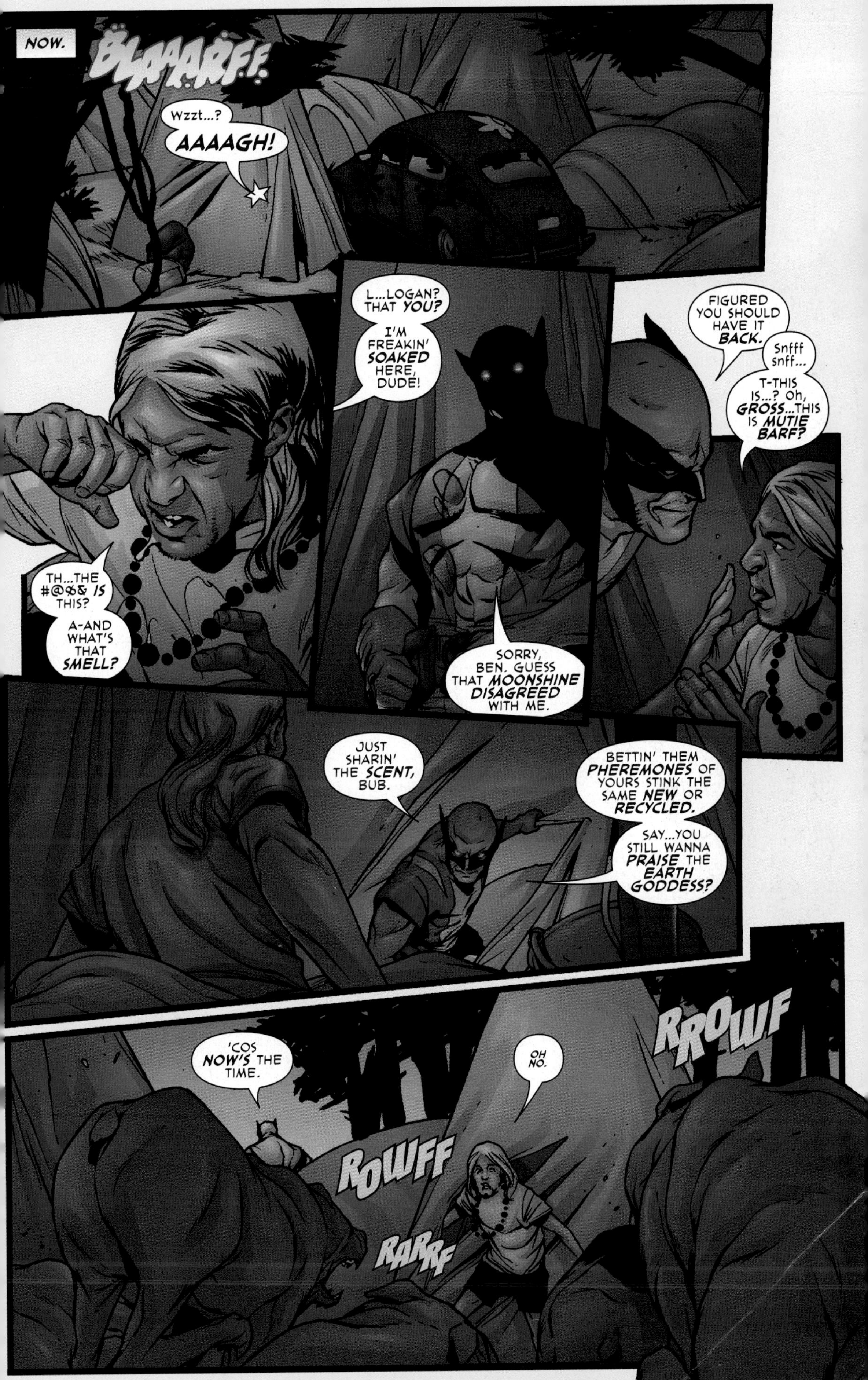
NOW.
BLAAARF.F.
Wzzt...?
AAAAGH!
L...LOGAN? THAT YOU?
I'M FREAKIN' SOAKED HERE, DUDE!
TH...THE #@%& IS THIS?
A-AND WHAT'S THAT SMELL?
SORRY, BEN. GUESS THAT MOONSHINE DISAGREED WITH ME.
FIGURED YOU SHOULD HAVE IT BACK.
Snfff snff...
T-THIS IS...? Oh, GROSS...THIS IS MUTIE BARF?
JUST SHARIN' THE SCENT, BUB.
BETTIN' THEM PHEREMONES OF YOURS STINK THE SAME NEW OR RECYCLED.
SAY...YOU STILL WANNA PRAISE THE EARTH GODDESS?
'COS NOW'S THE TIME.
OH NO.
RROWF
ROWFF
RARRF

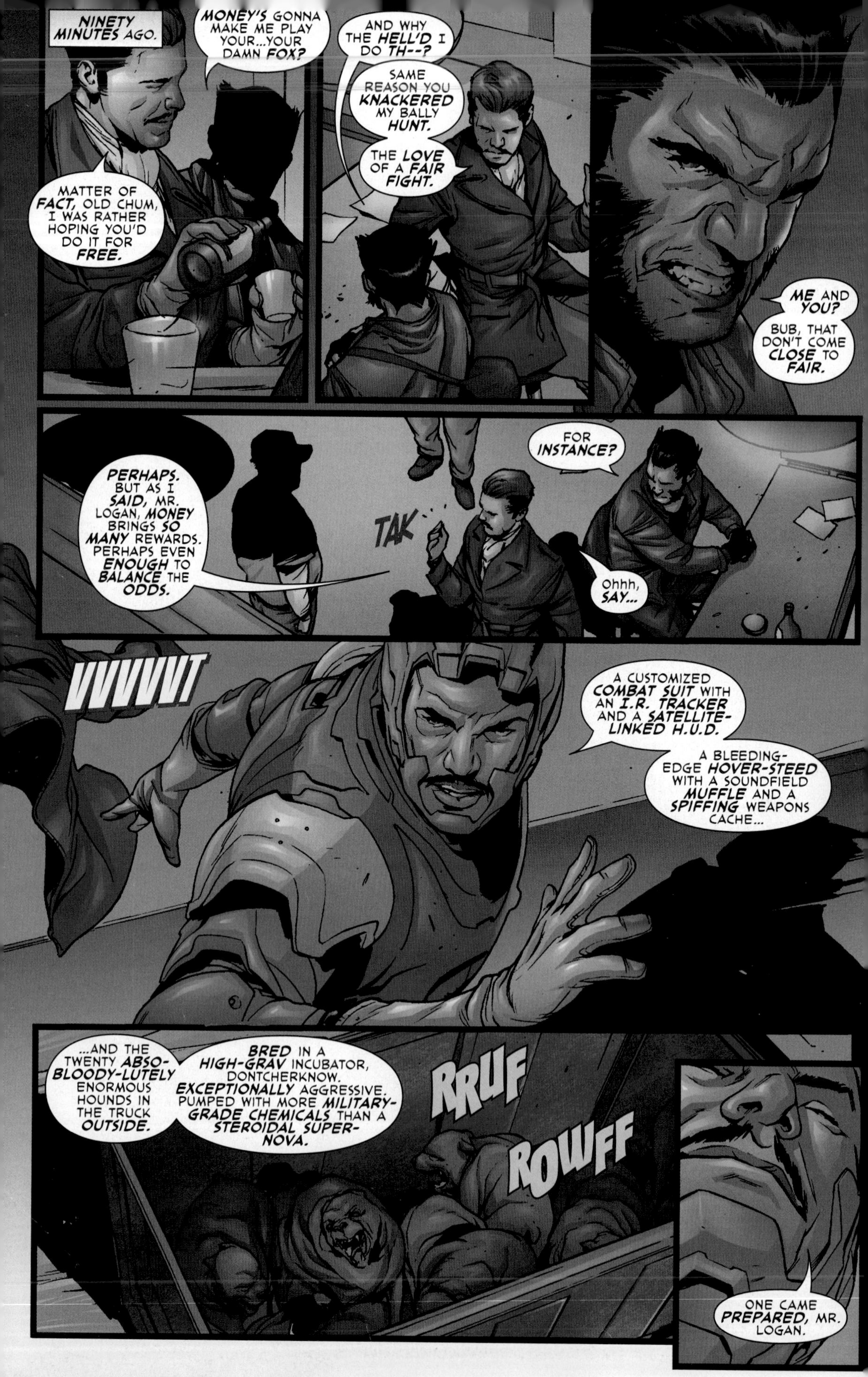
NINETY MINUTES AGO.
MONEY'S GONNA MAKE ME PLAY YOUR...YOUR DAMN FOX?
MATTER OF FACT, OLD CHUM, I WAS RATHER HOPING YOU'D DO IT FOR FREE.
AND WHY THE HELL'D I DO TH--?
SAME REASON YOU KNACKERED MY BALLY HUNT.
THE LOVE OF A FAIR FIGHT.
ME AND YOU?
BUB, THAT DON'T COME CLOSE TO FAIR.
PERHAPS. BUT AS I SAID, MR. LOGAN, MONEY BRINGS SO MANY REWARDS. PERHAPS EVEN ENOUGH TO BALANCE THE ODDS.
TAK
FOR INSTANCE?
Ohhh, SAY...
VVVVVVT
A CUSTOMIZED COMBAT SUIT WITH AN I.R. TRACKER AND A SATELLITE-LINKED H.U.D.
A BLEEDING-EDGE HOVER-STEED WITH A SOUNDFIELD MUFFLE AND A SPIFFING WEAPONS CACHE...
...AND THE TWENTY ABSO-BLOODY-LUTELY ENORMOUS HOUNDS IN THE TRUCK OUTSIDE.
BRED IN A HIGH-GRAV INCUBATOR, DONTCHERKNOW. EXCEPTIONALLY AGGRESSIVE. PUMPED WITH MORE MILITARY-GRADE CHEMICALS THAN A STEROIDAL SUPER-NOVA.
RRUF
ROWFF
ONE CAME PREPARED, MR. LOGAN.

... NO *DICE.* I AIN'T YOUR DAMN *TOY,* ENGLISH.

PITY. THEN I'M AFRAID YOU LEAVE ME NO *CHOICE,* OLD BEAN...

RUN, MR. LOGAN. RUN AS FAST YOU *CAN.*

K-CHKK

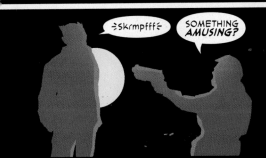

⋛Skrmpfff⋚

SOMETHING *AMUSING?*

Heh...THEM *AGENTS* OF YOURS'D *REALLY* DONE THEIR *HOMEWORK,* BUB, YOU'D KNOW A *GUN* AIN'T MUCH *INCENTIVE* T'ME.

I'M WILLING TO WAGER THERE ARE ONE OR TWO *SOFT PARTS* OF YOUR ANATOMY *LACKING A METAL CORE.*

GOIN' FOR A *LEAK. DON'T* BE HERE WHEN I GET *BACK.*

TRANQUILIZERS, YOU CANUCK *OIK.*

I'LL HAVE YOU COUNTING *SHEEP* BEFORE THOSE *TOOTHPICKS* OF YOURS ARE EVEN *BARED.*

THEY WON'T LOOK TOO *IMPRESSIVE* HUNG ABOVE MY *MANTEL,* NO DOUBT...

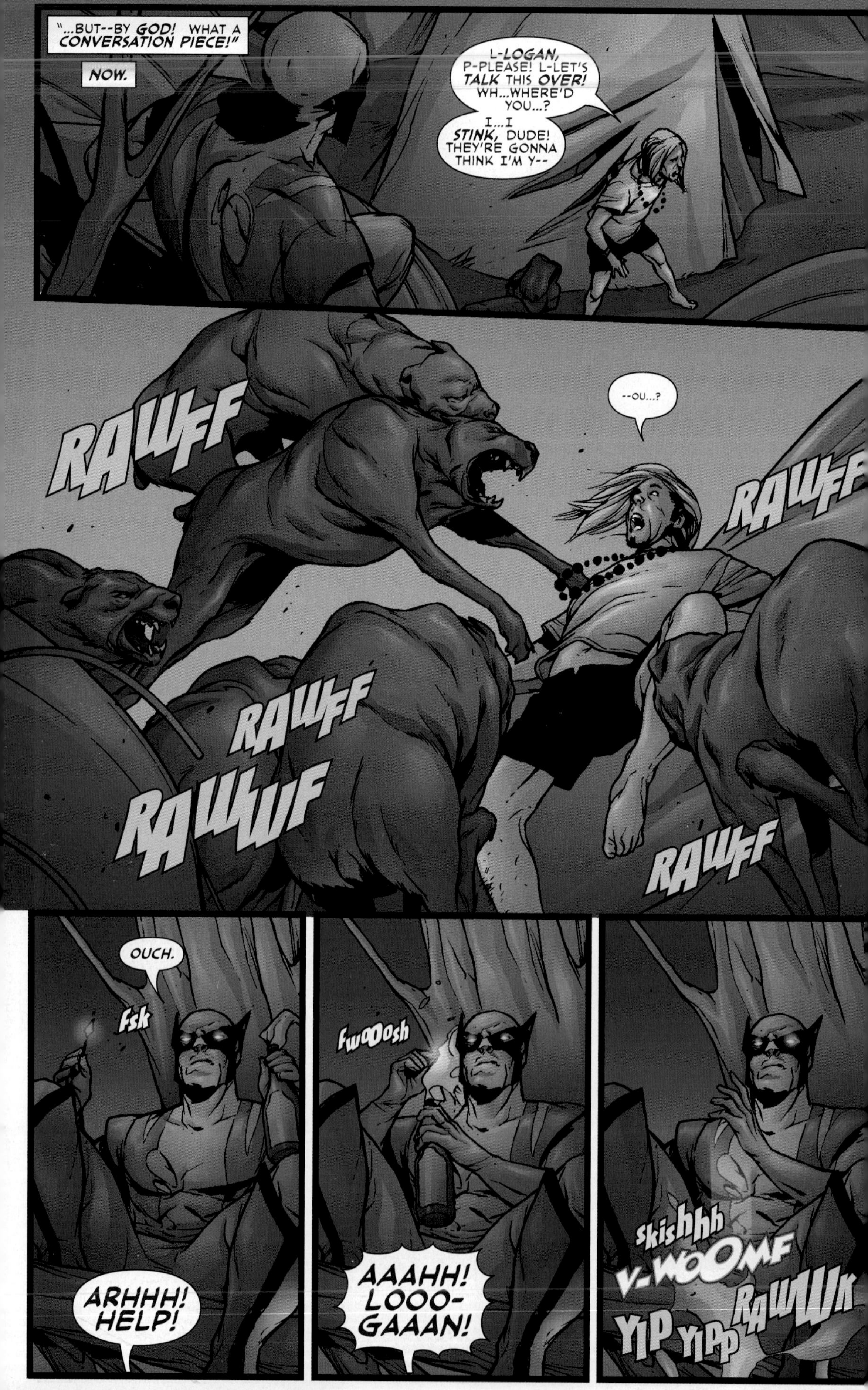

"...BUT--BY GOD! WHAT A CONVERSATION PIECE!"
NOW.
L-LOGAN, P-PLEASE! L-LET'S TALK THIS OVER! WH...WHERE'D YOU...?
I...I STINK, DUDE! THEY'RE GONNA THINK I'M Y--
RAWFF
--OU...?
RAWFF
RAWFF
RAWWF
RAWFF
OUCH.
Fsk
ARHHH! HELP!
fwoOosh
AAAHH! LOOO-GAAAN!
Skishhh
V-WOOMF
RAUWK
YIP YIPP

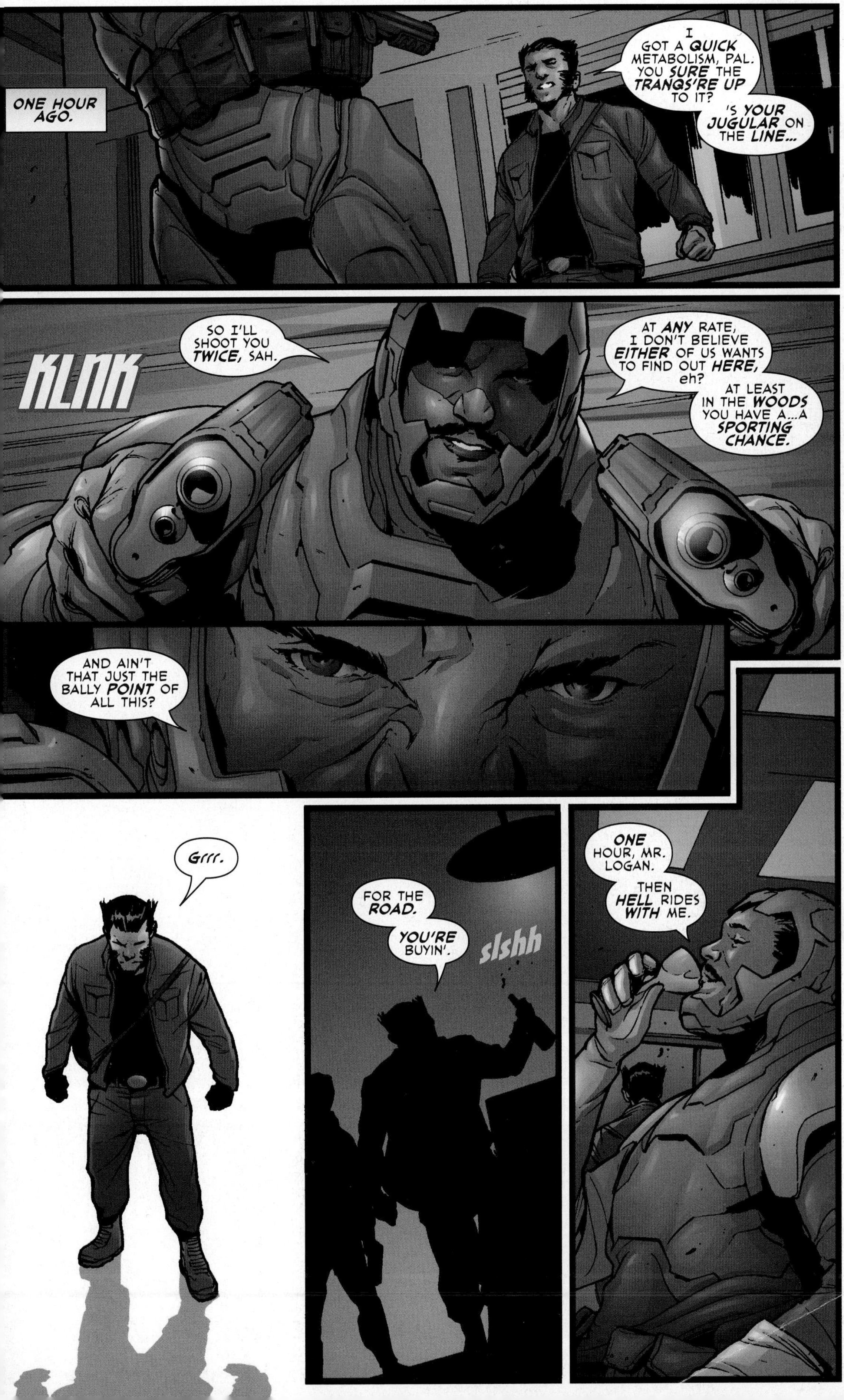
ONE HOUR AGO.
I GOT A QUICK METABOLISM, PAL. YOU SURE THE TRANQS'RE UP TO IT?
'S YOUR JUGULAR ON THE LINE...
KLNK
SO I'LL SHOOT YOU TWICE, SAH.
AT ANY RATE, I DON'T BELIEVE EITHER OF US WANTS TO FIND OUT HERE, eh?
AT LEAST IN THE WOODS YOU HAVE A...A SPORTING CHANCE.
AND AIN'T THAT JUST THE BALLY POINT OF ALL THIS?
Grrr.
FOR THE ROAD.
YOU'RE BUYIN'.
slshh
ONE HOUR, MR. LOGAN.
THEN HELL RIDES WITH ME.

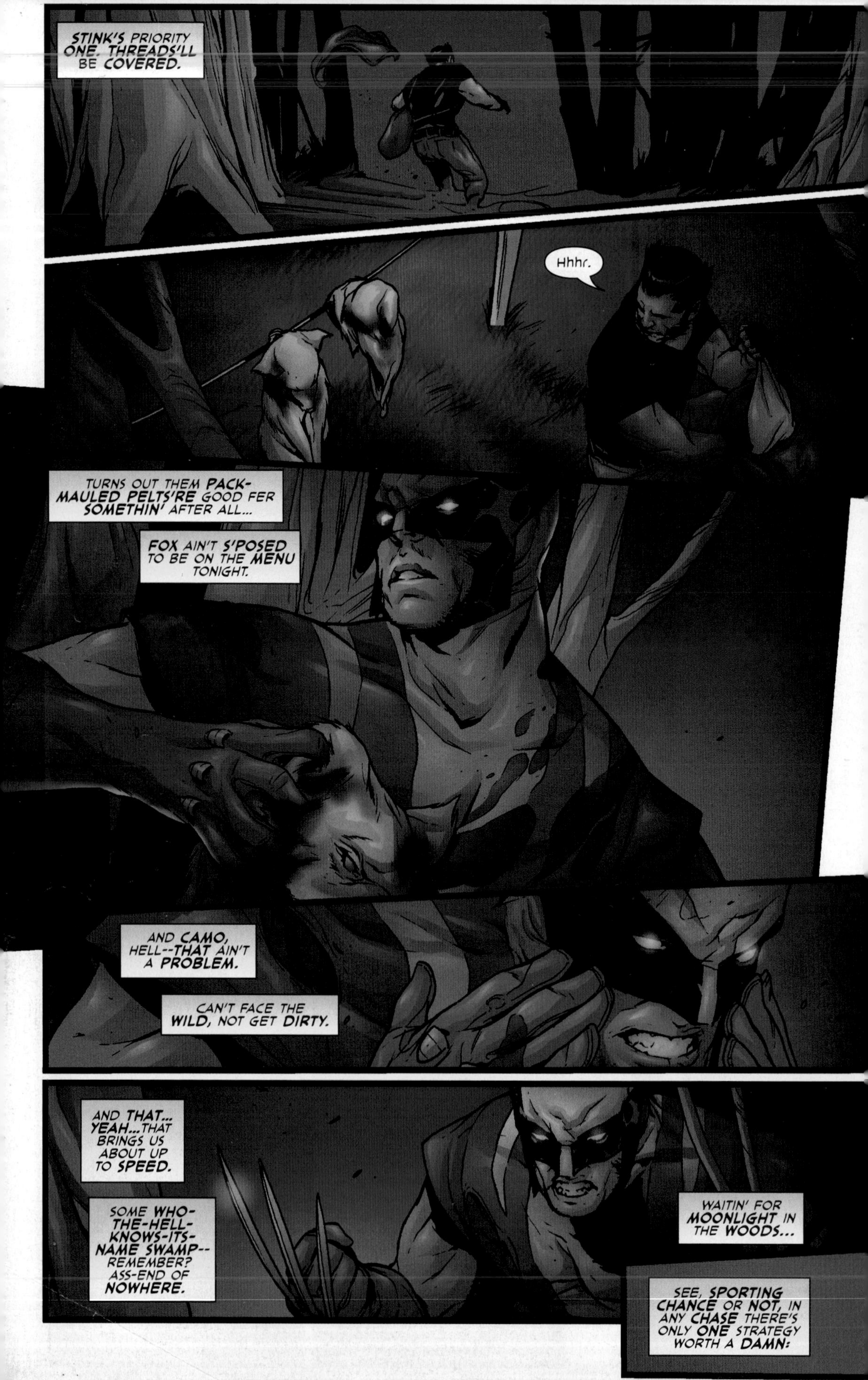

STINK'S PRIORITY ONE. THREADS'LL BE COVERED.
Hhhr.
TURNS OUT THEM PACK-MAULED PELTS'RE GOOD FER SOMETHIN' AFTER ALL...
FOX AIN'T S'POSED TO BE ON THE MENU TONIGHT.
AND CAMO, HELL--THAT AIN'T A PROBLEM.
CAN'T FACE THE WILD, NOT GET DIRTY.
AND THAT... YEAH...THAT BRINGS US ABOUT UP TO SPEED.
SOME WHO-THE-HELL-KNOWS-ITS-NAME SWAMP--REMEMBER? ASS-END OF NOWHERE.
WAITIN' FOR MOONLIGHT IN THE WOODS...
SEE, SPORTING CHANCE OR NOT, IN ANY CHASE THERE'S ONLY ONE STRATEGY WORTH A DAMN:

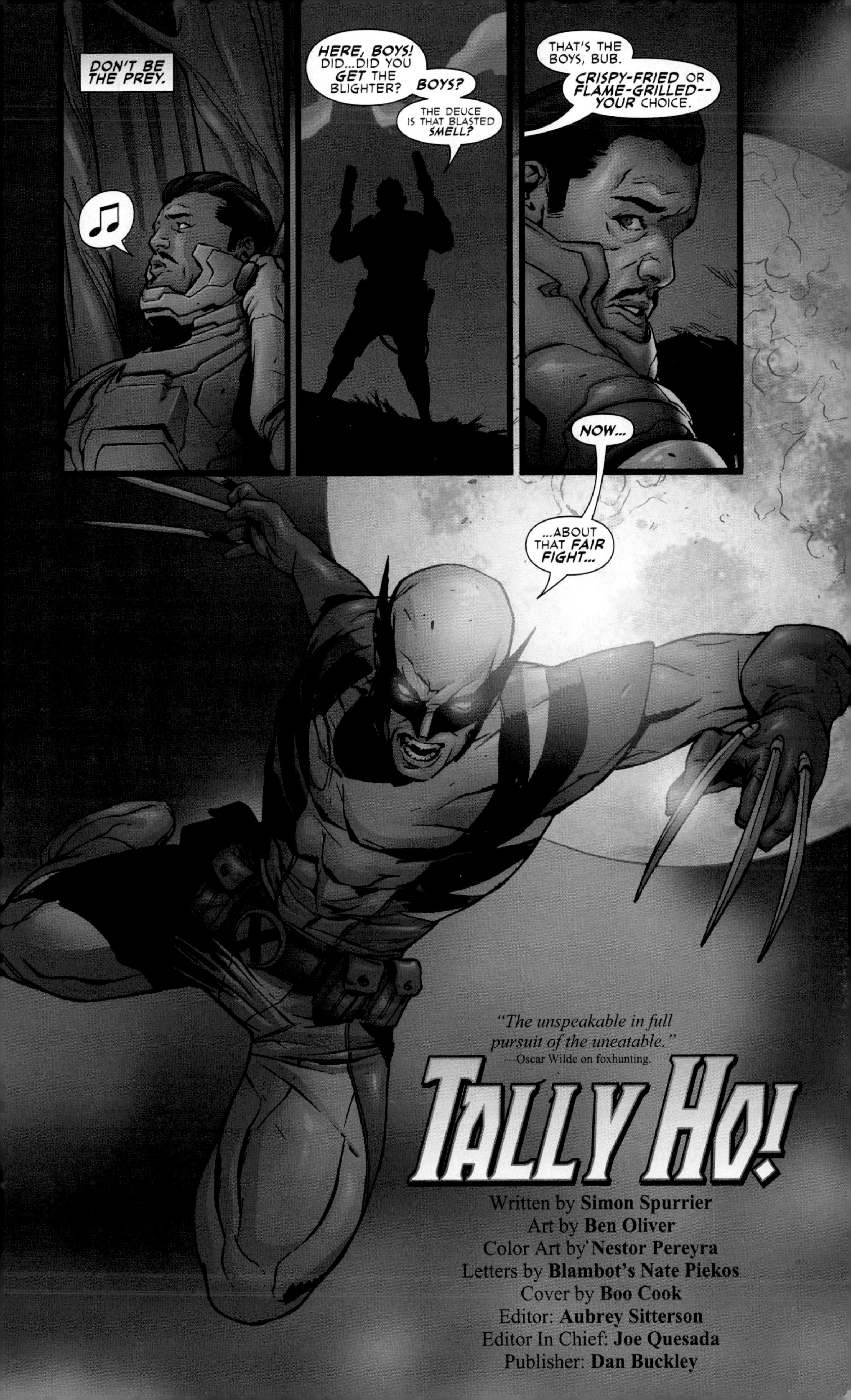
DON'T BE THE PREY.
♫
HERE, BOYS! DID...DID YOU GET THE BLIGHTER?
BOYS?
THE DEUCE IS THAT BLASTED SMELL?
THAT'S THE BOYS, BUB. CRISPY-FRIED OR FLAME-GRILLED-- YOUR CHOICE.
NOW...
...ABOUT THAT FAIR FIGHT...
"The unspeakable in full pursuit of the uneatable."
—Oscar Wilde on foxhunting.
TALLY HO!
Written by Simon Spurrier
Art by Ben Oliver
Color Art by Nestor Pereyra
Letters by Blambot's Nate Piekos
Cover by Boo Cook
Editor: Aubrey Sitterson
Editor In Chief: Joe Quesada
Publisher: Dan Buckley

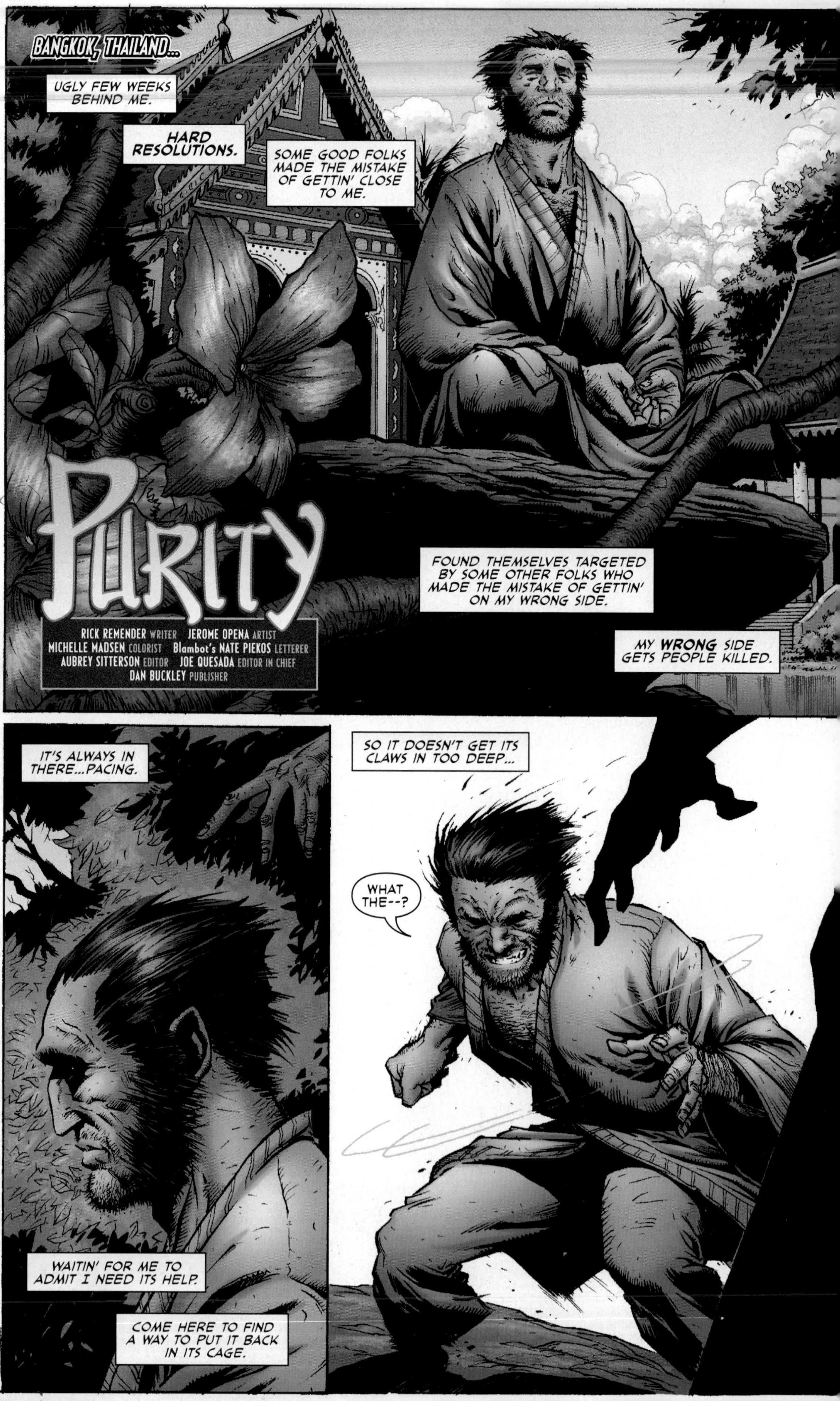

BANGKOK, THAILAND...
UGLY FEW WEEKS BEHIND ME.
HARD RESOLUTIONS.
SOME GOOD FOLKS MADE THE MISTAKE OF GETTIN' CLOSE TO ME.
PURITY
RICK REMENDER WRITER JEROME OPENA ARTIST
MICHELLE MADSEN COLORIST Blambot's NATE PIEKOS LETTERER
AUBREY SITTERSON EDITOR JOE QUESADA EDITOR IN CHIEF
DAN BUCKLEY PUBLISHER
FOUND THEMSELVES TARGETED BY SOME OTHER FOLKS WHO MADE THE MISTAKE OF GETTIN' ON MY WRONG SIDE.
MY WRONG SIDE GETS PEOPLE KILLED.
IT'S ALWAYS IN THERE...PACING.
WAITIN' FOR ME TO ADMIT I NEED ITS HELP.
COME HERE TO FIND A WAY TO PUT IT BACK IN ITS CAGE.
SO IT DOESN'T GET ITS CLAWS IN TOO DEEP...
WHAT THE--?

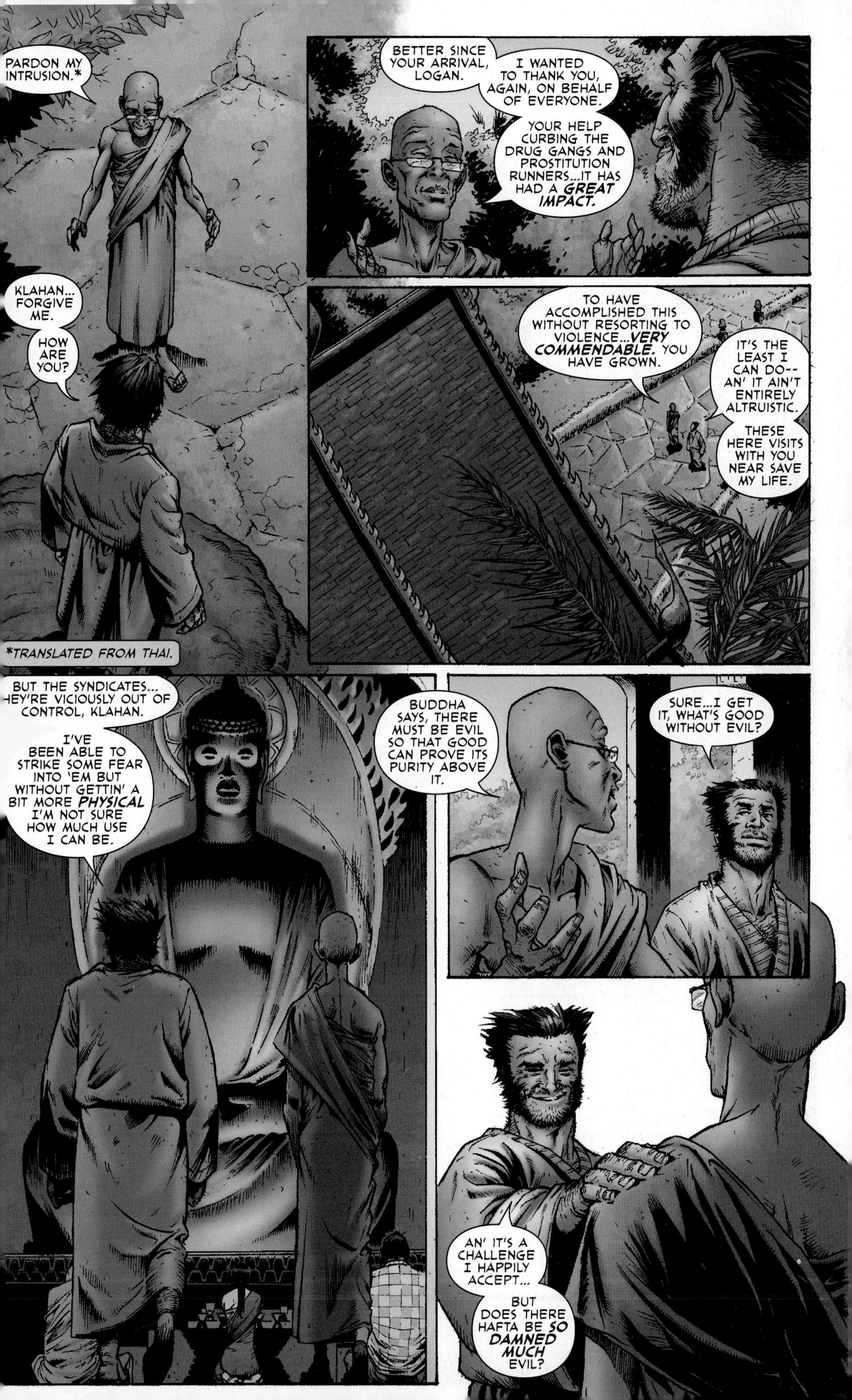
PARDON MY INTRUSION.*
KLAHAN... FORGIVE ME.
HOW ARE YOU?
*TRANSLATED FROM THAI.
BETTER SINCE YOUR ARRIVAL, LOGAN.
I WANTED TO THANK YOU, AGAIN, ON BEHALF OF EVERYONE.
YOUR HELP CURBING THE DRUG GANGS AND PROSTITUTION RUNNERS...IT HAS HAD A GREAT IMPACT.
TO HAVE ACCOMPLISHED THIS WITHOUT RESORTING TO VIOLENCE...VERY COMMENDABLE. YOU HAVE GROWN.
IT'S THE LEAST I CAN DO-- AN' IT AIN'T ENTIRELY ALTRUISTIC.
THESE HERE VISITS WITH YOU NEAR SAVE MY LIFE.
BUT THE SYNDICATES... HEY'RE VICIOUSLY OUT OF CONTROL, KLAHAN.
I'VE BEEN ABLE TO STRIKE SOME FEAR INTO 'EM BUT WITHOUT GETTIN' A BIT MORE PHYSICAL I'M NOT SURE HOW MUCH USE I CAN BE.
BUDDHA SAYS, THERE MUST BE EVIL SO THAT GOOD CAN PROVE ITS PURITY ABOVE IT.
SURE...I GET IT, WHAT'S GOOD WITHOUT EVIL?
AN' IT'S A CHALLENGE I HAPPILY ACCEPT...
BUT DOES THERE HAFTA BE SO DAMNED MUCH EVIL?

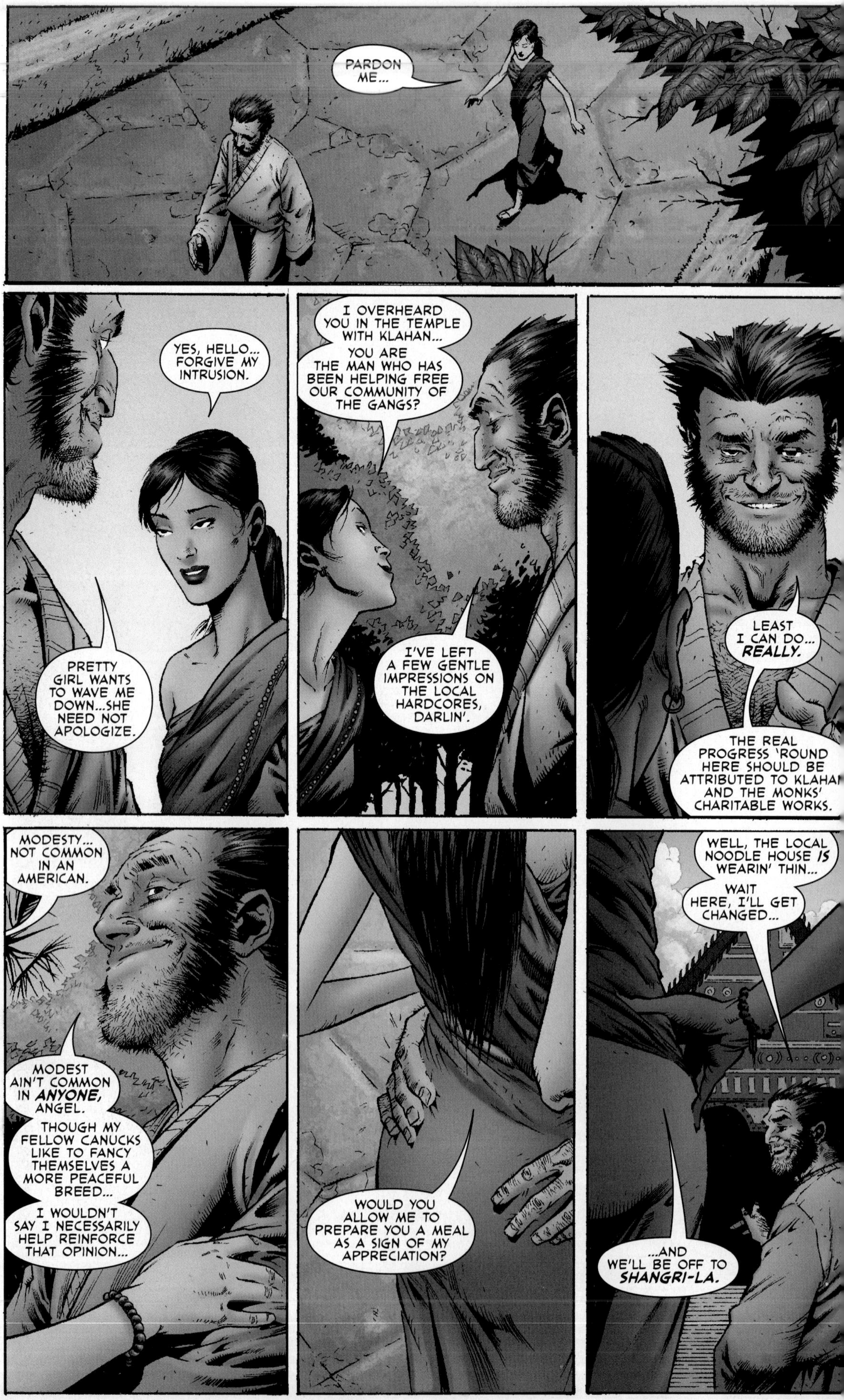
PARDON ME...
YES, HELLO... FORGIVE MY INTRUSION.
PRETTY GIRL WANTS TO WAVE ME DOWN...SHE NEED NOT APOLOGIZE.
I OVERHEARD YOU IN THE TEMPLE WITH KLAHAN...
YOU ARE THE MAN WHO HAS BEEN HELPING FREE OUR COMMUNITY OF THE GANGS?
I'VE LEFT A FEW GENTLE IMPRESSIONS ON THE LOCAL HARDCORES, DARLIN'.
LEAST I CAN DO... REALLY.
THE REAL PROGRESS 'ROUND HERE SHOULD BE ATTRIBUTED TO KLAHA
AND THE MONKS' CHARITABLE WORKS.
MODESTY... NOT COMMON IN AN AMERICAN.
MODEST AIN'T COMMON IN ANYONE, ANGEL.
THOUGH MY FELLOW CANUCKS LIKE TO FANCY THEMSELVES A MORE PEACEFUL BREED...
I WOULDN'T SAY I NECESSARILY HELP REINFORCE THAT OPINION...
WOULD YOU ALLOW ME TO PREPARE YOU A MEAL AS A SIGN OF MY APPRECIATION?
WELL, THE LOCAL NOODLE HOUSE IS WEARIN' THIN...
WAIT HERE, I'LL GET CHANGED...
...AND WE'LL BE OFF TO SHANGRI-LA.

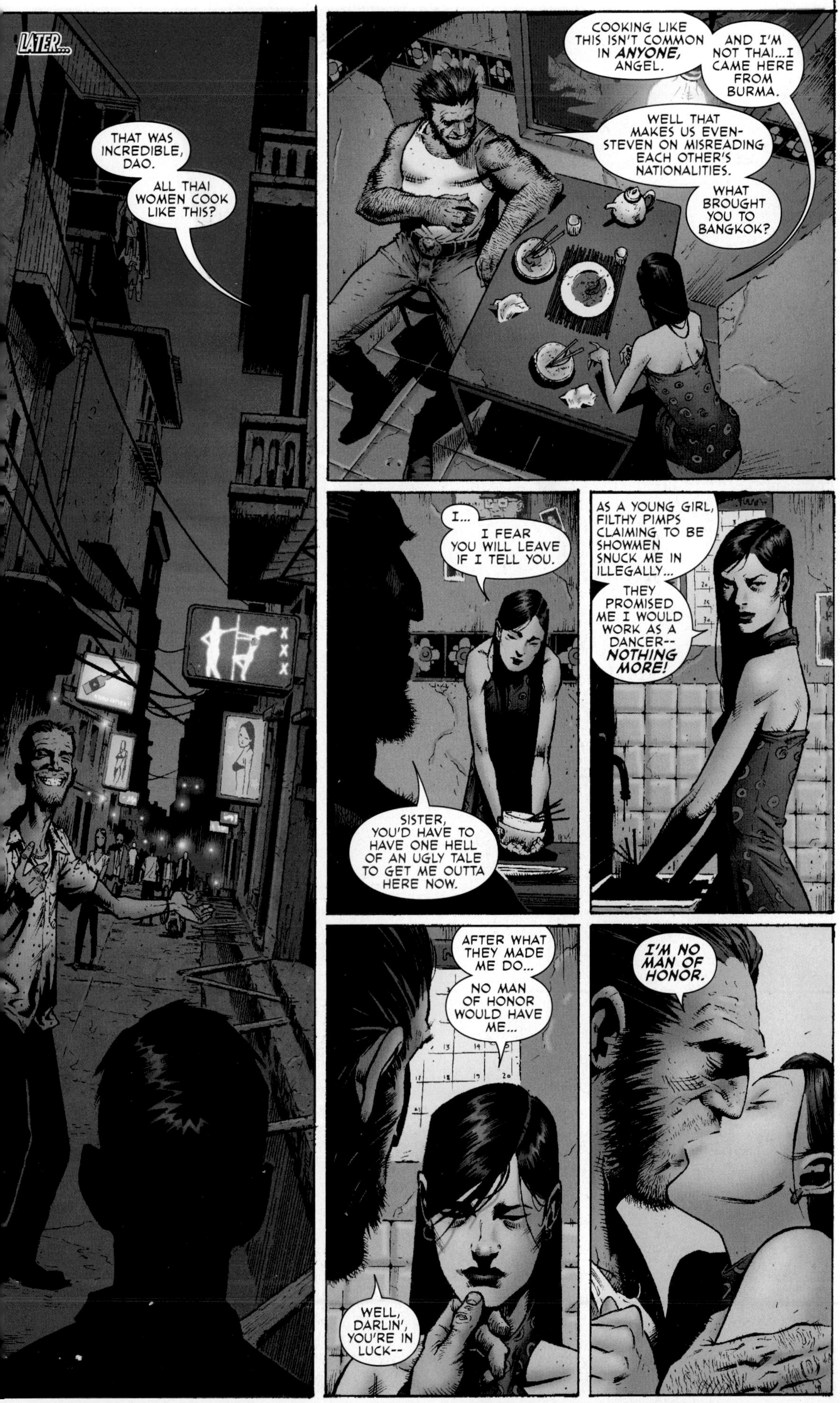
LATER...
THAT WAS INCREDIBLE, DAO.
ALL THAI WOMEN COOK LIKE THIS?
COOKING LIKE THIS ISN'T COMMON IN ANYONE, ANGEL.
AND I'M NOT THAI...I CAME HERE FROM BURMA.
WELL THAT MAKES US EVEN-STEVEN ON MISREADING EACH OTHER'S NATIONALITIES.
WHAT BROUGHT YOU TO BANGKOK?
I...
I FEAR YOU WILL LEAVE IF I TELL YOU.
SISTER, YOU'D HAVE TO HAVE ONE HELL OF AN UGLY TALE TO GET ME OUTTA HERE NOW.
AS A YOUNG GIRL, FILTHY PIMPS CLAIMING TO BE SHOWMEN SNUCK ME IN ILLEGALLY...
THEY PROMISED ME I WOULD WORK AS A DANCER--NOTHING MORE!
AFTER WHAT THEY MADE ME DO...
NO MAN OF HONOR WOULD HAVE ME...
WELL, DARLIN', YOU'RE IN LUCK--
I'M NO MAN OF HONOR.

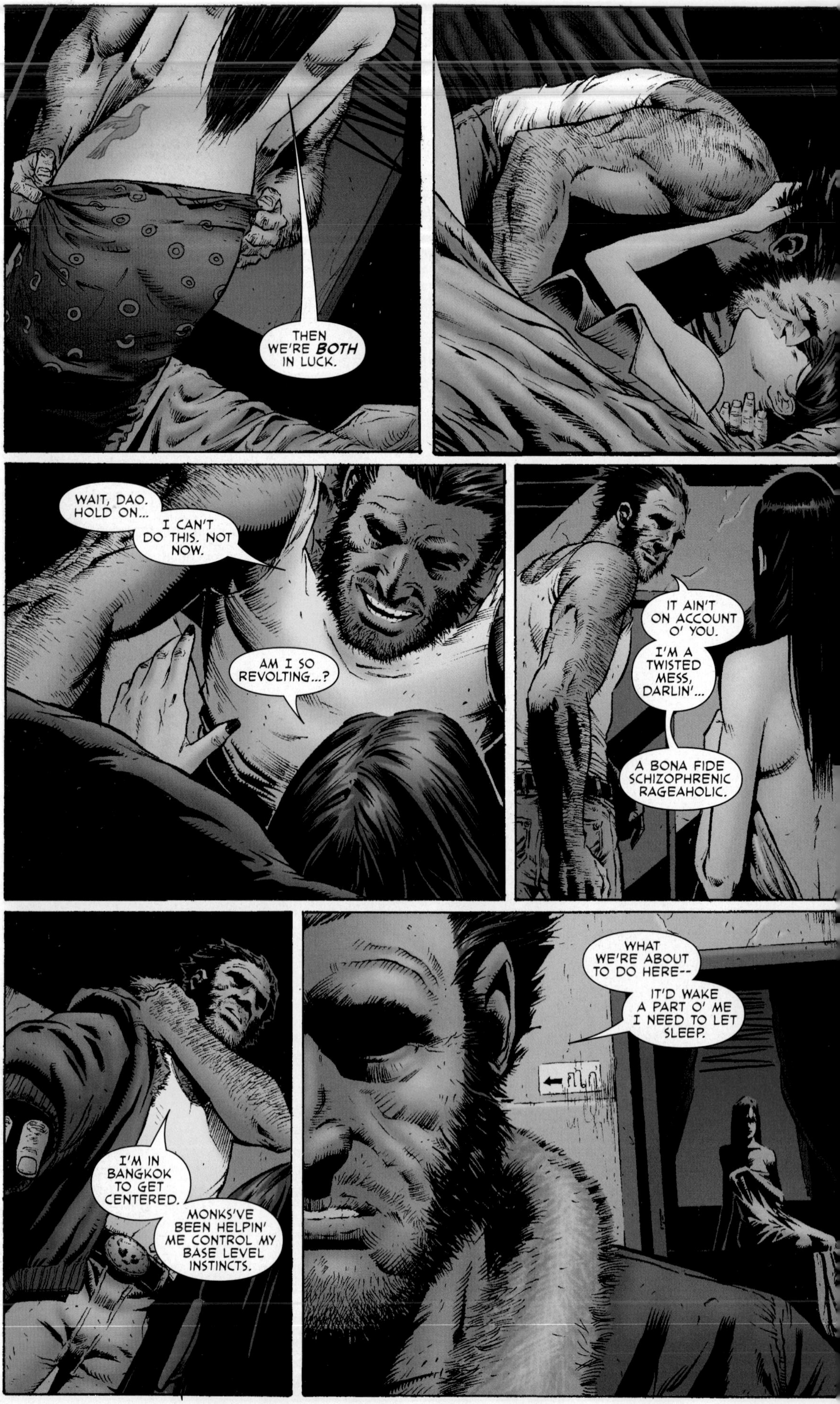
THEN WE'RE *BOTH* IN LUCK.
WAIT, DAO. HOLD ON...
I CAN'T DO THIS. NOT NOW.
AM I SO REVOLTING...?
IT AIN'T ON ACCOUNT O' YOU.
I'M A TWISTED MESS, DARLIN'...
A BONA FIDE SCHIZOPHRENIC RAGEAHOLIC.
I'M IN BANGKOK TO GET CENTERED.
MONKS'VE BEEN HELPIN' ME CONTROL MY BASE LEVEL INSTINCTS.
WHAT WE'RE ABOUT TO DO HERE--
IT'D WAKE A PART O' ME I NEED TO LET SLEEP.

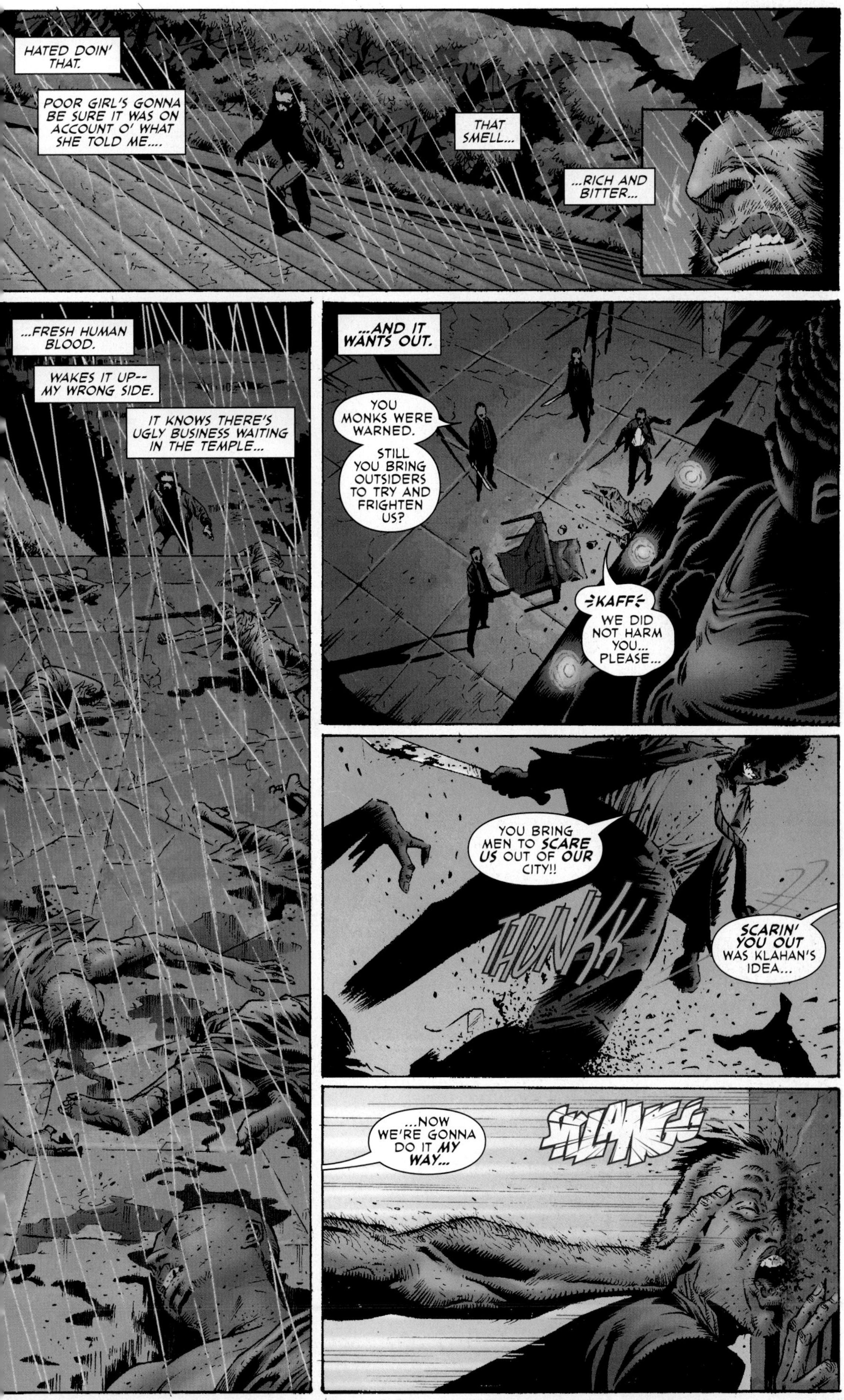
HATED DOIN' THAT.
POOR GIRL'S GONNA BE SURE IT WAS ON ACCOUNT O' WHAT SHE TOLD ME....
THAT SMELL...
...RICH AND BITTER...
...FRESH HUMAN BLOOD.
WAKES IT UP-- MY WRONG SIDE.
IT KNOWS THERE'S UGLY BUSINESS WAITING IN THE TEMPLE...
...AND IT WANTS OUT.
YOU MONKS WERE WARNED.
STILL YOU BRING OUTSIDERS TO TRY AND FRIGHTEN US?
KAFF WE DID NOT HARM YOU... PLEASE...
YOU BRING MEN TO SCARE US OUT OF OUR CITY!!
THUNKK
SCARIN' YOU OUT WAS KLAHAN'S IDEA...
...NOW WE'RE GONNA DO IT MY WAY...
SHLANGG

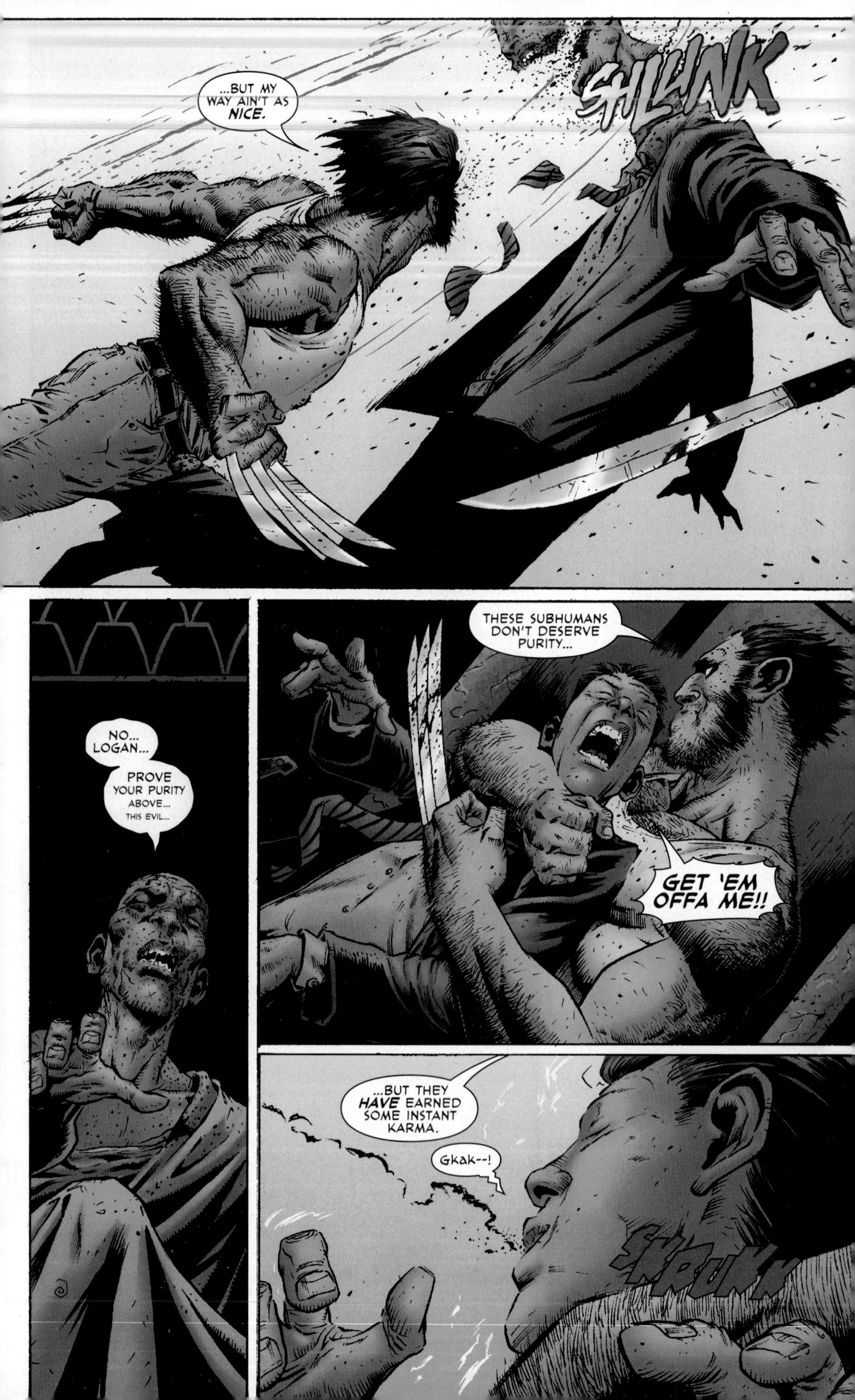
...BUT MY WAY AIN'T AS NICE.
SHLUNK
NO... LOGAN...
PROVE YOUR PURITY ABOVE... THIS EVIL...
THESE SUBHUMANS DON'T DESERVE PURITY...
GET 'EM OFFA ME!!
...BUT THEY HAVE EARNED SOME INSTANT KARMA.
Gkak--!

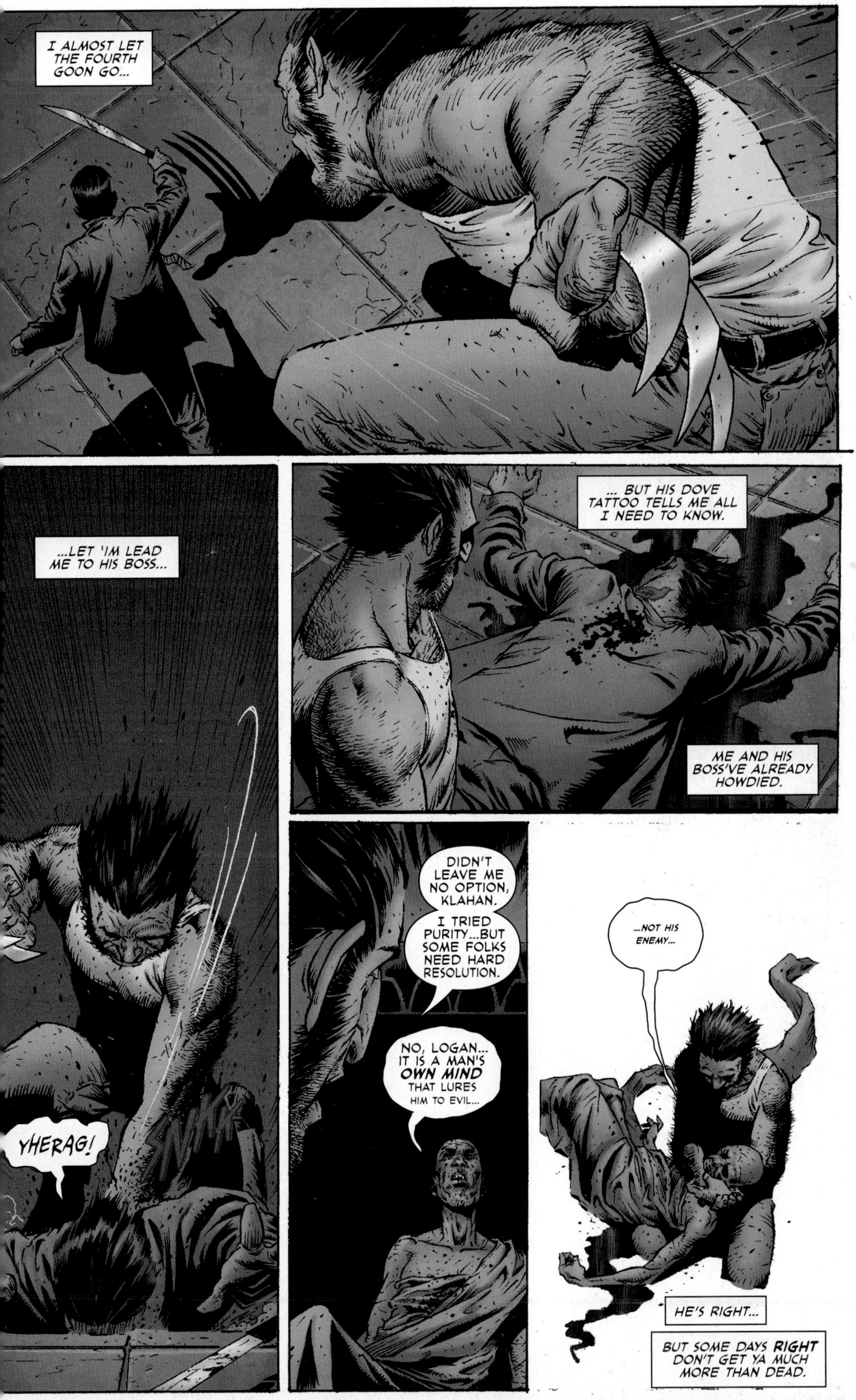
I ALMOST LET THE FOURTH GOON GO...
...LET 'IM LEAD ME TO HIS BOSS...
YHERAG!
... BUT HIS DOVE TATTOO TELLS ME ALL I NEED TO KNOW.
ME AND HIS BOSS'VE ALREADY HOWDIED.
DIDN'T LEAVE ME NO OPTION, KLAHAN.
I TRIED PURITY...BUT SOME FOLKS NEED HARD RESOLUTION.
NO, LOGAN... IT IS A MAN'S OWN MIND THAT LURES HIM TO EVIL...
...NOT HIS ENEMY...
HE'S RIGHT...
BUT SOME DAYS RIGHT DON'T GET YA MUCH MORE THAN DEAD.

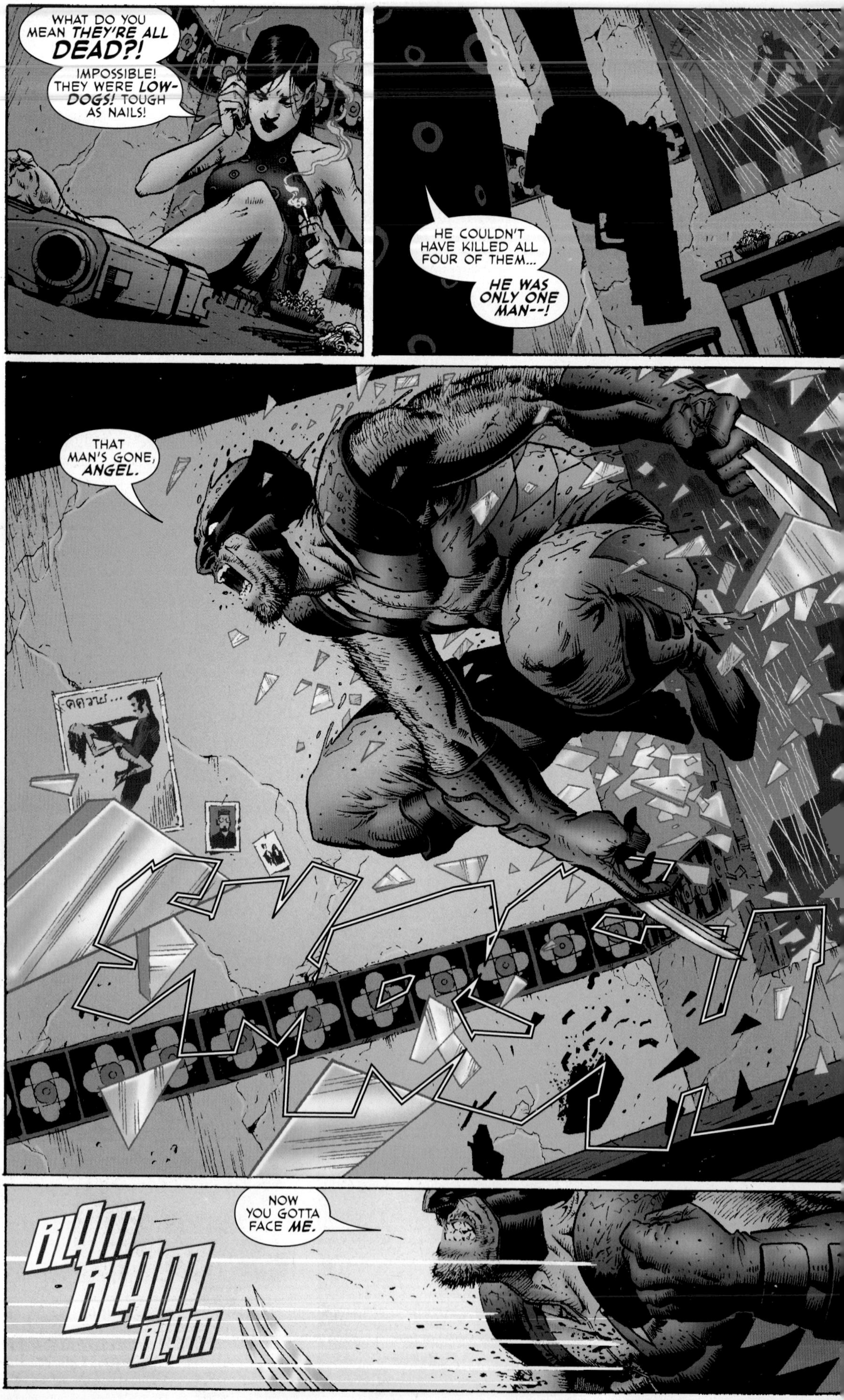

WHAT DO YOU MEAN THEY'RE ALL DEAD?!
IMPOSSIBLE! THEY WERE LOW-DOGS! TOUGH AS NAILS!
HE COULDN'T HAVE KILLED ALL FOUR OF THEM...
HE WAS ONLY ONE MAN--!
THAT MAN'S GONE, ANGEL.
BLAM BLAM BLAM
NOW YOU GOTTA FACE ME.

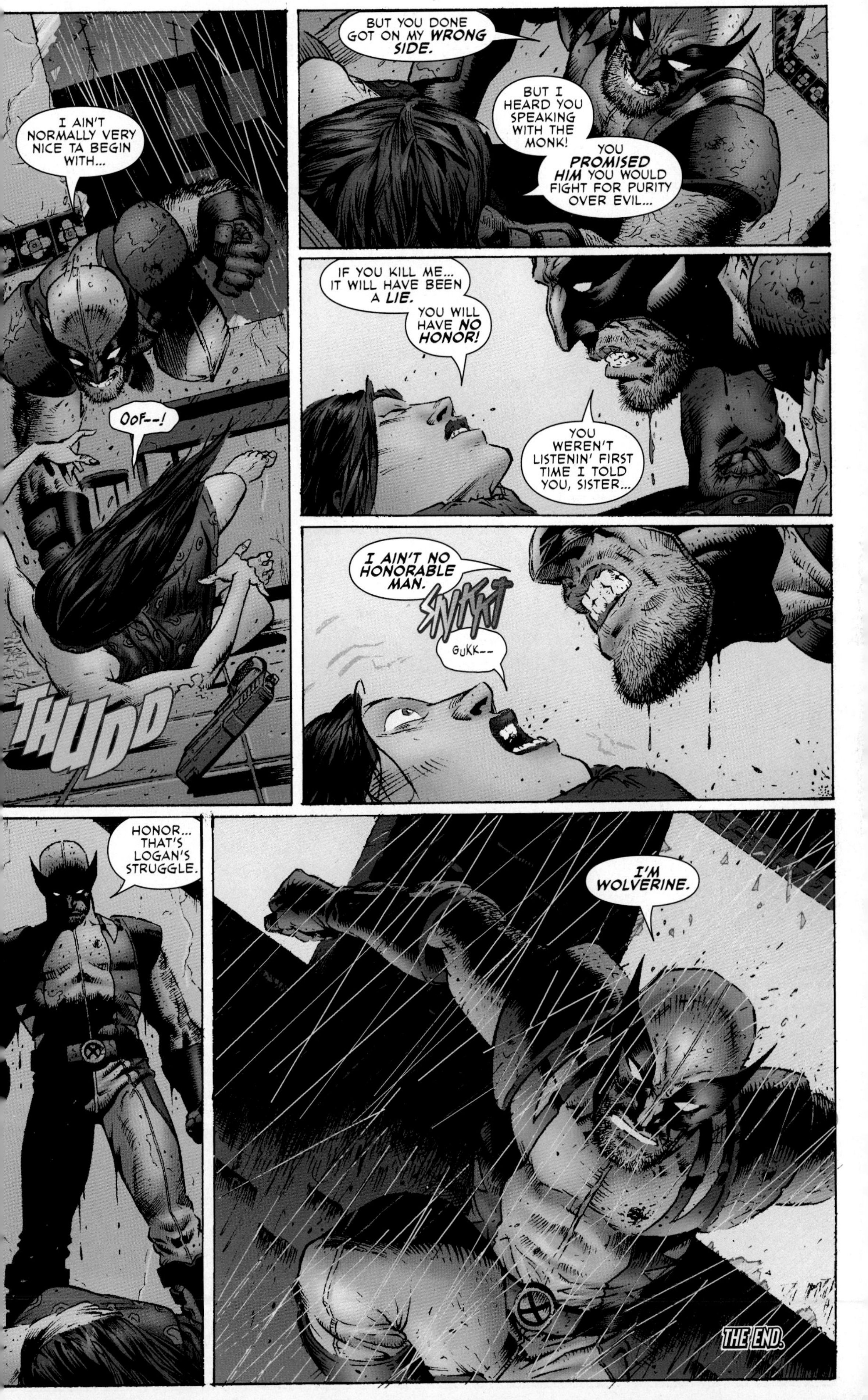
I AIN'T NORMALLY VERY NICE TA BEGIN WITH...
OOF--!
THUDD
BUT YOU DONE GOT ON MY WRONG SIDE.
BUT I HEARD YOU SPEAKING WITH THE MONK!
YOU PROMISED HIM YOU WOULD FIGHT FOR PURITY OVER EVIL...
IF YOU KILL ME... IT WILL HAVE BEEN A LIE.
YOU WILL HAVE NO HONOR!
YOU WEREN'T LISTENIN' FIRST TIME I TOLD YOU, SISTER...
I AIN'T NO HONORABLE MAN.
SNIKKT
GUKK--
HONOR... THAT'S LOGAN'S STRUGGLE.
I'M WOLVERINE.
THE END.

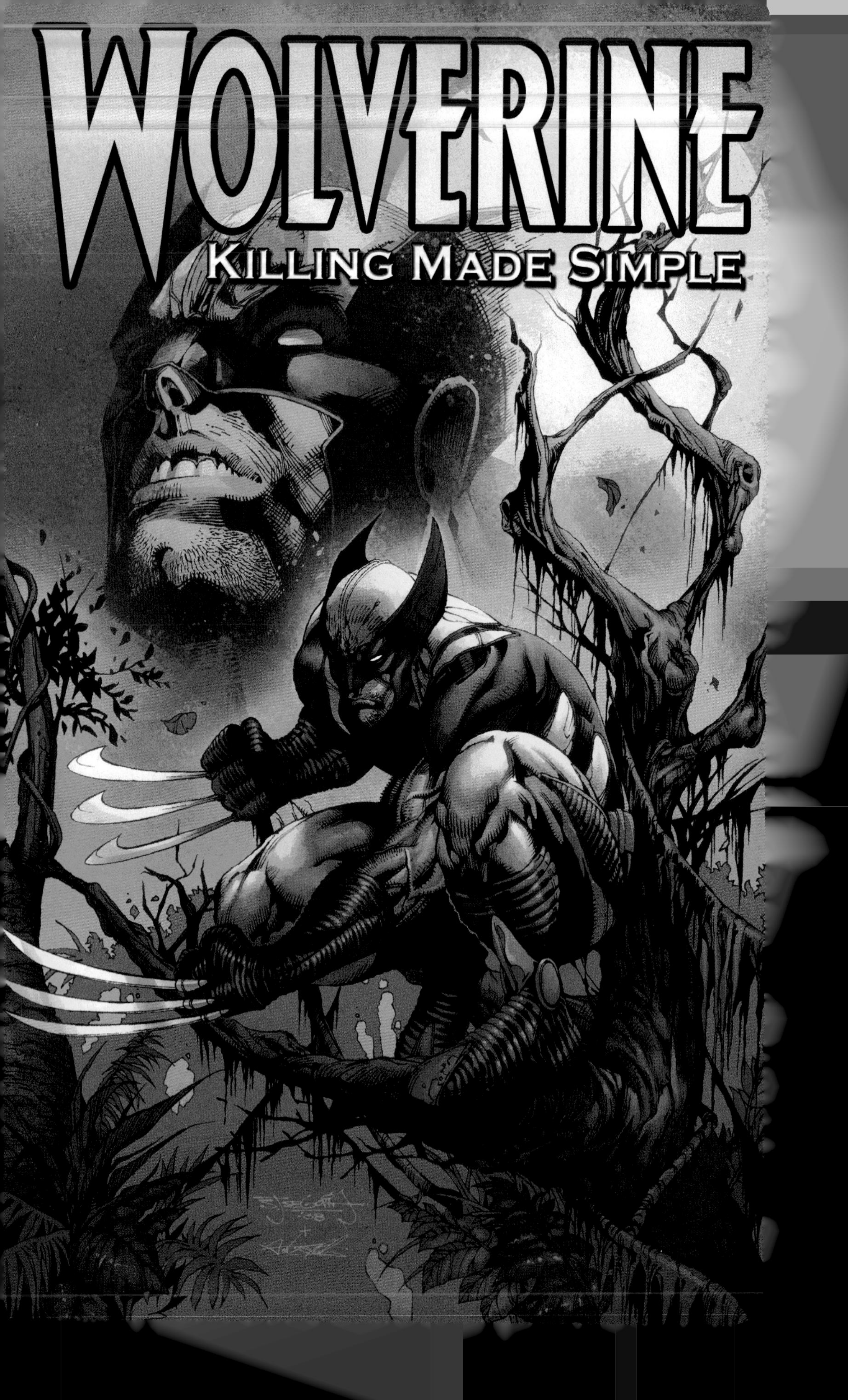
WOLVERINE
KILLING MADE SIMPLE

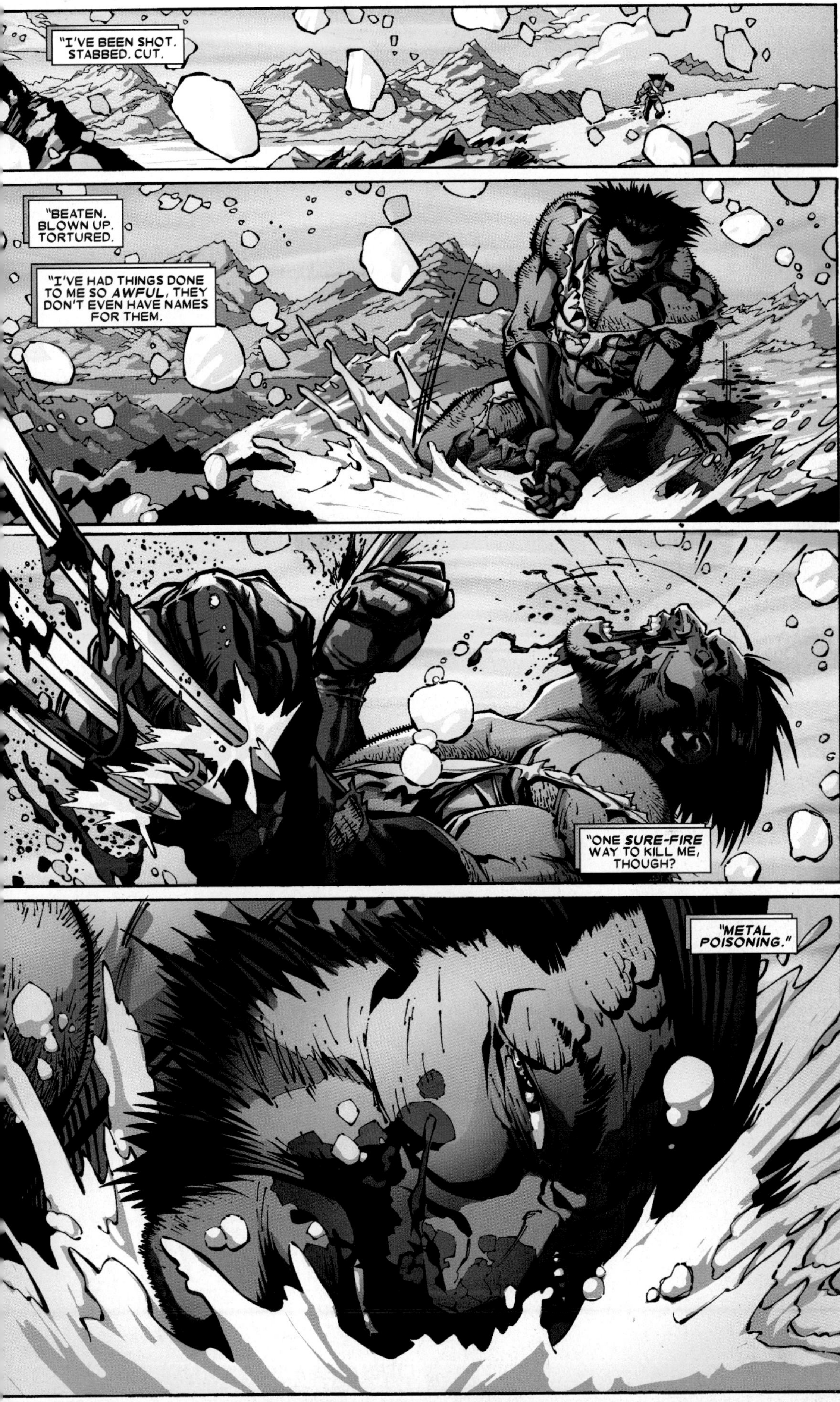
"I'VE BEEN SHOT. STABBED. CUT.
"BEATEN. BLOWN UP. TORTURED.
"I'VE HAD THINGS DONE TO ME SO AWFUL, THEY DON'T EVEN HAVE NAMES FOR THEM.
"ONE SURE-FIRE WAY TO KILL ME, THOUGH?
"METAL POISONING."

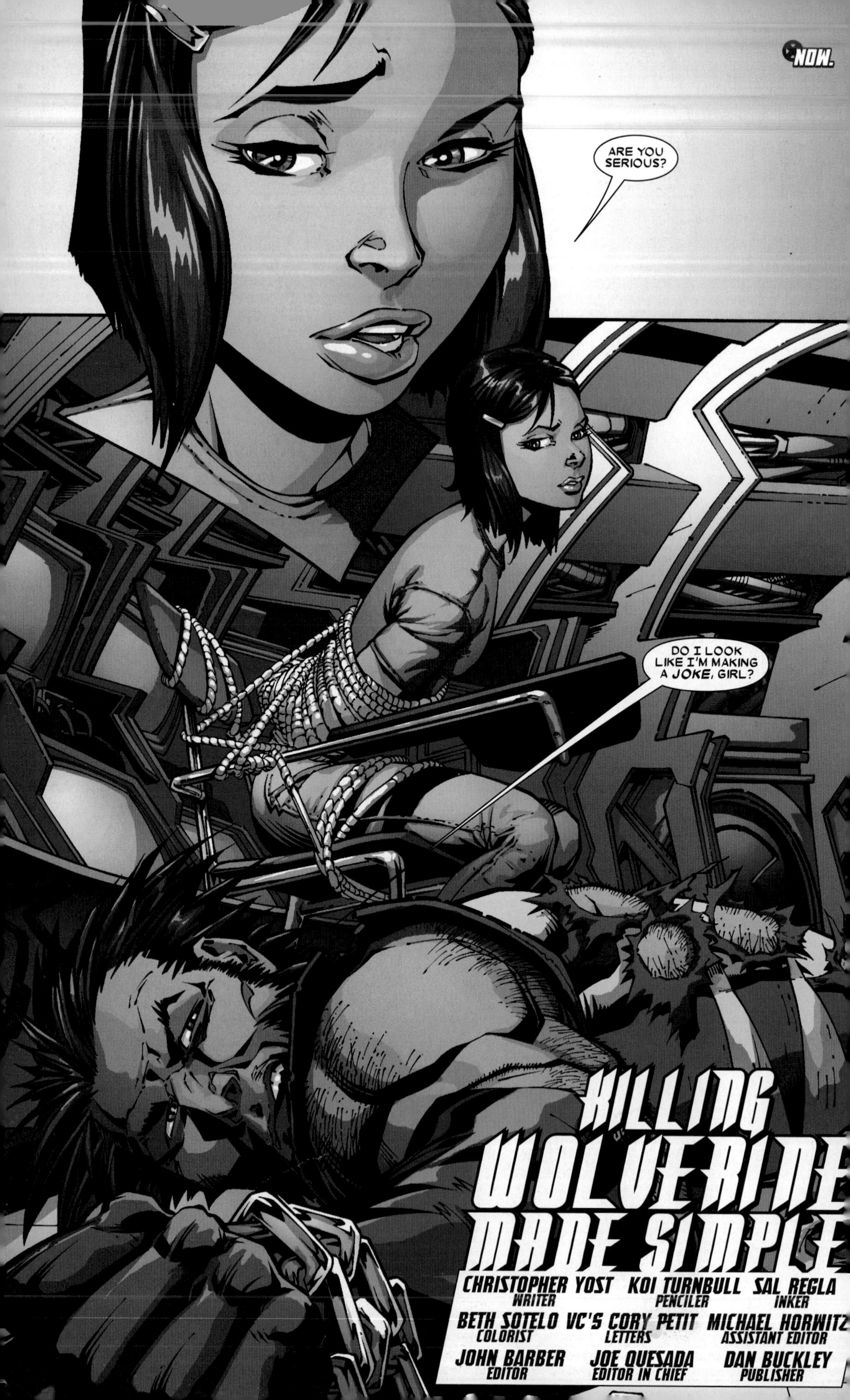
NOW.
ARE YOU SERIOUS?
DO I LOOK LIKE I'M MAKING A JOKE, GIRL?
KILLING WOLVERINE MADE SIMPLE
CHRISTOPHER YOST WRITER
KOI TURNBULL PENCILER
SAL REGLA INKER
BETH SOTELO COLORIST
VC'S CORY PETIT LETTERS
MICHAEL HORWITZ ASSISTANT EDITOR
JOHN BARBER EDITOR
JOE QUESADA EDITOR IN CHIEF
DAN BUCKLEY PUBLISHER

YOU WANTED TO KNOW, SO I'M *TELLING* YOU.
TAKE AWAY MY POWERS, I'M *DEAD*. THE METAL ON MY BONES, IT'LL KILL ME.
I'VE BEEN PRETTY CLOSE THAT WAY A TIME OR TWO. IT FEELS LIKE SOMEONE COATED YOUR SKELETON WITH *GUNPOWDER*, THEN LIT A MATCH.
UGH!
THE GIRL'S NAME IS *HOPE ABBOTT*. THEY CALL HER *TRANCE*. SHE WAS A STUDENT AT THE *XAVIER INSTITUTE* UNTIL RECENTLY.
SHE JUST GOT *KIDNAPPED.*
I TAKE IT BACK, I *DON'T* WANT TO KNOW.
I CAME TO SAVE HER.
LUCKY ME.
SWEETHEART, I JUST GOT STARTED.

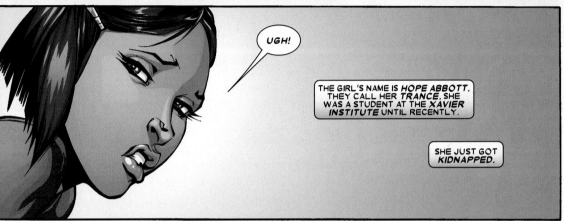

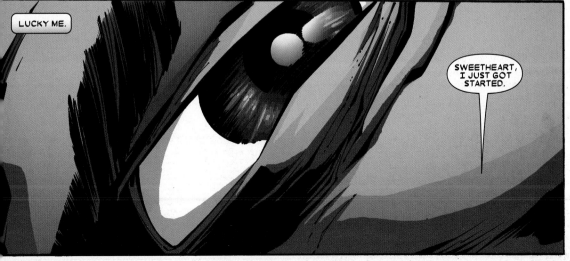

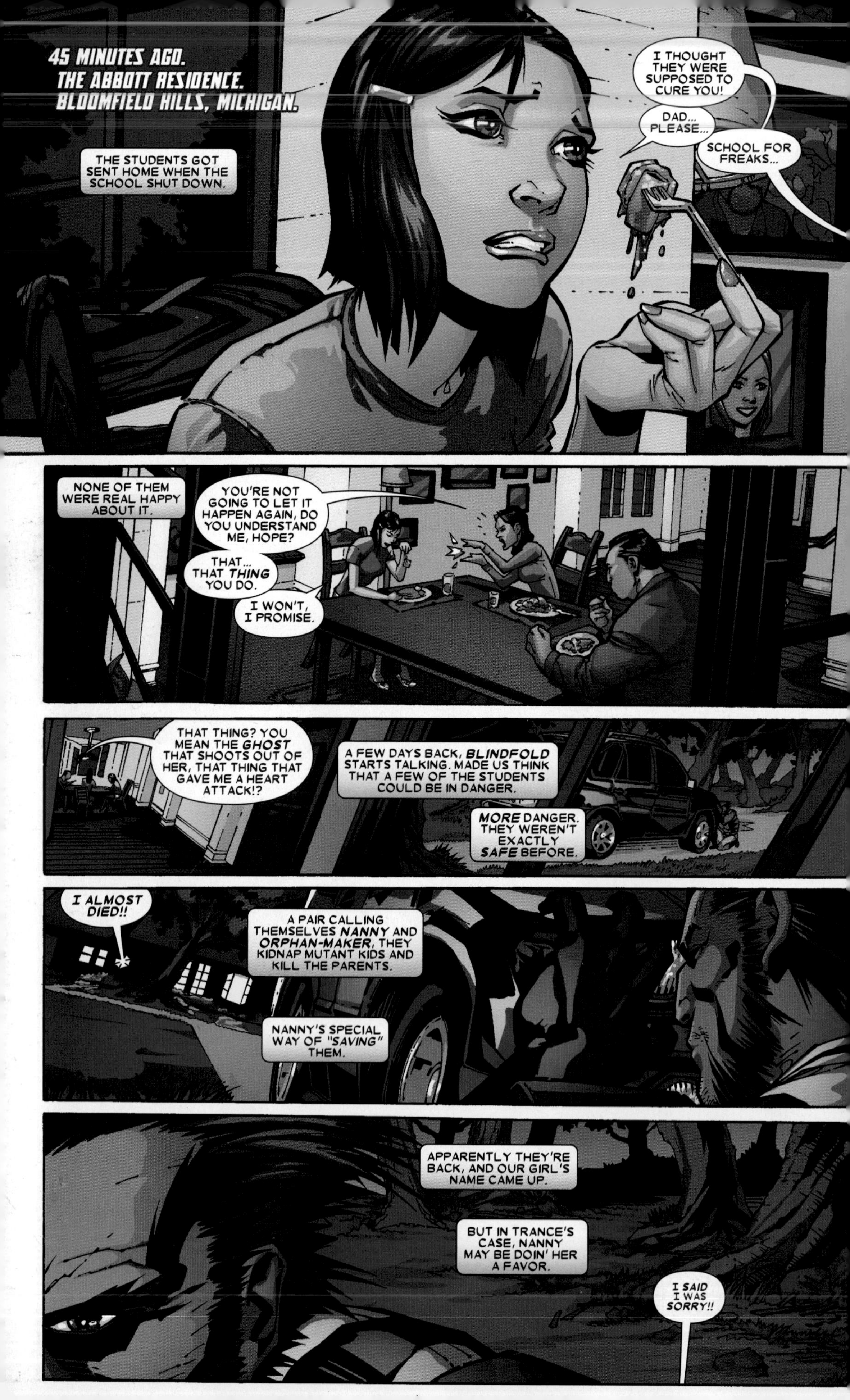
45 MINUTES AGO.
THE ABBOTT RESIDENCE.
BLOOMFIELD HILLS, MICHIGAN.
THE STUDENTS GOT SENT HOME WHEN THE SCHOOL SHUT DOWN.
SCHOOL FOR FREAKS...
I THOUGHT THEY WERE SUPPOSED TO CURE YOU!
DAD... PLEASE...
NONE OF THEM WERE REAL HAPPY ABOUT IT.
YOU'RE NOT GOING TO LET IT HAPPEN AGAIN, DO YOU UNDERSTAND ME, HOPE?
THAT... THAT THING YOU DO.
I WON'T, I PROMISE.
THAT THING? YOU MEAN THE GHOST THAT SHOOTS OUT OF HER, THAT THING THAT GAVE ME A HEART ATTACK!?
A FEW DAYS BACK, BLINDFOLD STARTS TALKING. MADE US THINK THAT A FEW OF THE STUDENTS COULD BE IN DANGER.
MORE DANGER. THEY WEREN'T EXACTLY SAFE BEFORE.
I ALMOST DIED!!
A PAIR CALLING THEMSELVES NANNY AND ORPHAN-MAKER, THEY KIDNAP MUTANT KIDS AND KILL THE PARENTS.
NANNY'S SPECIAL WAY OF "SAVING" THEM.
APPARENTLY THEY'RE BACK, AND OUR GIRL'S NAME CAME UP.
BUT IN TRANCE'S CASE, NANNY MAY BE DOIN' HER A FAVOR.
I SAID I WAS SORRY!!

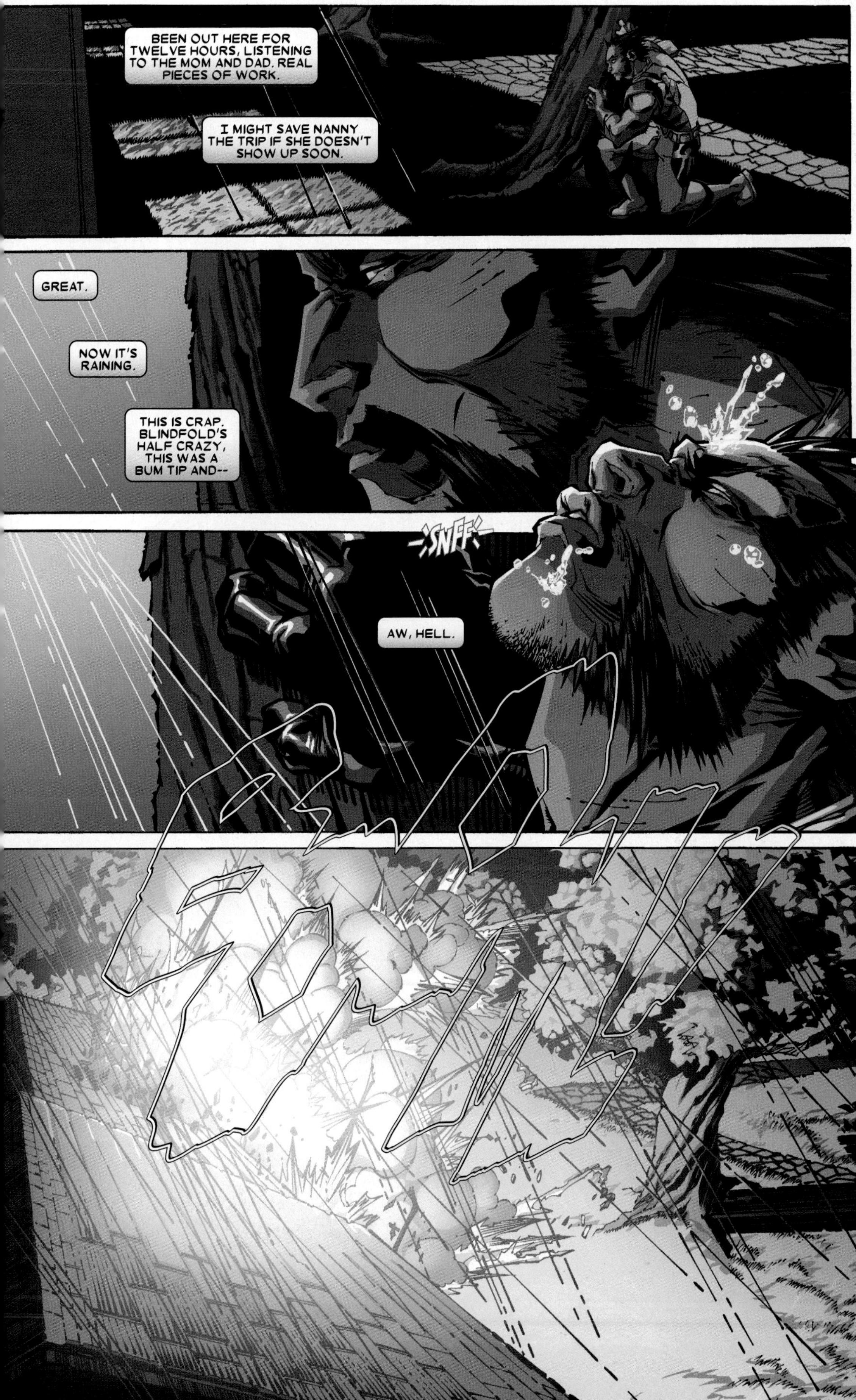
BEEN OUT HERE FOR TWELVE HOURS, LISTENING TO THE MOM AND DAD. REAL PIECES OF WORK.
I MIGHT SAVE NANNY THE TRIP IF SHE DOESN'T SHOW UP SOON.
GREAT.
NOW IT'S RAINING.
THIS IS CRAP. BLINDFOLD'S HALF CRAZY, THIS WAS A BUM TIP AND--
SNFF
AW, HELL.

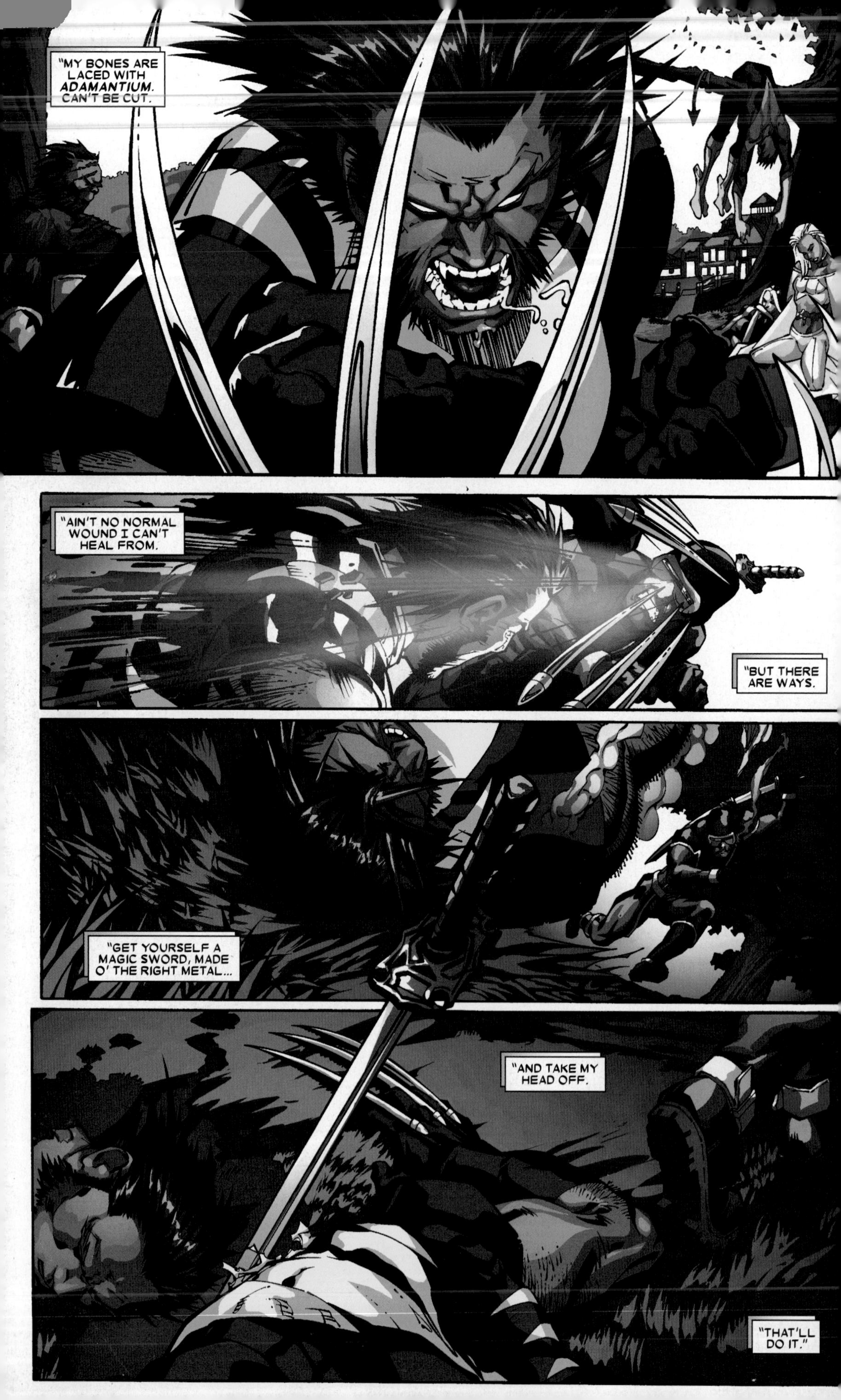
"MY BONES ARE LACED WITH *ADAMANTIUM*. CAN'T BE CUT.
"AIN'T NO NORMAL WOUND I CAN'T HEAL FROM.
"BUT THERE ARE WAYS.
"GET YOURSELF A MAGIC SWORD, MADE O' THE RIGHT METAL...
"AND TAKE MY HEAD OFF.
"THAT'LL DO IT."

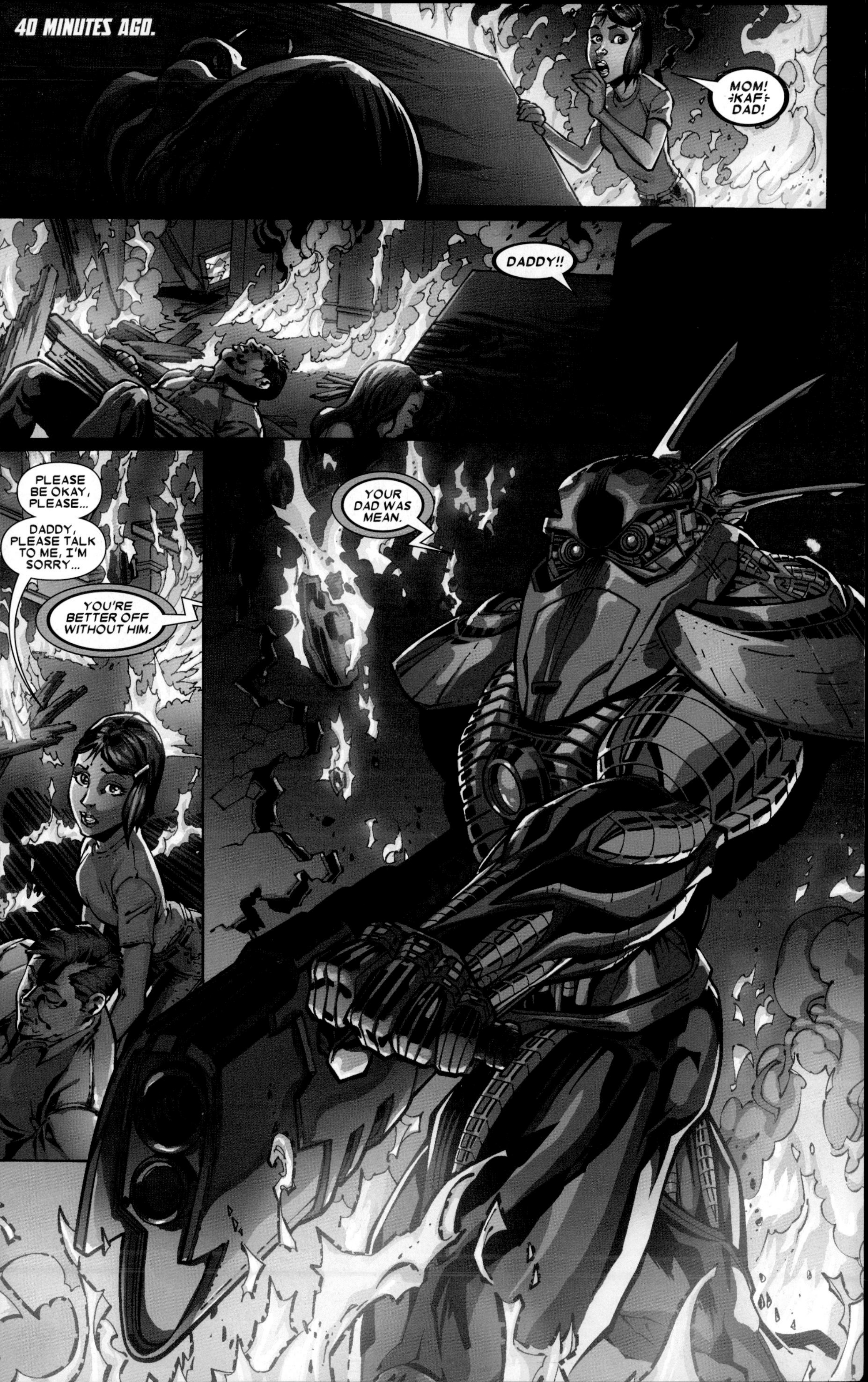
40 MINUTES AGO.
MOM! *KAF* DAD!
DADDY!!
PLEASE BE OKAY, PLEASE...
DADDY, PLEASE TALK TO ME, I'M SORRY...
YOU'RE BETTER OFF WITHOUT HIM.
YOUR DAD WAS MEAN.

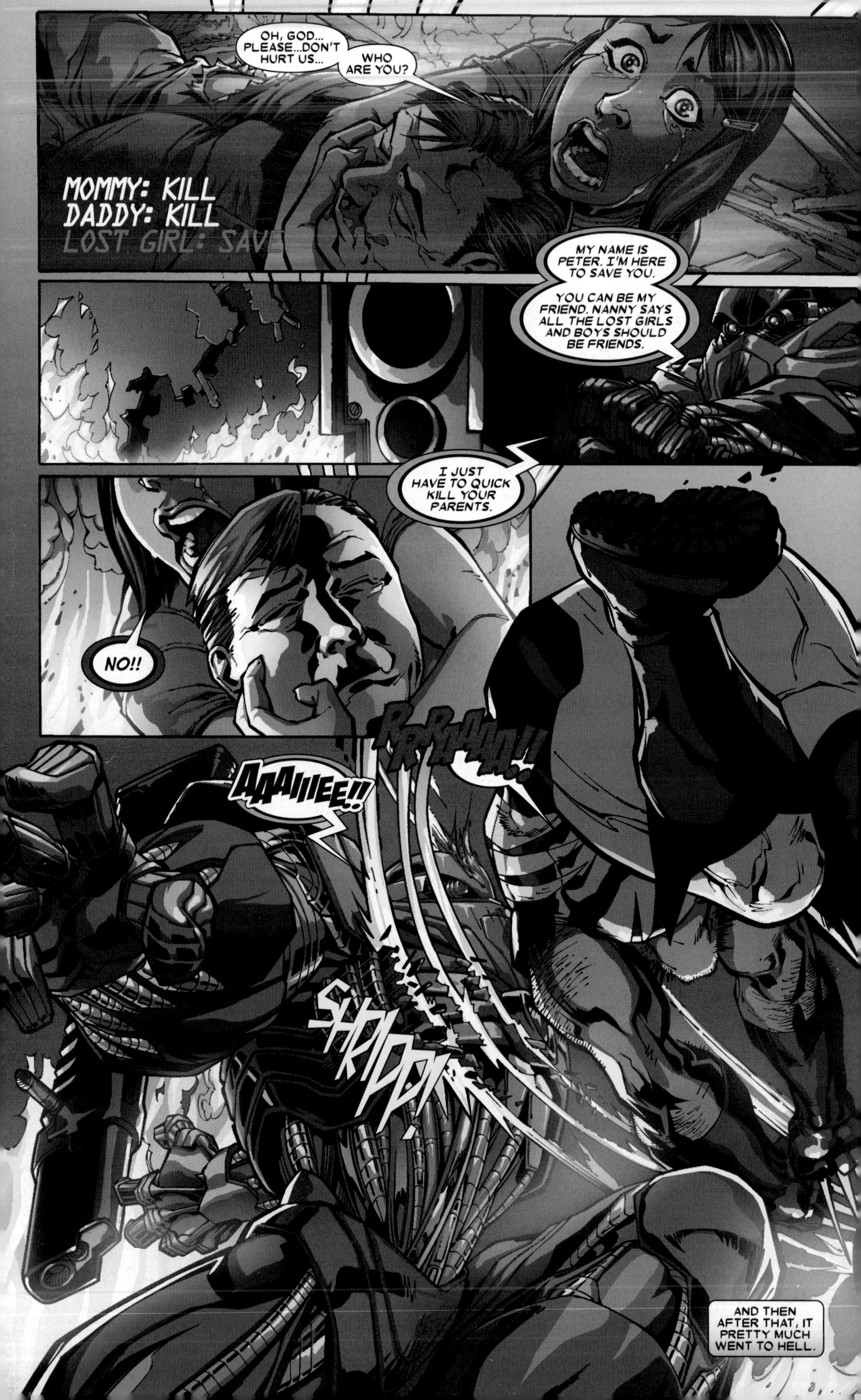

OH, GOD... PLEASE...DON'T HURT US...
WHO ARE YOU?
MOMMY: KILL
DADDY: KILL
LOST GIRL: SAVE
MY NAME IS PETER. I'M HERE TO SAVE YOU.
YOU CAN BE MY FRIEND. NANNY SAYS ALL THE LOST GIRLS AND BOYS SHOULD BE FRIENDS.
I JUST HAVE TO QUICK KILL YOUR PARENTS.
NO!!
RRRAAAA!!
AAAIIIEE!!
SKRIDD!
AND THEN AFTER THAT, IT PRETTY MUCH WENT TO HELL.

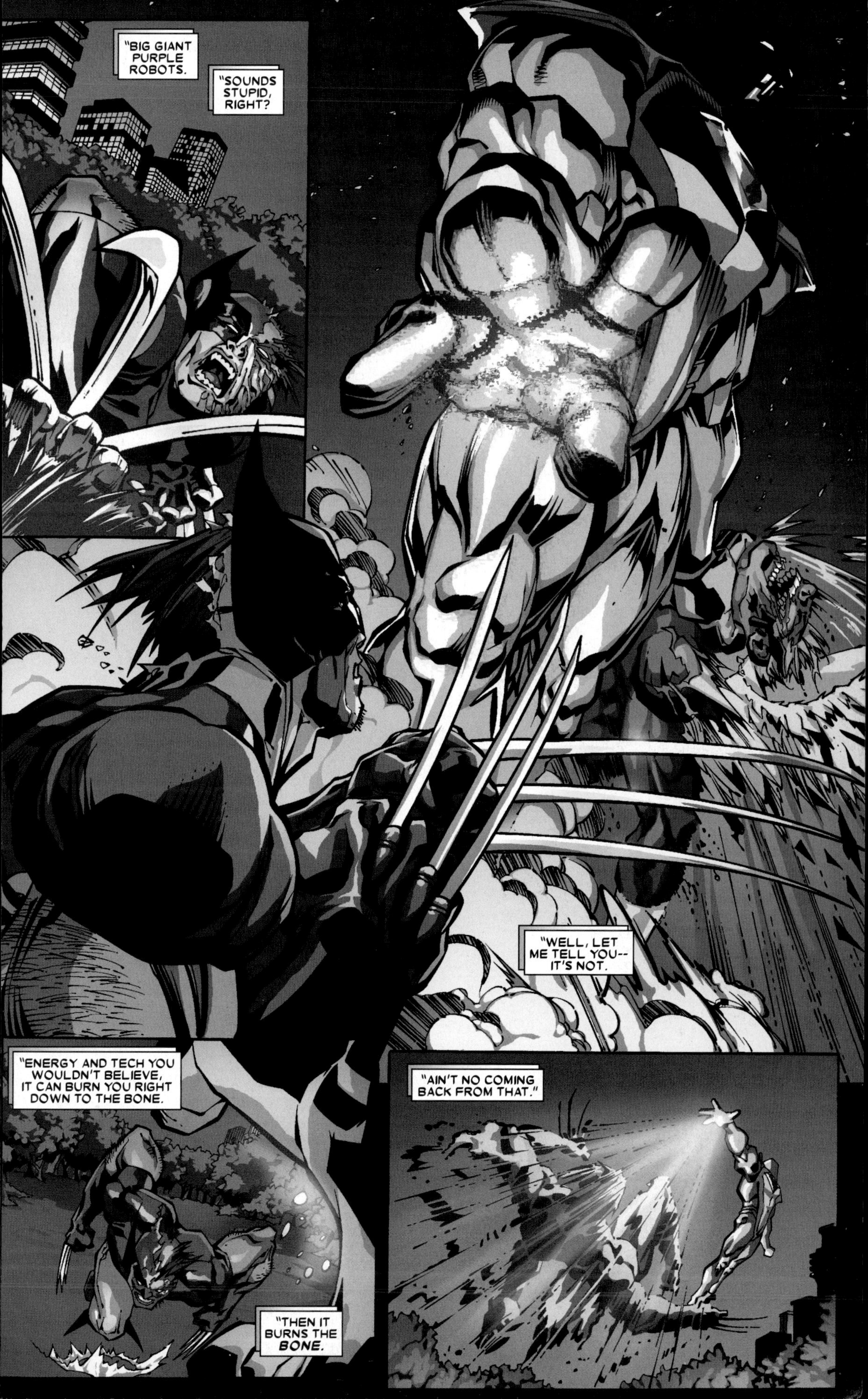
"BIG GIANT PURPLE ROBOTS.
"SOUNDS STUPID, RIGHT?
"WELL, LET ME TELL YOU-- IT'S NOT.
"ENERGY AND TECH YOU WOULDN'T BELIEVE, IT CAN BURN YOU RIGHT DOWN TO THE BONE.
"THEN IT BURNS THE *BONE*.
"AIN'T NO COMING BACK FROM THAT."

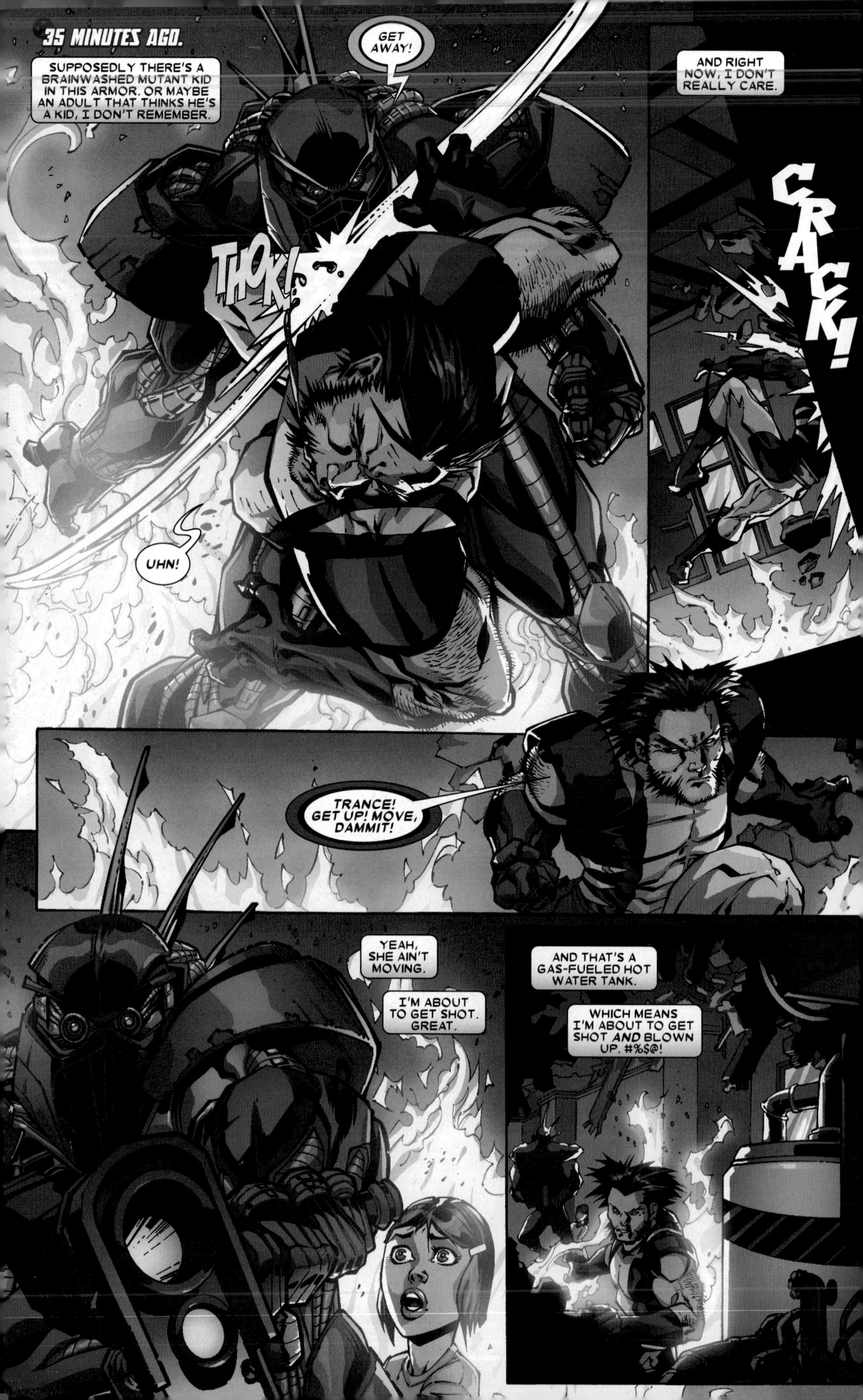
35 MINUTES AGO.
SUPPOSEDLY THERE'S A BRAINWASHED MUTANT KID IN THIS ARMOR. OR MAYBE AN ADULT THAT THINKS HE'S A KID, I DON'T REMEMBER.
GET AWAY!
AND RIGHT NOW, I DON'T REALLY CARE.
THOK!
CRACK!
UHN!
TRANCE! GET UP! MOVE, DAMMIT!
YEAH, SHE AIN'T MOVING.
I'M ABOUT TO GET SHOT. GREAT.
AND THAT'S A GAS-FUELED HOT WATER TANK.
WHICH MEANS I'M ABOUT TO GET SHOT AND BLOWN UP. #%$@!

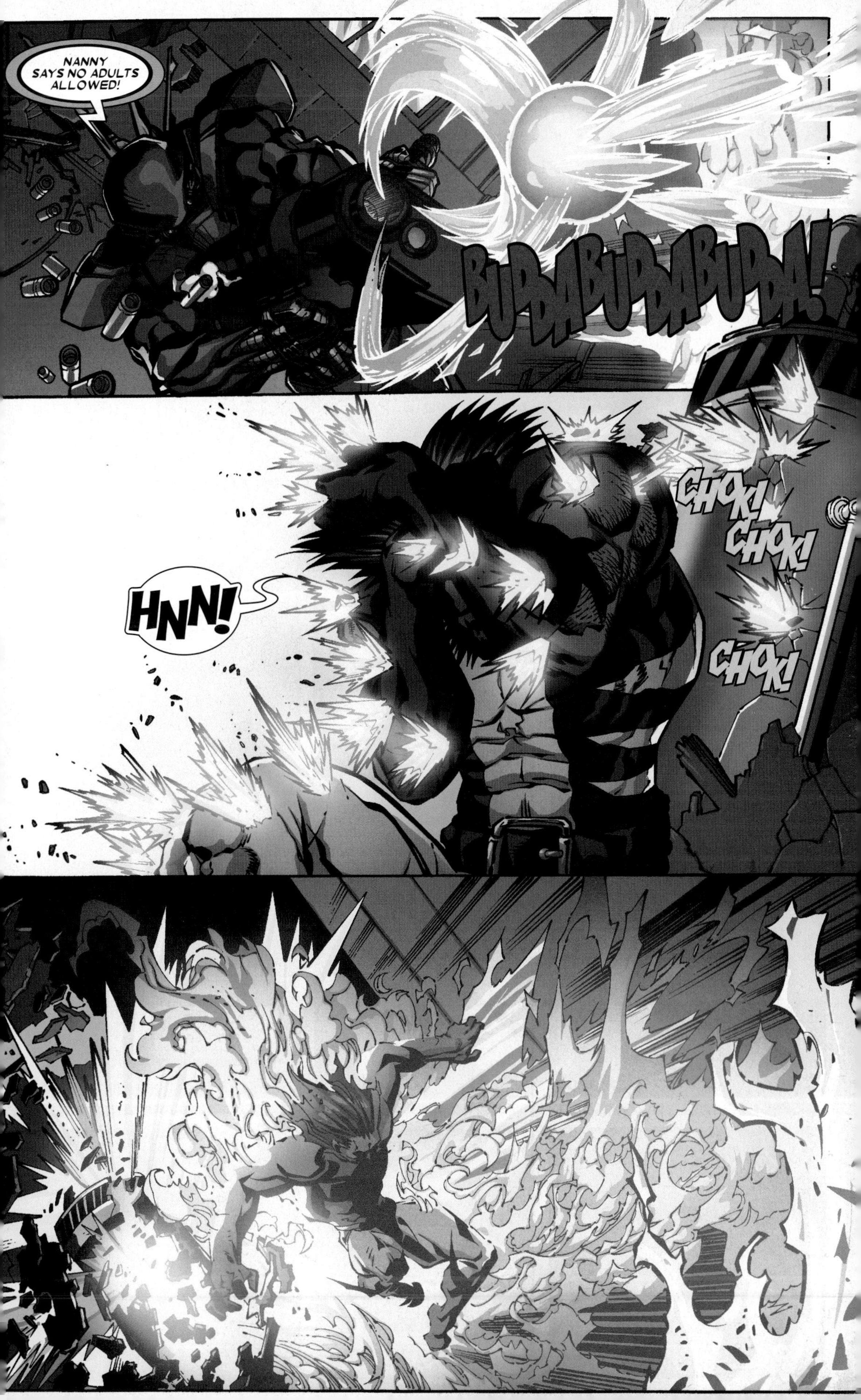
NANNY SAYS NO ADULTS ALLOWED!
BUDDABUDDABUDDA!
HNN!
CHOK!
CHOK!
CHOK!

PETER... PETER, ARE YOU OKAY? WHAT HAPPENED, BOY?

PETER, ARE YOU THERE?

I'M HERE, NANNY.

I HAVE HOPE HERE WITH ME, BUT THERE WAS A PROBLEM.

AND NOW I HAVE TO KILL WOLVERINE.

WHAT? PETER, NO!

WE CAN USE HIM! LEAVE THE PARENTS, JUST BRING HIM AND THE GIRL TO ME RIGHT NOW!

ARE YOU SURE, NANNY? WOLVERINE HURT ME. HE HURT ME BAD.

I THINK HE NEEDS TO BE PUNISHED.

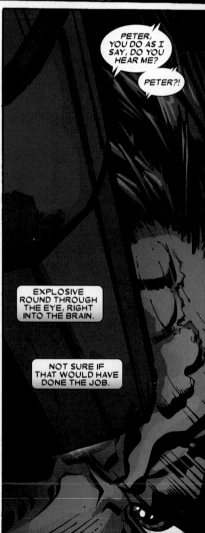

PETER, YOU DO AS I SAY, DO YOU HEAR ME?

PETER?!

EXPLOSIVE ROUND THROUGH THE EYE, RIGHT INTO THE BRAIN.

NOT SURE IF THAT WOULD HAVE DONE THE JOB.

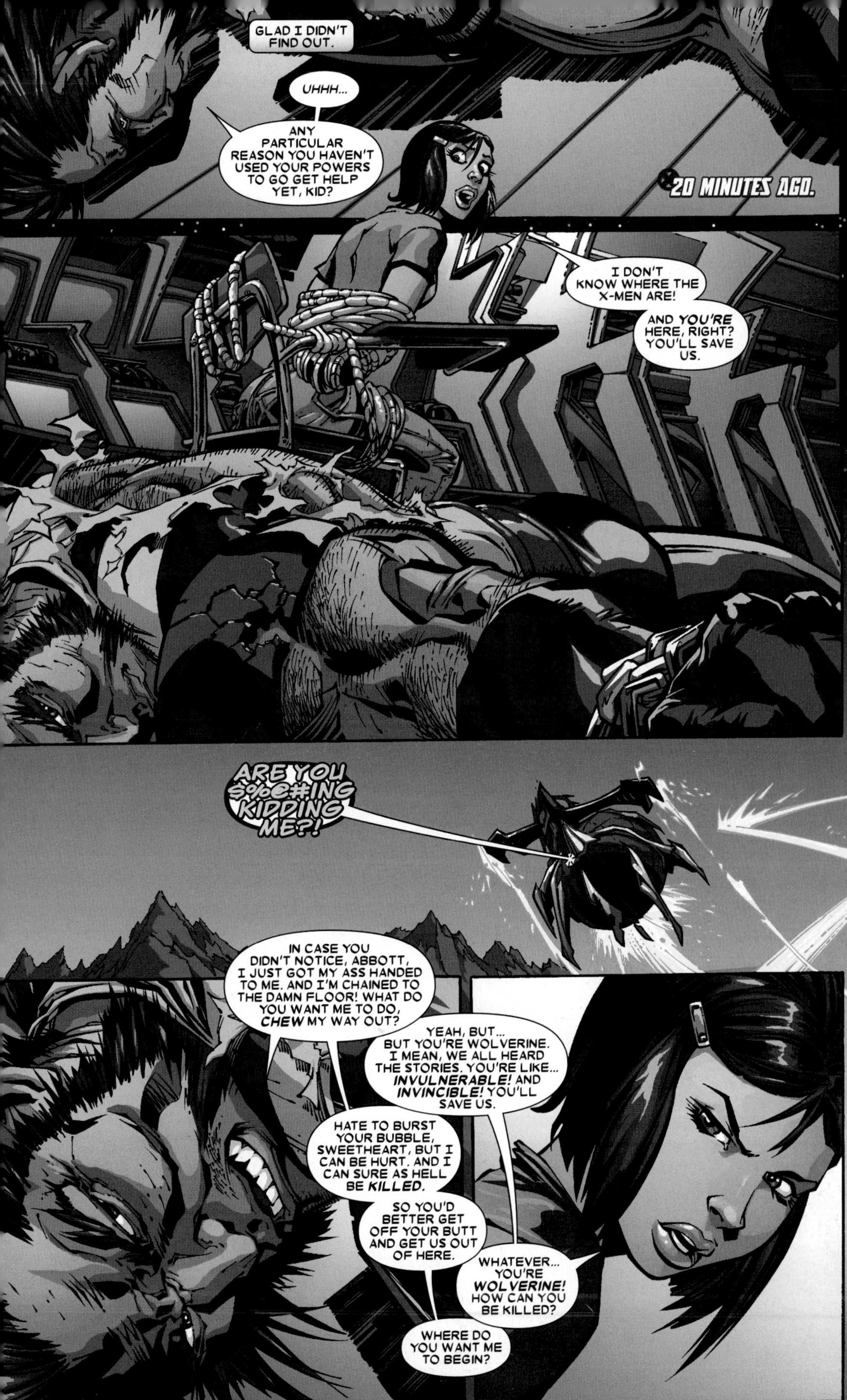
GLAD I DIDN'T FIND OUT.
UHHH...
ANY PARTICULAR REASON YOU HAVEN'T USED YOUR POWERS TO GO GET HELP YET, KID?
20 MINUTES AGO.
I DON'T KNOW WHERE THE X-MEN ARE!
AND YOU'RE HERE, RIGHT? YOU'LL SAVE US.
ARE YOU $%@#ING KIDDING ME?!
IN CASE YOU DIDN'T NOTICE, ABBOTT, I JUST GOT MY ASS HANDED TO ME. AND I'M CHAINED TO THE DAMN FLOOR! WHAT DO YOU WANT ME TO DO, CHEW MY WAY OUT?
YEAH, BUT... BUT YOU'RE WOLVERINE. I MEAN, WE ALL HEARD THE STORIES. YOU'RE LIKE... INVULNERABLE! AND INVINCIBLE! YOU'LL SAVE US.
HATE TO BURST YOUR BUBBLE, SWEETHEART, BUT I CAN BE HURT. AND I CAN SURE AS HELL BE KILLED.
SO YOU'D BETTER GET OFF YOUR BUTT AND GET US OUT OF HERE.
WHATEVER... YOU'RE WOLVERINE! HOW CAN YOU BE KILLED?
WHERE DO YOU WANT ME TO BEGIN?

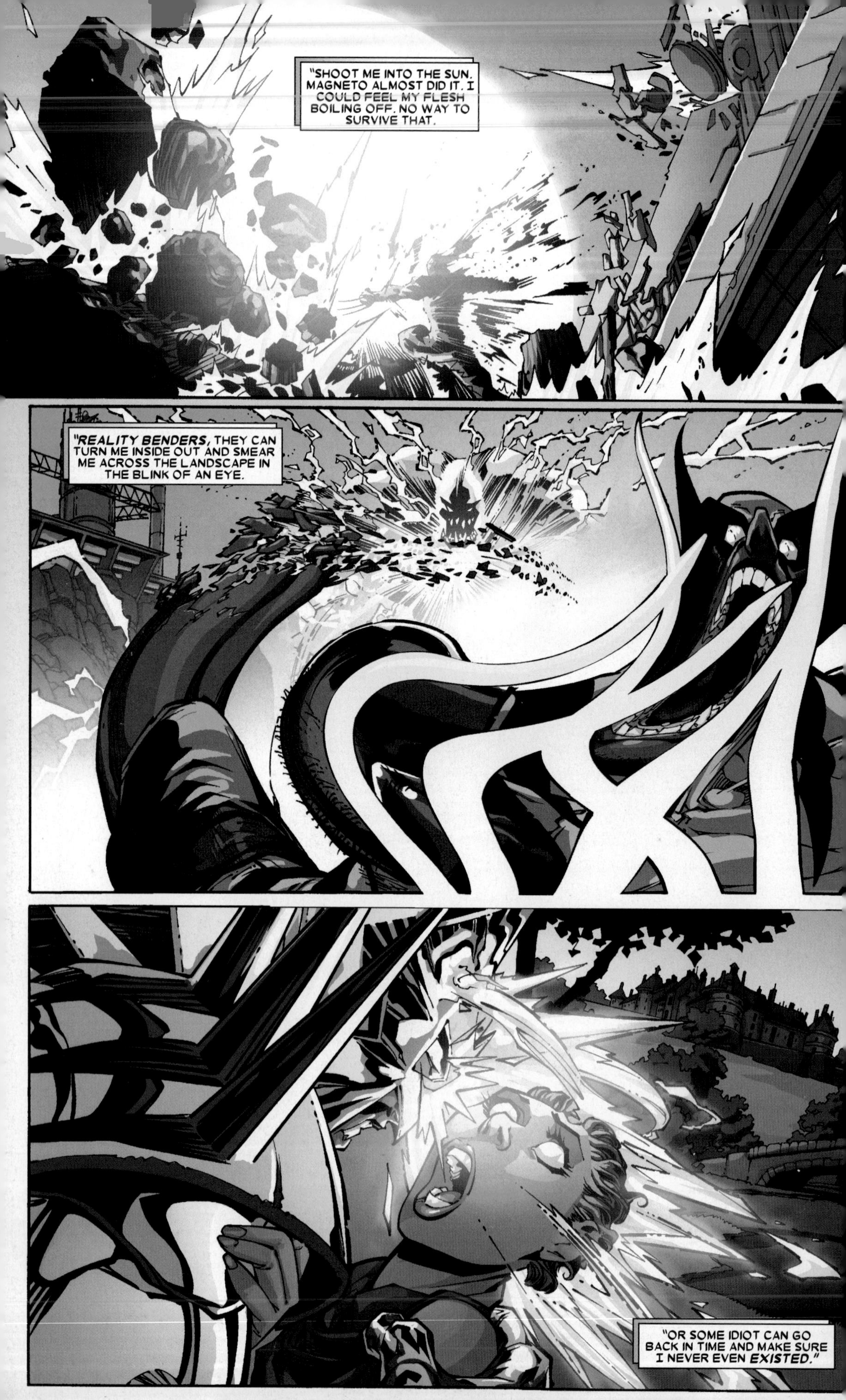
"SHOOT ME INTO THE SUN. MAGNETO ALMOST DID IT. I COULD FEEL MY FLESH BOILING OFF. NO WAY TO SURVIVE THAT.
"REALITY BENDERS, THEY CAN TURN ME INSIDE OUT AND SMEAR ME ACROSS THE LANDSCAPE IN THE BLINK OF AN EYE.
"OR SOME IDIOT CAN GO BACK IN TIME AND MAKE SURE I NEVER EVEN EXISTED."

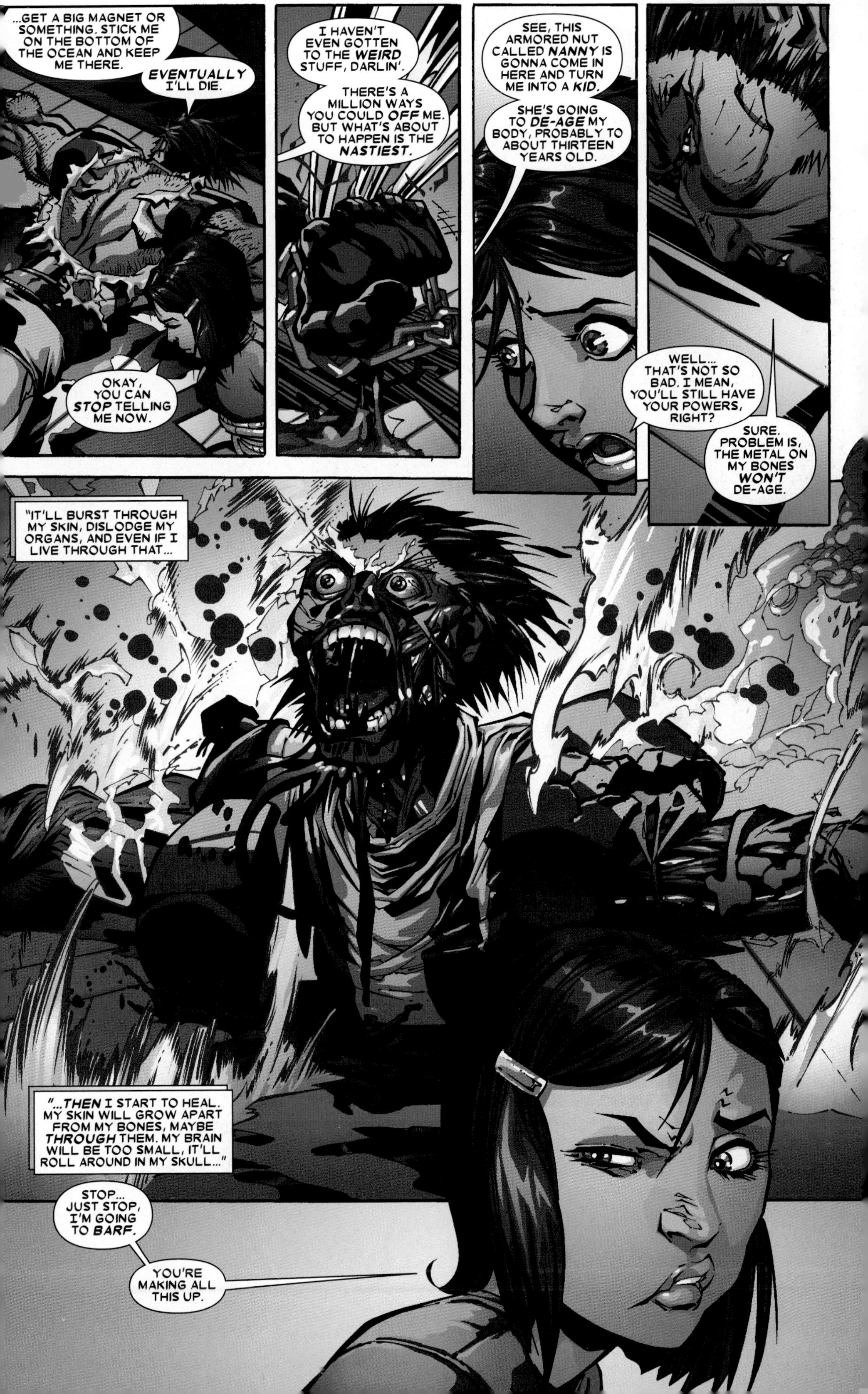
...GET A BIG MAGNET OR SOMETHING. STICK ME ON THE BOTTOM OF THE OCEAN AND KEEP ME THERE.
EVENTUALLY I'LL DIE.
OKAY, YOU CAN STOP TELLING ME NOW.
I HAVEN'T EVEN GOTTEN TO THE WEIRD STUFF, DARLIN'.
THERE'S A MILLION WAYS YOU COULD OFF ME. BUT WHAT'S ABOUT TO HAPPEN IS THE NASTIEST.
SEE, THIS ARMORED NUT CALLED NANNY IS GONNA COME IN HERE AND TURN ME INTO A KID.
SHE'S GOING TO DE-AGE MY BODY, PROBABLY TO ABOUT THIRTEEN YEARS OLD.
WELL... THAT'S NOT SO BAD. I MEAN, YOU'LL STILL HAVE YOUR POWERS, RIGHT?
SURE. PROBLEM IS, THE METAL ON MY BONES WON'T DE-AGE.
"IT'LL BURST THROUGH MY SKIN, DISLODGE MY ORGANS, AND EVEN IF I LIVE THROUGH THAT...
"...THEN I START TO HEAL. MY SKIN WILL GROW APART FROM MY BONES, MAYBE THROUGH THEM. MY BRAIN WILL BE TOO SMALL, IT'LL ROLL AROUND IN MY SKULL..."
STOP... JUST STOP, I'M GOING TO BARF.
YOU'RE MAKING ALL THIS UP.

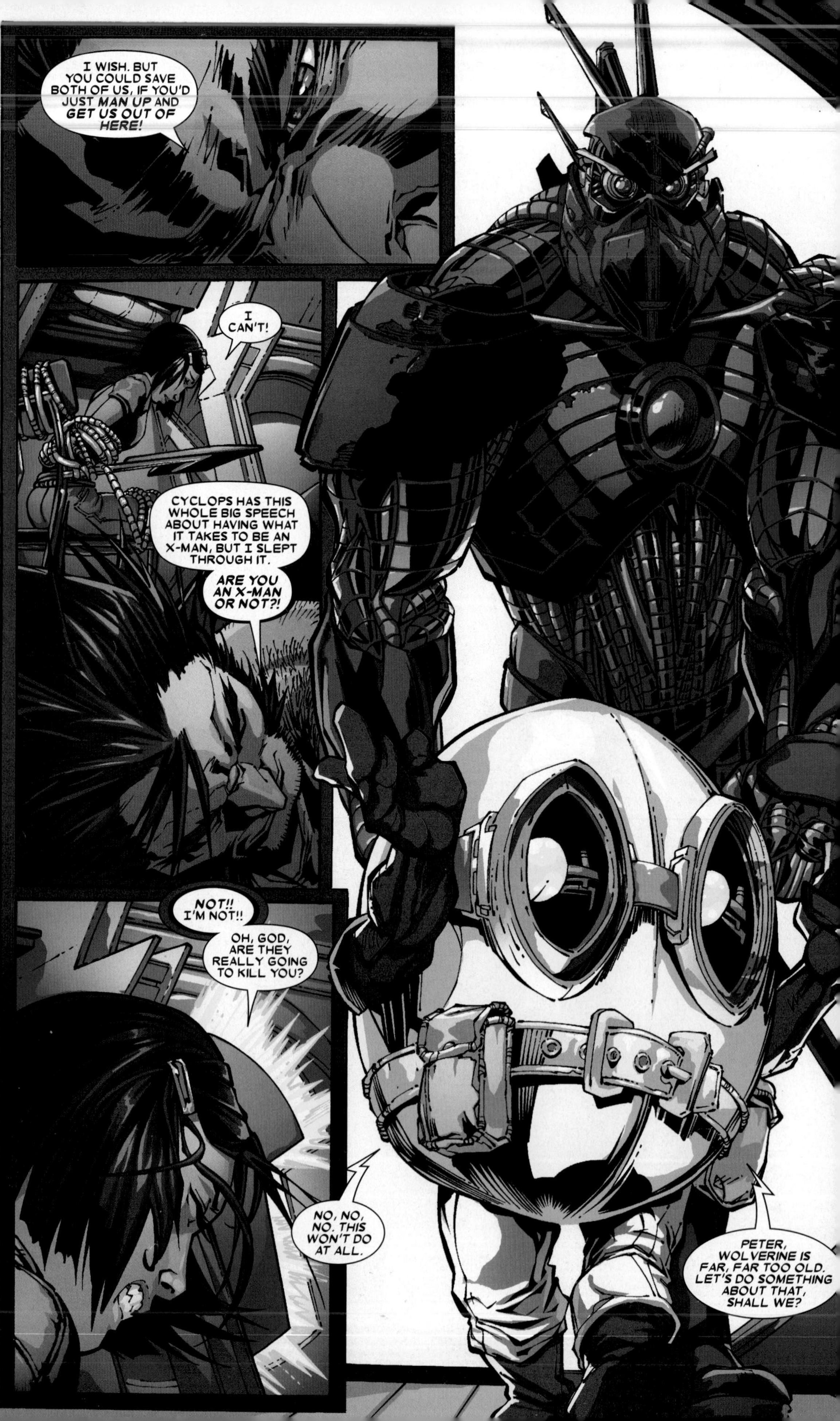
I WISH. BUT YOU COULD SAVE BOTH OF US, IF YOU'D JUST MAN UP AND GET US OUT OF HERE!
I CAN'T!
CYCLOPS HAS THIS WHOLE BIG SPEECH ABOUT HAVING WHAT IT TAKES TO BE AN X-MAN, BUT I SLEPT THROUGH IT.
ARE YOU AN X-MAN OR NOT?!
NOT!! I'M NOT!!
OH, GOD, ARE THEY REALLY GOING TO KILL YOU?
NO, NO, NO. THIS WON'T DO AT ALL.
PETER, WOLVERINE IS FAR, FAR TOO OLD. LET'S DO SOMETHING ABOUT THAT, SHALL WE?

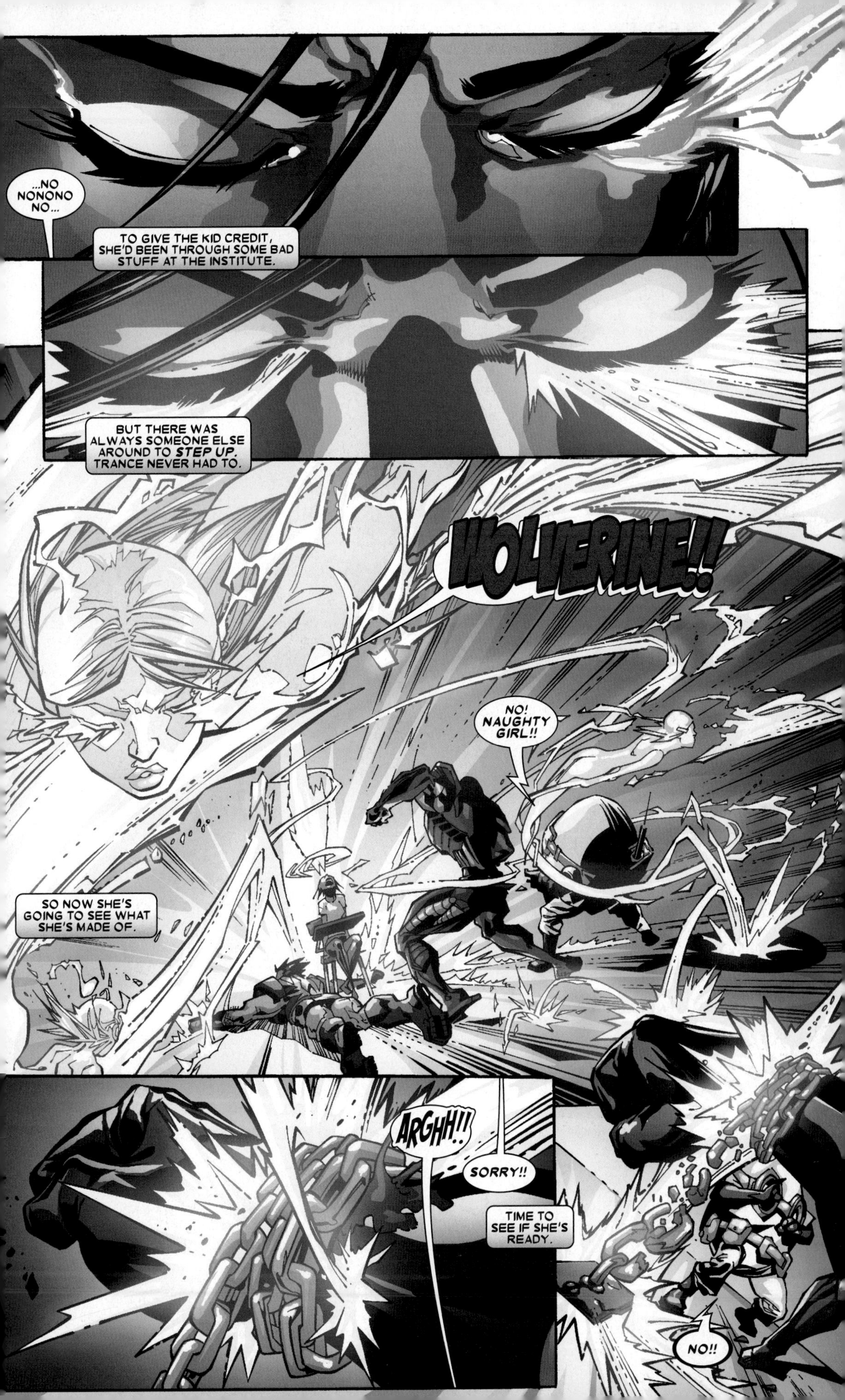

...NO NONONO NO...
TO GIVE THE KID CREDIT, SHE'D BEEN THROUGH SOME BAD STUFF AT THE INSTITUTE.
BUT THERE WAS ALWAYS SOMEONE ELSE AROUND TO STEP UP. TRANCE NEVER HAD TO.
WOLVERINE!!
NO! NAUGHTY GIRL!!
SO NOW SHE'S GOING TO SEE WHAT SHE'S MADE OF.
ARGHH!!
SORRY!!
TIME TO SEE IF SHE'S READY.
NO!!

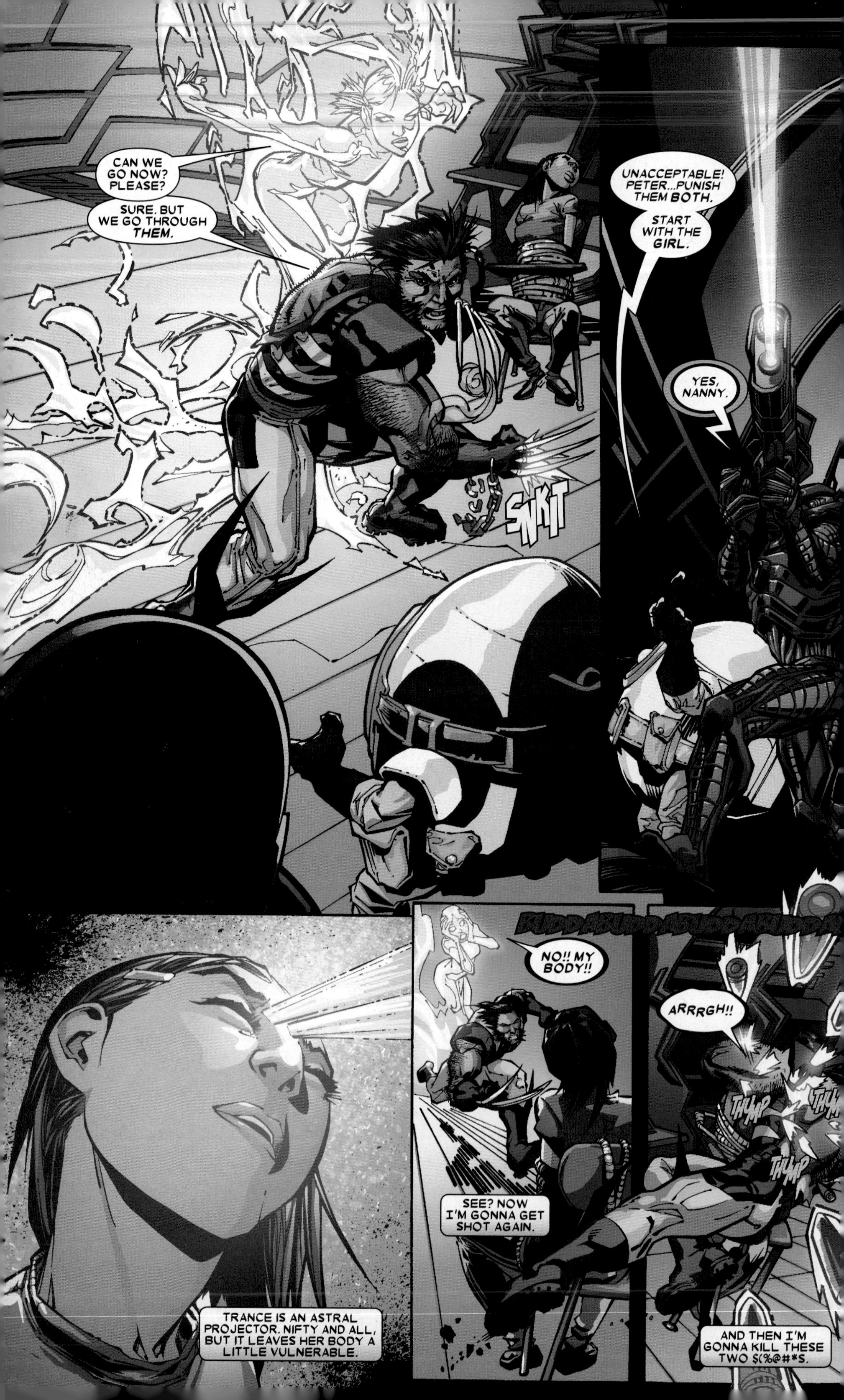
CAN WE GO NOW? PLEASE?
SURE. BUT WE GO THROUGH THEM.
UNACCEPTABLE! PETER...PUNISH THEM BOTH.
START WITH THE GIRL.
YES, NANNY.
SNIKT
TRANCE IS AN ASTRAL PROJECTOR. NIFTY AND ALL, BUT IT LEAVES HER BODY A LITTLE VULNERABLE.
NO!! MY BODY!!
SEE? NOW I'M GONNA GET SHOT AGAIN.
ARRRGH!!
THUMP
THUMP
AND THEN I'M GONNA KILL THESE TWO $(%@#*S.

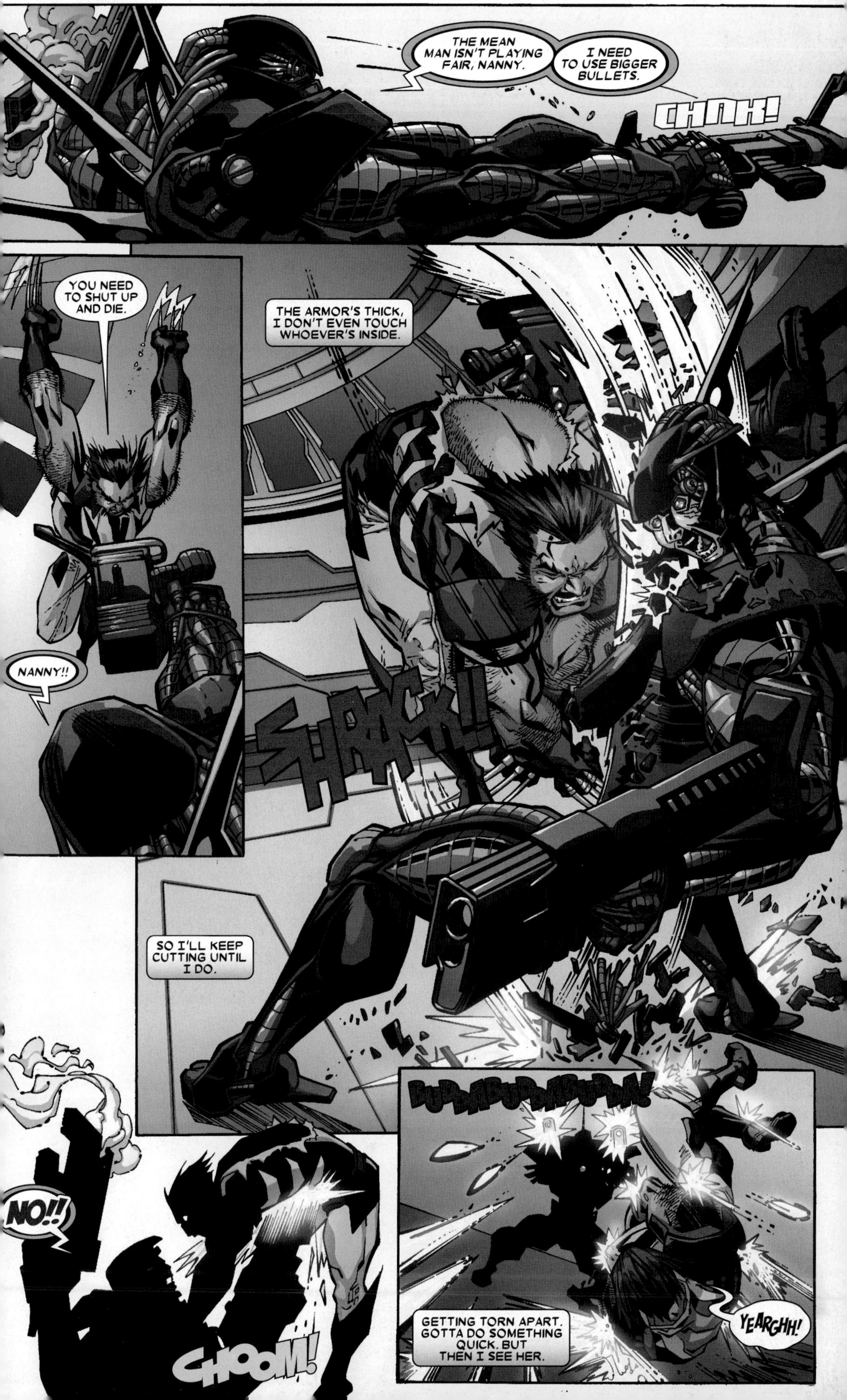
THE MEAN MAN ISN'T PLAYING FAIR, NANNY.
I NEED TO USE BIGGER BULLETS.
CHNK!
YOU NEED TO SHUT UP AND DIE.
THE ARMOR'S THICK, I DON'T EVEN TOUCH WHOEVER'S INSIDE.
NANNY!!
SHRACK!!
SO I'LL KEEP CUTTING UNTIL I DO.
NO!!
CHOOM!
BUDDABUDDABUDDA!
GETTING TORN APART. GOTTA DO SOMETHING QUICK. BUT THEN I SEE HER.
YEARGHH!

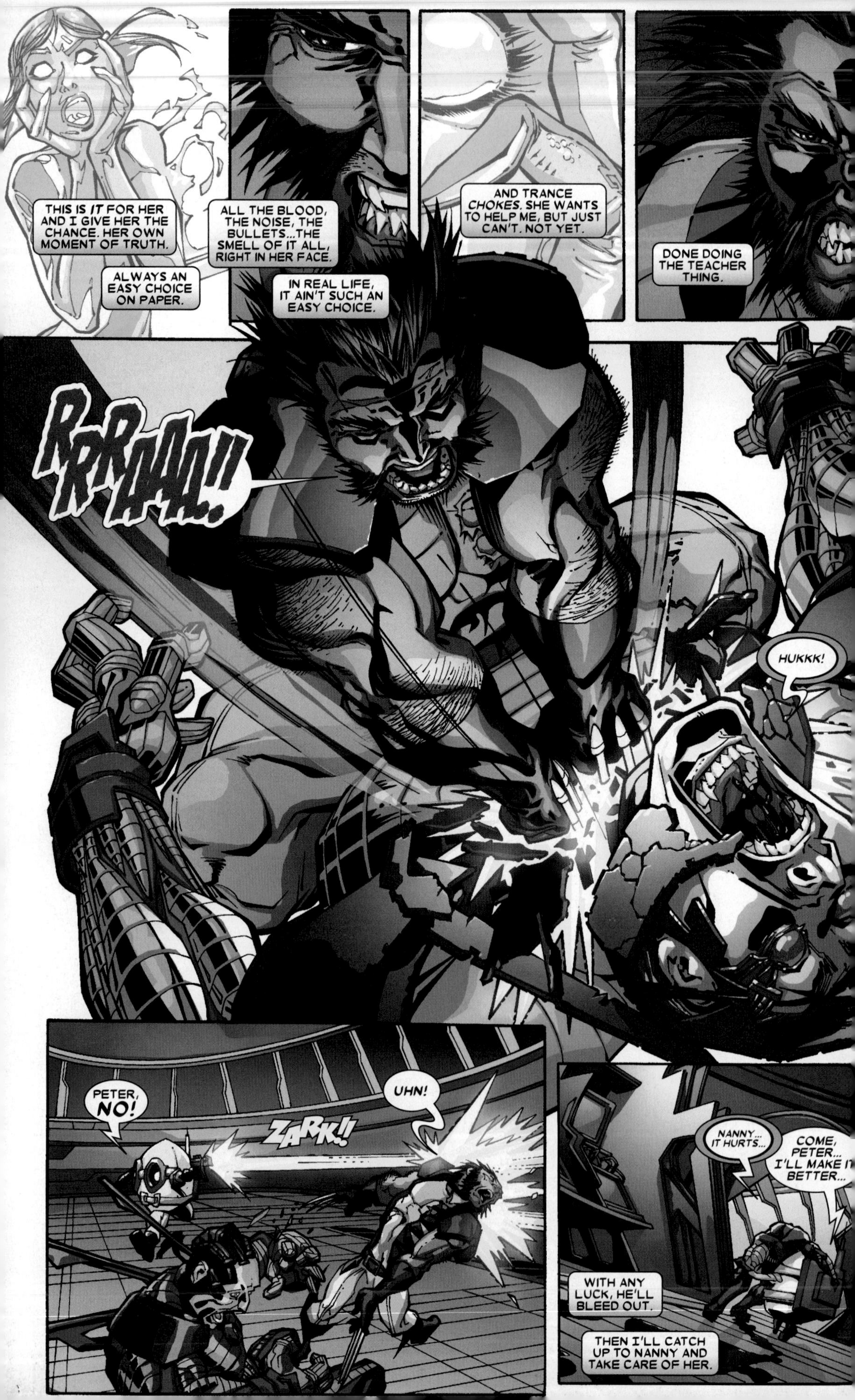
THIS IS *IT* FOR HER AND I GIVE HER THE CHANCE. HER OWN MOMENT OF TRUTH.
ALWAYS AN EASY CHOICE ON PAPER.
ALL THE BLOOD, THE NOISE, THE BULLETS...THE SMELL OF IT ALL, RIGHT IN HER FACE.
IN REAL LIFE, IT AIN'T SUCH AN EASY CHOICE.
AND TRANCE *CHOKES*. SHE WANTS TO HELP ME, BUT JUST CAN'T. NOT YET.
DONE DOING THE TEACHER THING.
RRRAAA!!
HUKKK!
PETER, NO!
UHN!
ZARK!!
NANNY... IT HURTS...
COME, PETER... I'LL MAKE IT BETTER...
WITH ANY LUCK, HE'LL BLEED OUT.
THEN I'LL CATCH UP TO NANNY AND TAKE CARE OF HER.

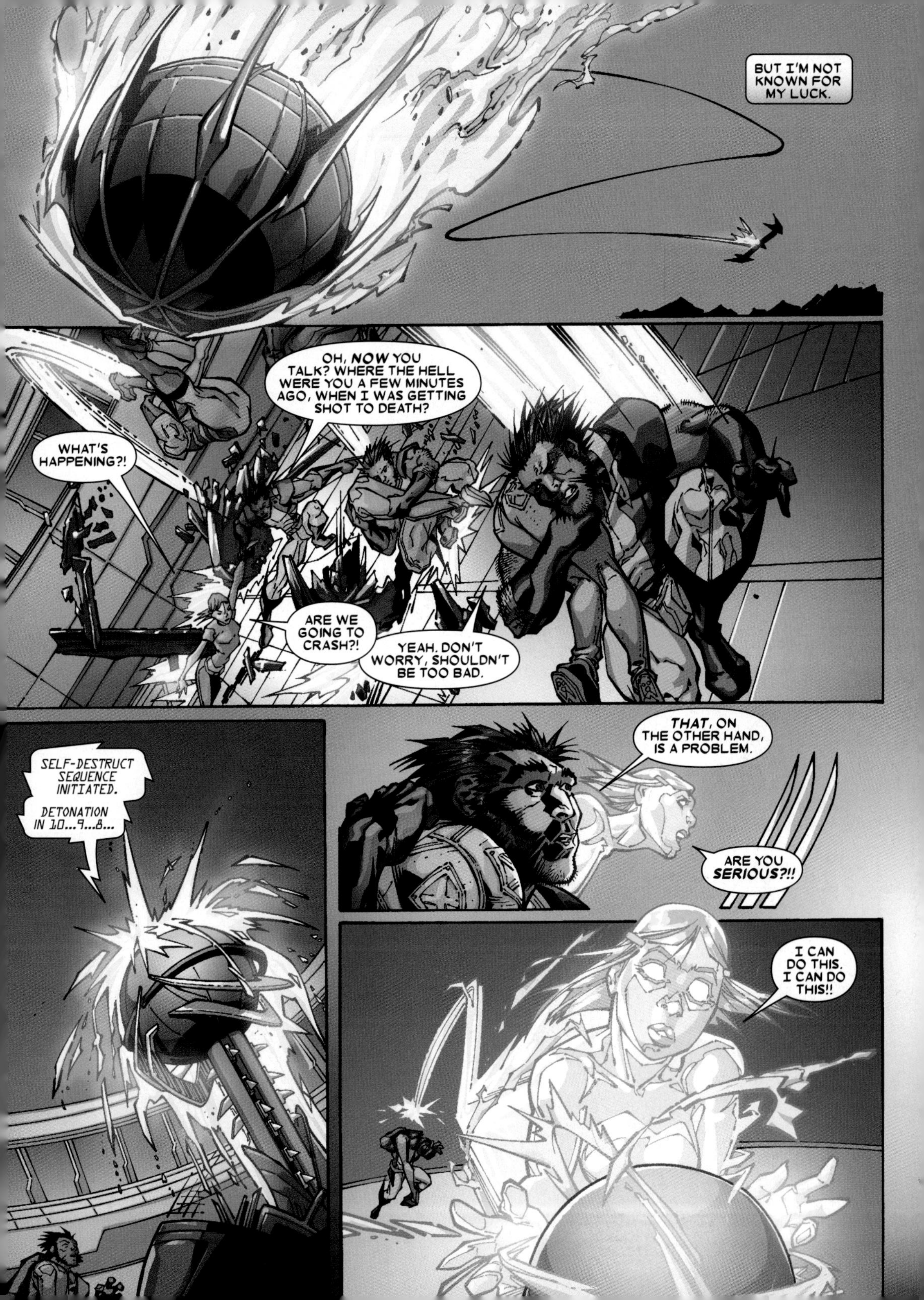

BUT I'M NOT KNOWN FOR MY LUCK.
WHAT'S HAPPENING?!
OH, NOW YOU TALK? WHERE THE HELL WERE YOU A FEW MINUTES AGO, WHEN I WAS GETTING SHOT TO DEATH?
ARE WE GOING TO CRASH?!
YEAH. DON'T WORRY, SHOULDN'T BE TOO BAD.
SELF-DESTRUCT SEQUENCE INITIATED.
DETONATION IN 10...9...8...
THAT, ON THE OTHER HAND, IS A PROBLEM.
ARE YOU SERIOUS?!!
I CAN DO THIS. I CAN DO THIS!!

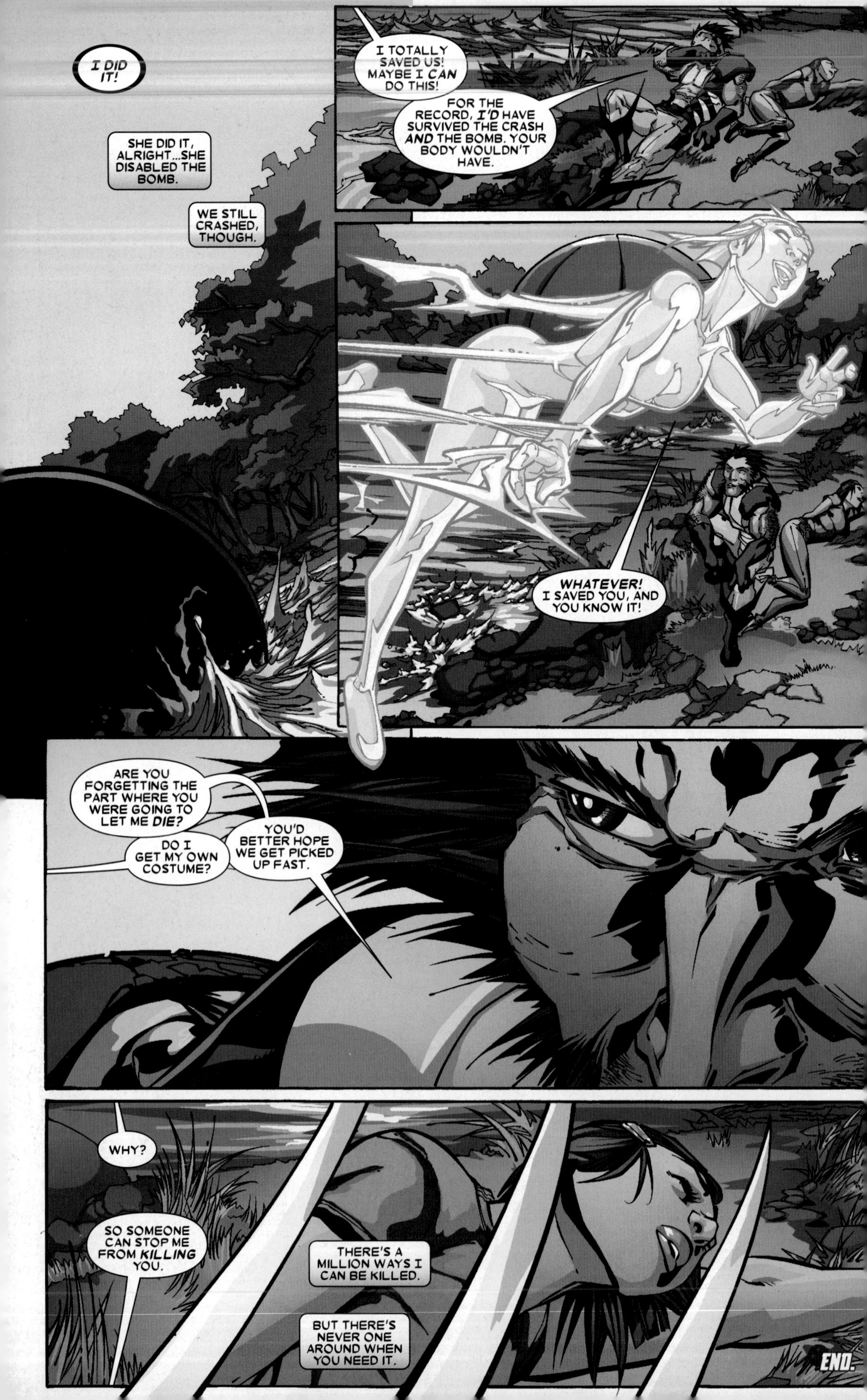
I DID IT!
SHE DID IT, ALRIGHT...SHE DISABLED THE BOMB.
WE STILL CRASHED, THOUGH.
I TOTALLY SAVED US! MAYBE I CAN DO THIS!
FOR THE RECORD, I'D HAVE SURVIVED THE CRASH AND THE BOMB. YOUR BODY WOULDN'T HAVE.
WHATEVER! I SAVED YOU, AND YOU KNOW IT!
ARE YOU FORGETTING THE PART WHERE YOU WERE GOING TO LET ME DIE?
DO I GET MY OWN COSTUME?
YOU'D BETTER HOPE WE GET PICKED UP FAST.
WHY?
SO SOMEONE CAN STOP ME FROM KILLING YOU.
THERE'S A MILLION WAYS I CAN BE KILLED.
BUT THERE'S NEVER ONE AROUND WHEN YOU NEED IT.
END.

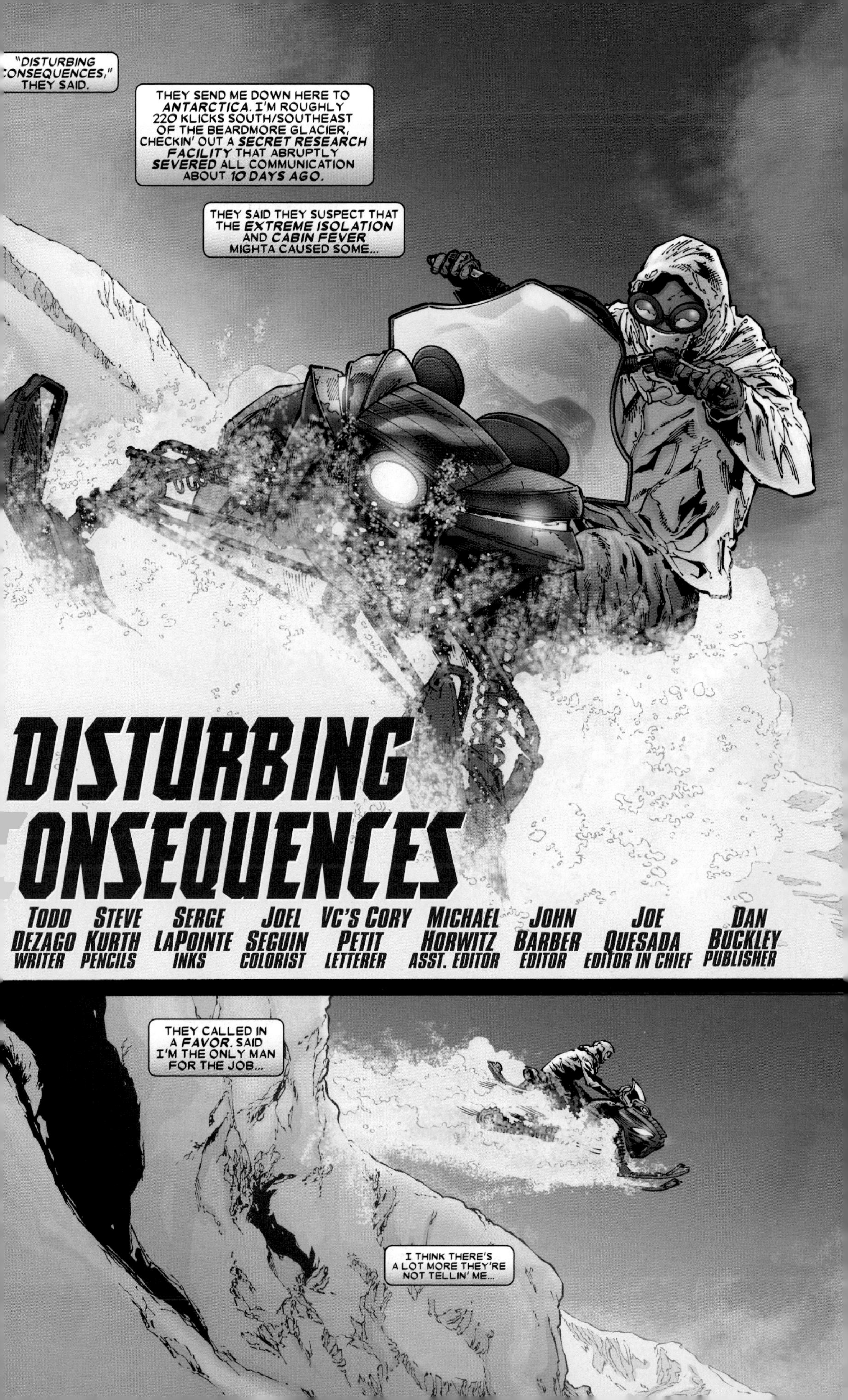
"DISTURBING ONSEQUENCES," THEY SAID.
THEY SEND ME DOWN HERE TO ANTARCTICA. I'M ROUGHLY 220 KLICKS SOUTH/SOUTHEAST OF THE BEARDMORE GLACIER, CHECKIN' OUT A SECRET RESEARCH FACILITY THAT ABRUPTLY SEVERED ALL COMMUNICATION ABOUT 10 DAYS AGO.
THEY SAID THEY SUSPECT THAT THE EXTREME ISOLATION AND CABIN FEVER MIGHTA CAUSED SOME...
DISTURBING ONSEQUENCES
TODD DEZAGO WRITER
STEVE KURTH PENCILS
SERGE LaPOINTE INKS
JOEL SEGUIN COLORIST
VC'S CORY PETIT LETTERER
MICHAEL HORWITZ ASST. EDITOR
JOHN BARBER EDITOR
JOE QUESADA EDITOR IN CHIEF
DAN BUCKLEY PUBLISHER
THEY CALLED IN A FAVOR. SAID I'M THE ONLY MAN FOR THE JOB...
I THINK THERE'S A LOT MORE THEY'RE NOT TELLIN' ME...

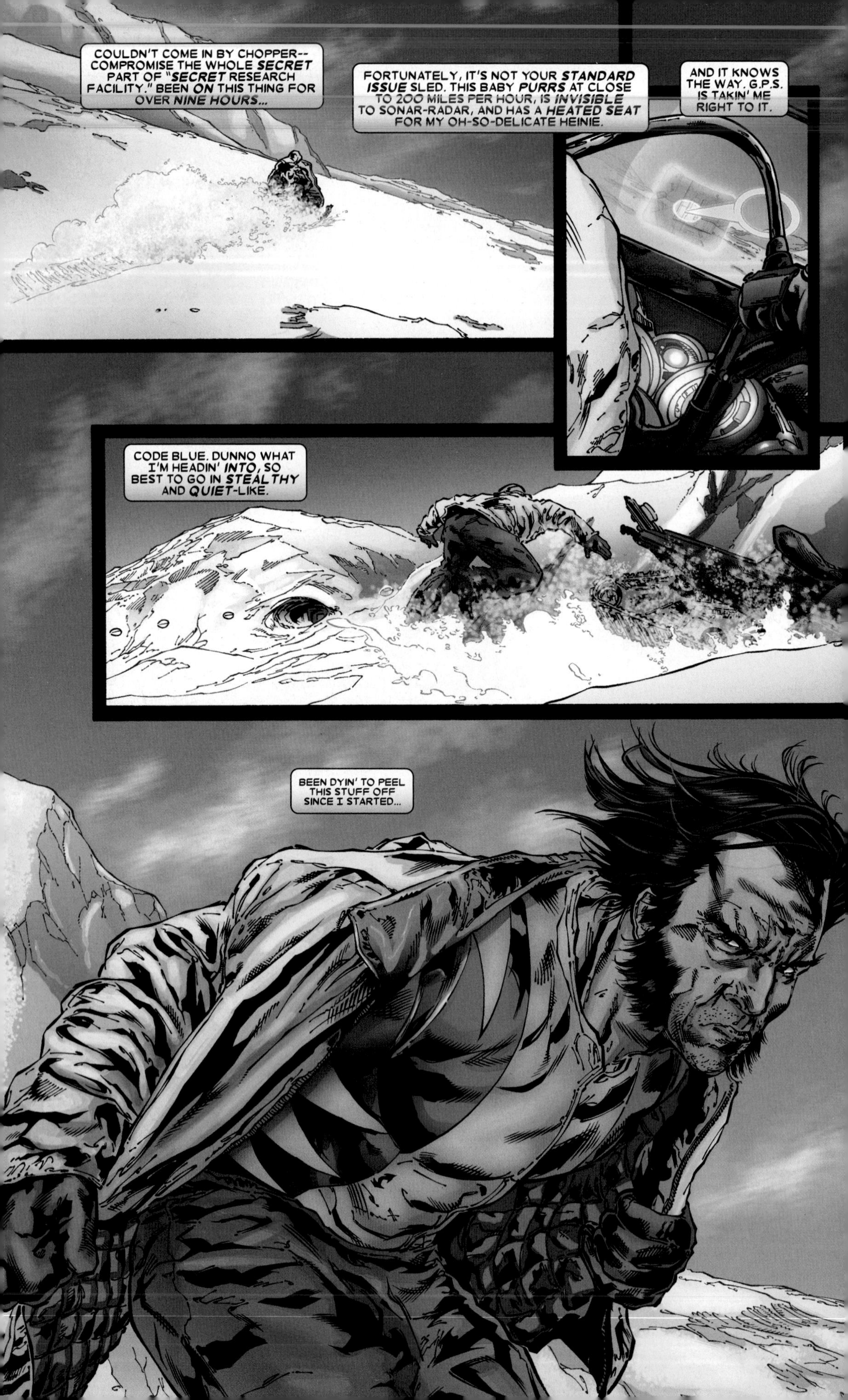
COULDN'T COME IN BY CHOPPER-- COMPROMISE THE WHOLE *SECRET* PART OF "*SECRET* RESEARCH FACILITY." BEEN *ON* THIS THING FOR OVER *NINE HOURS...*
FORTUNATELY, IT'S NOT YOUR *STANDARD ISSUE* SLED. THIS BABY *PURRS* AT CLOSE TO 200 MILES PER HOUR, IS *INVISIBLE* TO SONAR-RADAR, AND HAS A *HEATED SEAT* FOR MY OH-SO-DELICATE HEINIE.
AND IT KNOWS THE WAY. G.P.S. IS TAKIN' ME RIGHT TO IT.
CODE BLUE. DUNNO WHAT I'M HEADIN' *INTO*, SO BEST TO GO IN *STEALTHY* AND *QUIET*-LIKE.
BEEN DYIN' TO PEEL THIS STUFF OFF SINCE I STARTED...

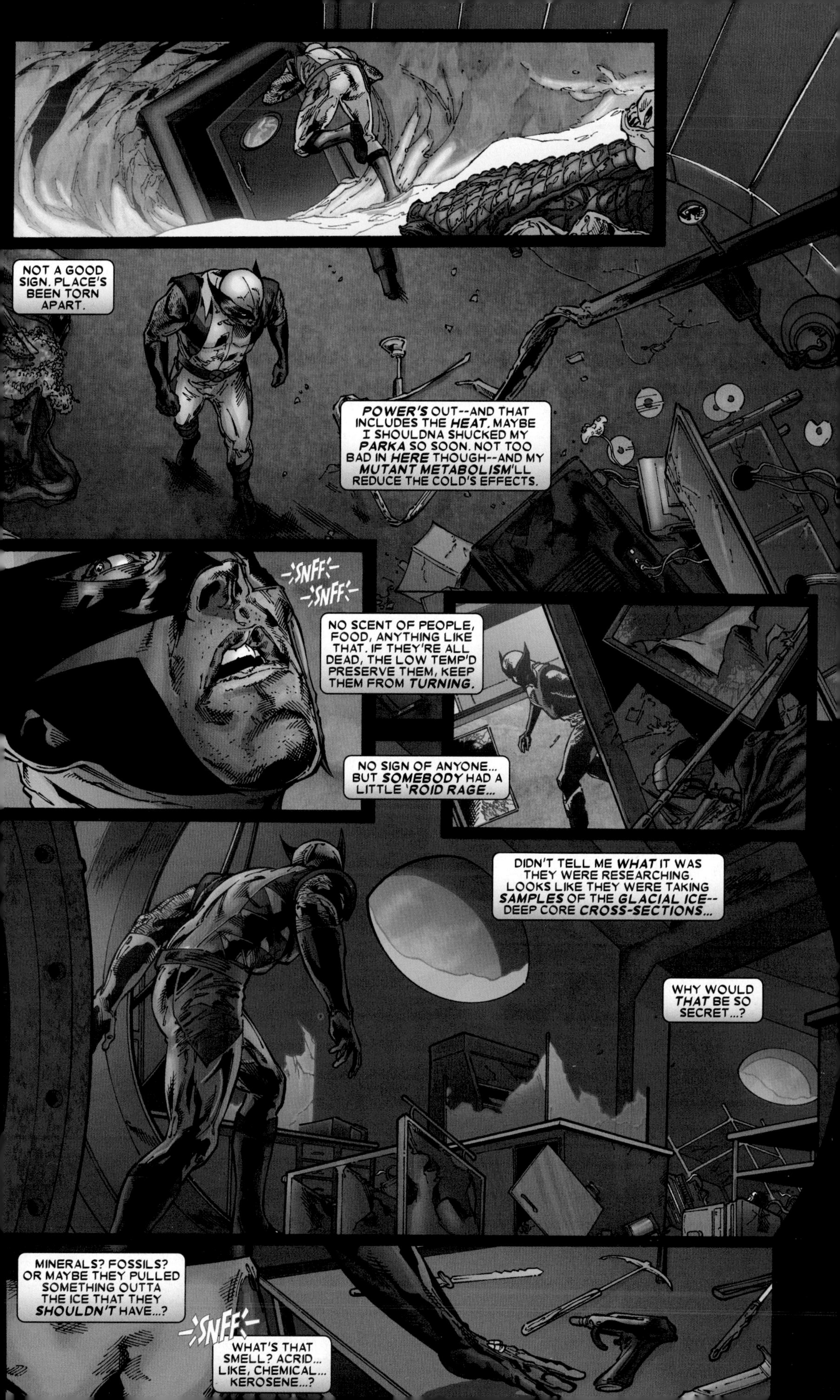
NOT A GOOD SIGN. PLACE'S BEEN TORN APART.
POWER'S OUT--AND THAT INCLUDES THE HEAT. MAYBE I SHOULDNA SHUCKED MY PARKA SO SOON. NOT TOO BAD IN HERE THOUGH--AND MY MUTANT METABOLISM'LL REDUCE THE COLD'S EFFECTS.
-SNFF-
-SNFF-
NO SCENT OF PEOPLE, FOOD, ANYTHING LIKE THAT. IF THEY'RE ALL DEAD, THE LOW TEMP'D PRESERVE THEM, KEEP THEM FROM TURNING.
NO SIGN OF ANYONE... BUT SOMEBODY HAD A LITTLE 'ROID RAGE...
DIDN'T TELL ME WHAT IT WAS THEY WERE RESEARCHING. LOOKS LIKE THEY WERE TAKING SAMPLES OF THE GLACIAL ICE--DEEP CORE CROSS-SECTIONS...
WHY WOULD THAT BE SO SECRET...?
MINERALS? FOSSILS? OR MAYBE THEY PULLED SOMETHING OUTTA THE ICE THAT THEY SHOULDN'T HAVE...?
-SNFF-
WHAT'S THAT SMELL? ACRID... LIKE, CHEMICAL... KEROSENE...?

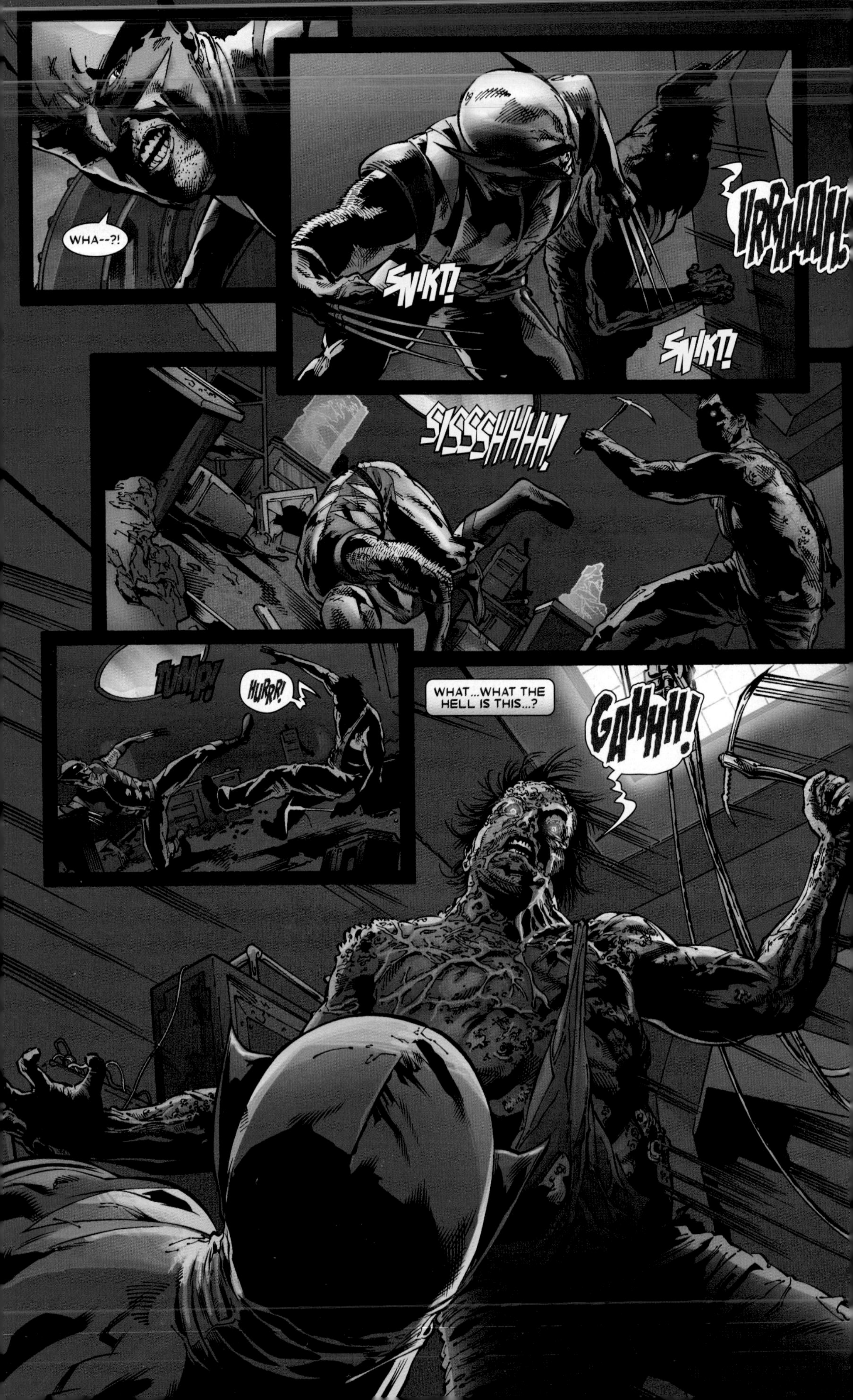
WHA--?!
SNIKT!
VRROAAH!
SNIKT!
SISSSHHHH!
TUMP!
HURRR!
WHAT...WHAT THE HELL IS THIS...?
GAHHH!

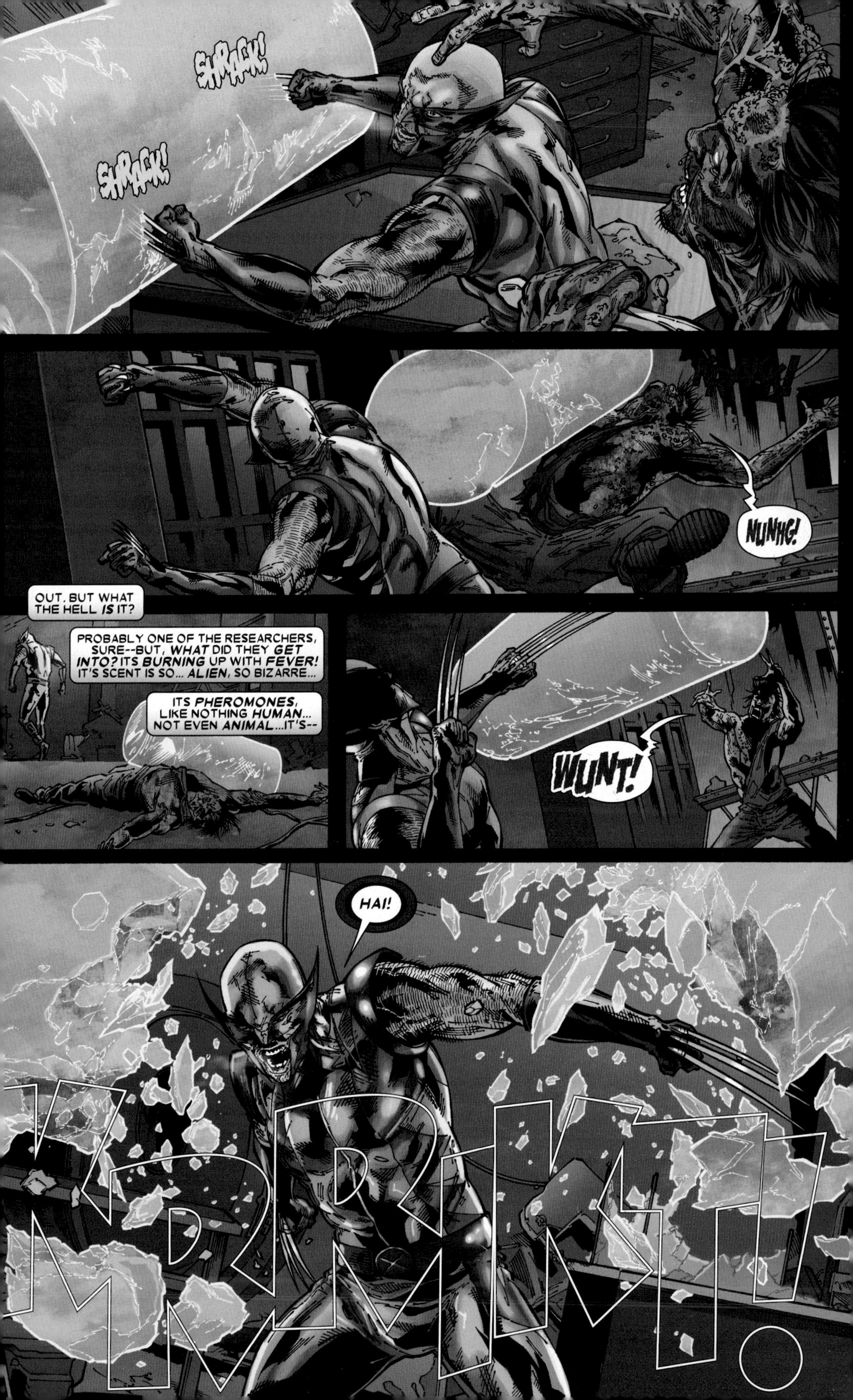
SHRACK!
SHRACK!
NUNHG!
OUT. BUT WHAT THE HELL IS IT?
PROBABLY ONE OF THE RESEARCHERS, SURE--BUT, WHAT DID THEY GET INTO? ITS BURNING UP WITH FEVER! IT'S SCENT IS SO... ALIEN, SO BIZARRE...
ITS PHEROMONES, LIKE NOTHING HUMAN... NOT EVEN ANIMAL...IT'S--
WUNT!
HAI!

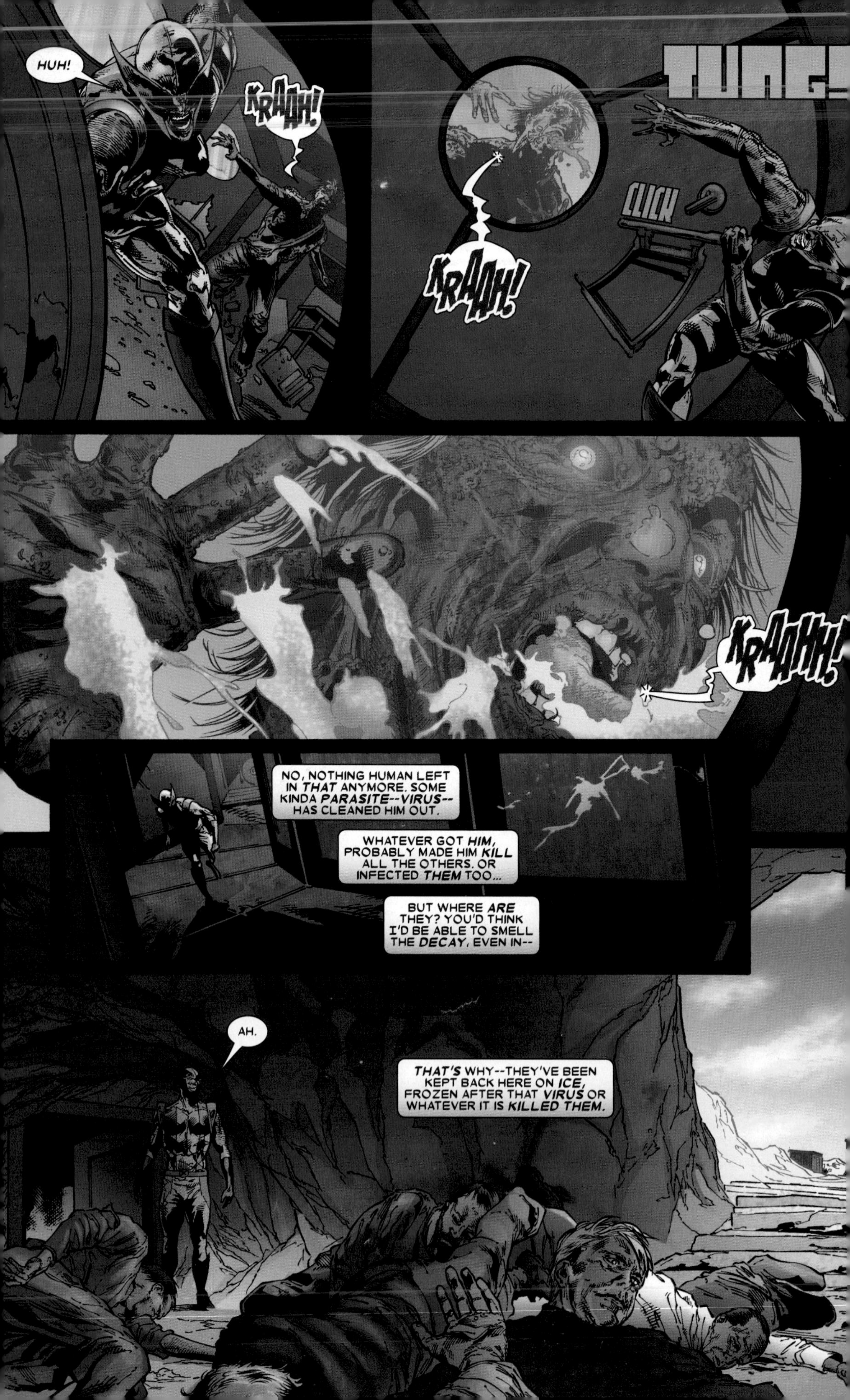
HUH!
KRAAH!
TUNG!
KRAAH!
CLICK
KRAAHH!
NO, NOTHING HUMAN LEFT IN *THAT* ANYMORE. SOME KINDA *PARASITE--VIRUS--* HAS CLEANED HIM OUT.
WHATEVER GOT *HIM*, PROBABLY MADE HIM *KILL* ALL THE OTHERS. OR INFECTED *THEM* TOO...
BUT WHERE *ARE* THEY? YOU'D THINK I'D BE ABLE TO SMELL THE *DECAY*, EVEN IN--
AH.
THAT'S WHY--THEY'VE BEEN KEPT BACK HERE ON *ICE*, FROZEN AFTER THAT *VIRUS* OR WHATEVER IT IS *KILLED THEM.*

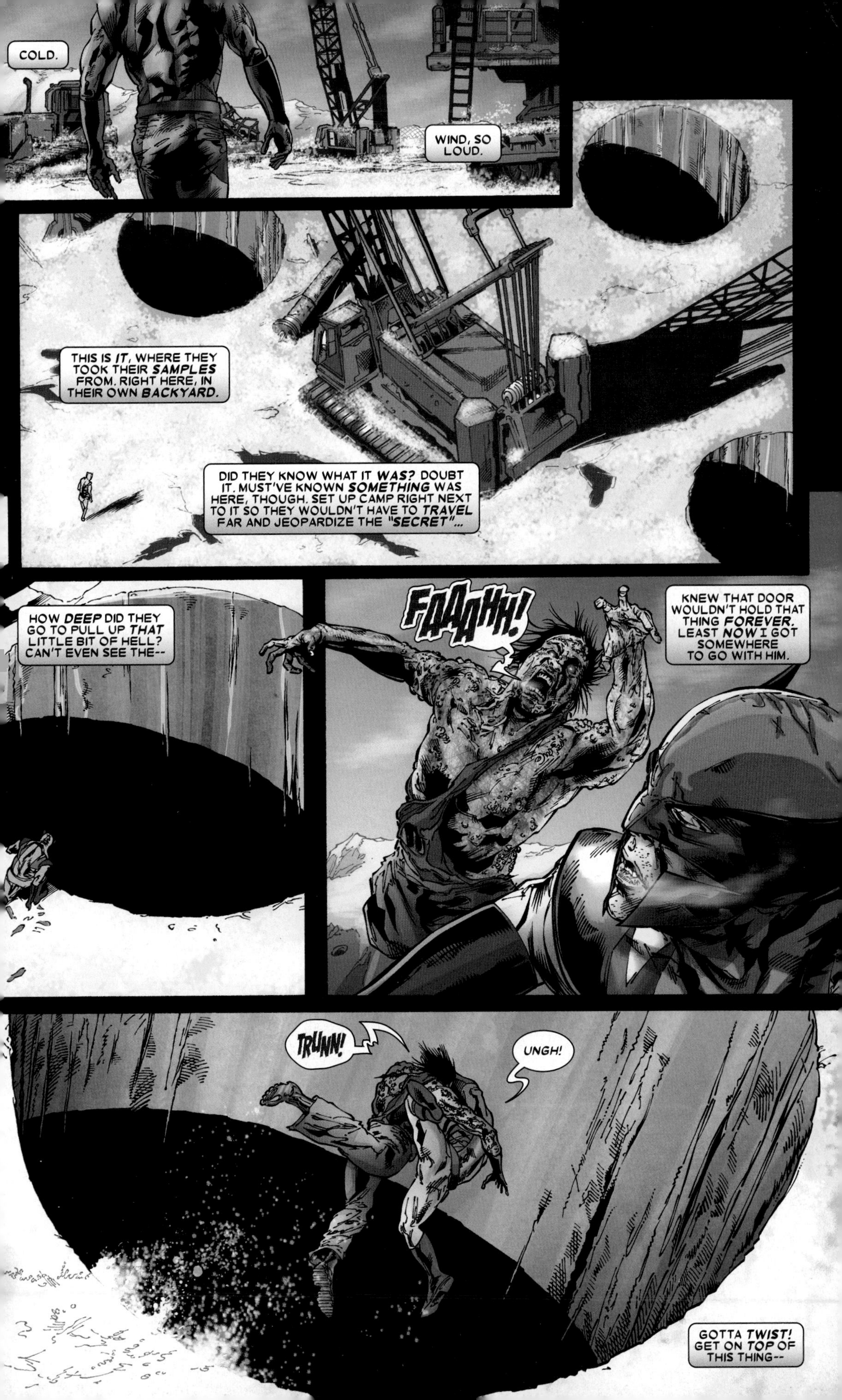

COLD.
WIND, SO LOUD.
THIS IS *IT*, WHERE THEY TOOK THEIR *SAMPLES* FROM. RIGHT HERE, IN THEIR OWN *BACKYARD*.
DID THEY KNOW WHAT IT *WAS?* DOUBT IT. MUST'VE KNOWN *SOMETHING* WAS HERE, THOUGH. SET UP CAMP RIGHT NEXT TO IT SO THEY WOULDN'T HAVE TO *TRAVEL* FAR AND JEOPARDIZE THE *"SECRET"*...
HOW *DEEP* DID THEY GO TO PULL UP *THAT* LITTLE BIT OF HELL? CAN'T EVEN SEE THE--
FAAAHH!
KNEW THAT DOOR WOULDN'T HOLD THAT THING *FOREVER.* LEAST *NOW* I GOT SOMEWHERE TO GO WITH HIM.
TRUNN!
UNGH!
GOTTA *TWIST!* GET ON *TOP* OF THIS THING--

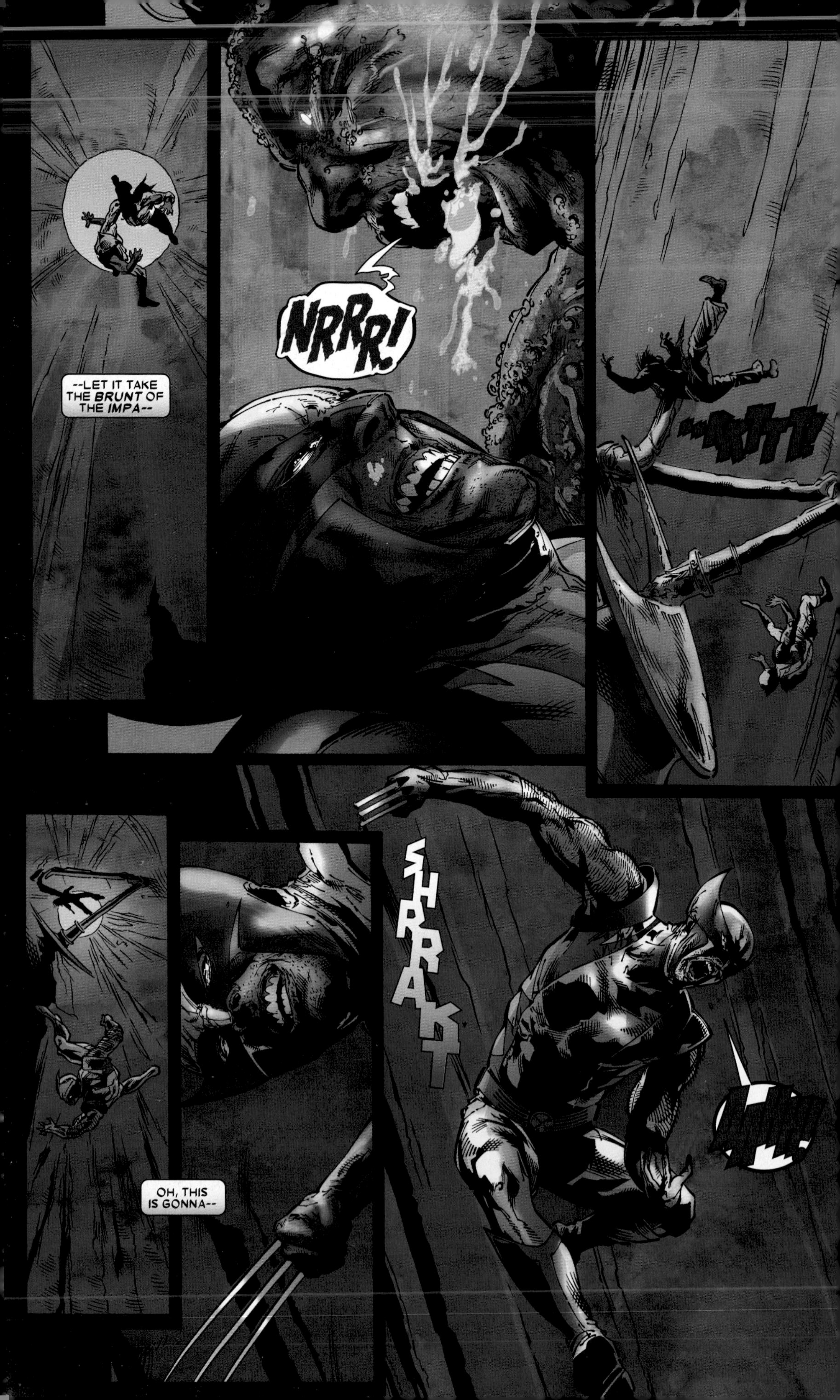
--LET IT TAKE THE BRUNT OF THE IMPA--
NRRR!
OH, THIS IS GONNA--
SHRRAKT

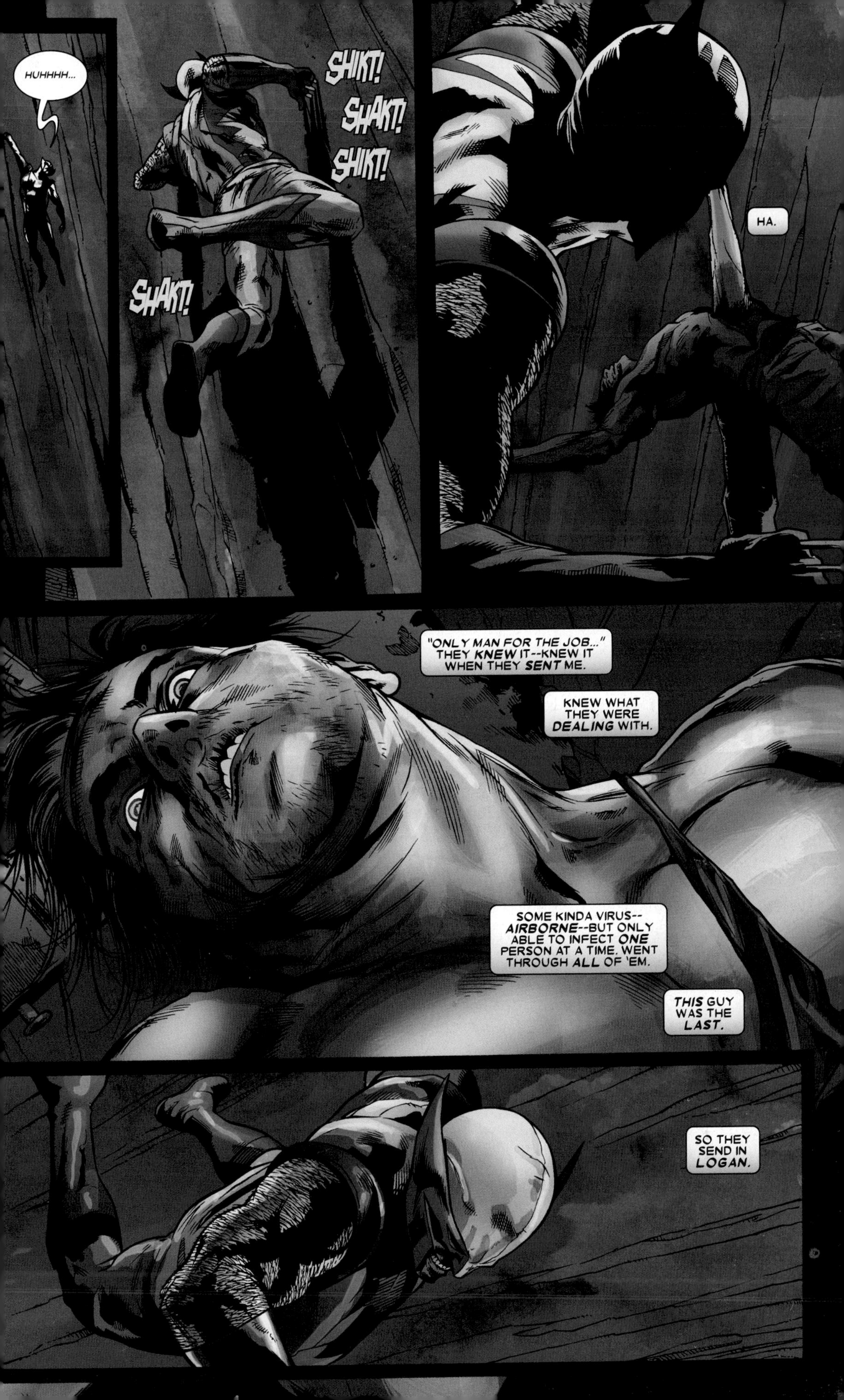
HUHHHH...
SHIKT!
SHAKT!
SHIKT!
SHAKT!
HA.
"ONLY MAN FOR THE JOB..." THEY KNEW IT--KNEW IT WHEN THEY SENT ME.
KNEW WHAT THEY WERE DEALING WITH.
SOME KINDA VIRUS--AIRBORNE--BUT ONLY ABLE TO INFECT ONE PERSON AT A TIME. WENT THROUGH ALL OF 'EM.
THIS GUY WAS THE LAST.
SO THEY SEND IN LOGAN.

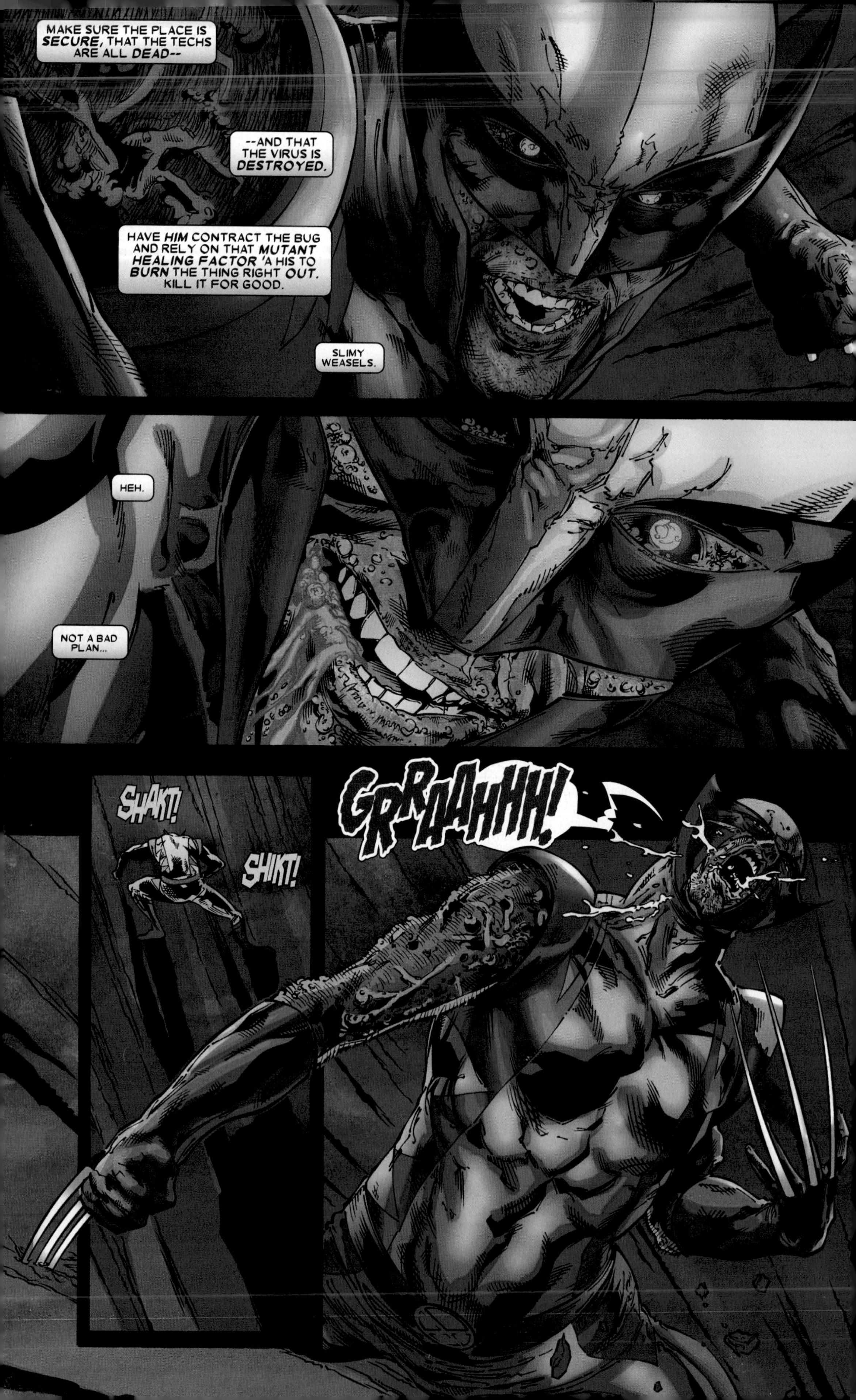
MAKE SURE THE PLACE IS SECURE, THAT THE TECHS ARE ALL DEAD--
--AND THAT THE VIRUS IS DESTROYED.
HAVE HIM CONTRACT THE BUG AND RELY ON THAT MUTANT HEALING FACTOR 'A HIS TO BURN THE THING RIGHT OUT. KILL IT FOR GOOD.
SLIMY WEASELS.
HEH.
NOT A BAD PLAN...
SHAKT!
SHIKT!
GRRAAHHH!

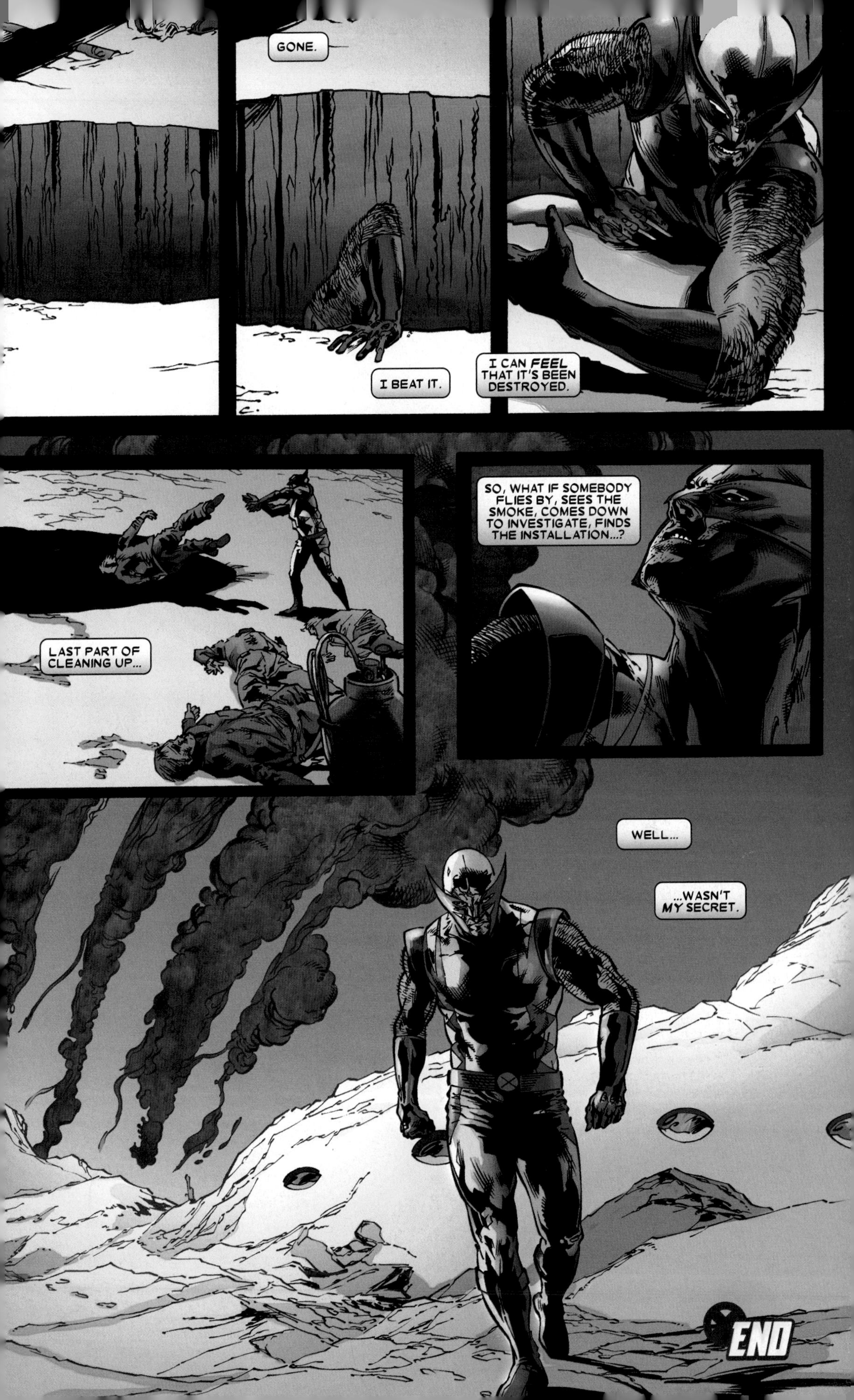
GONE.
I BEAT IT.
I CAN FEEL THAT IT'S BEEN DESTROYED.
LAST PART OF CLEANING UP...
SO, WHAT IF SOMEBODY FLIES BY, SEES THE SMOKE, COMES DOWN TO INVESTIGATE, FINDS THE INSTALLATION...?
WELL...
...WASN'T MY SECRET.
END

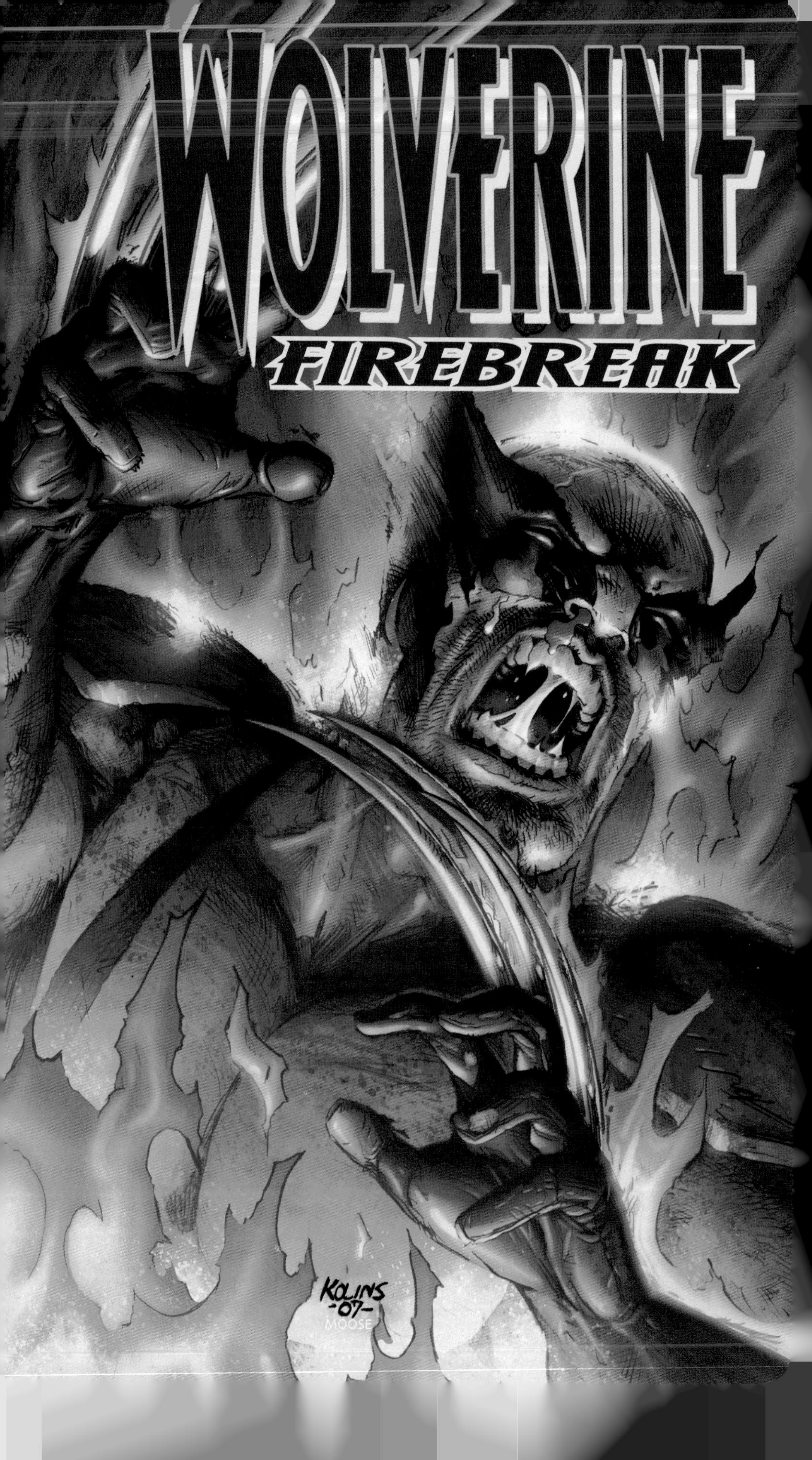
WOLVERINE
FIREBREAK
KOLINS
-07-
MOOSE

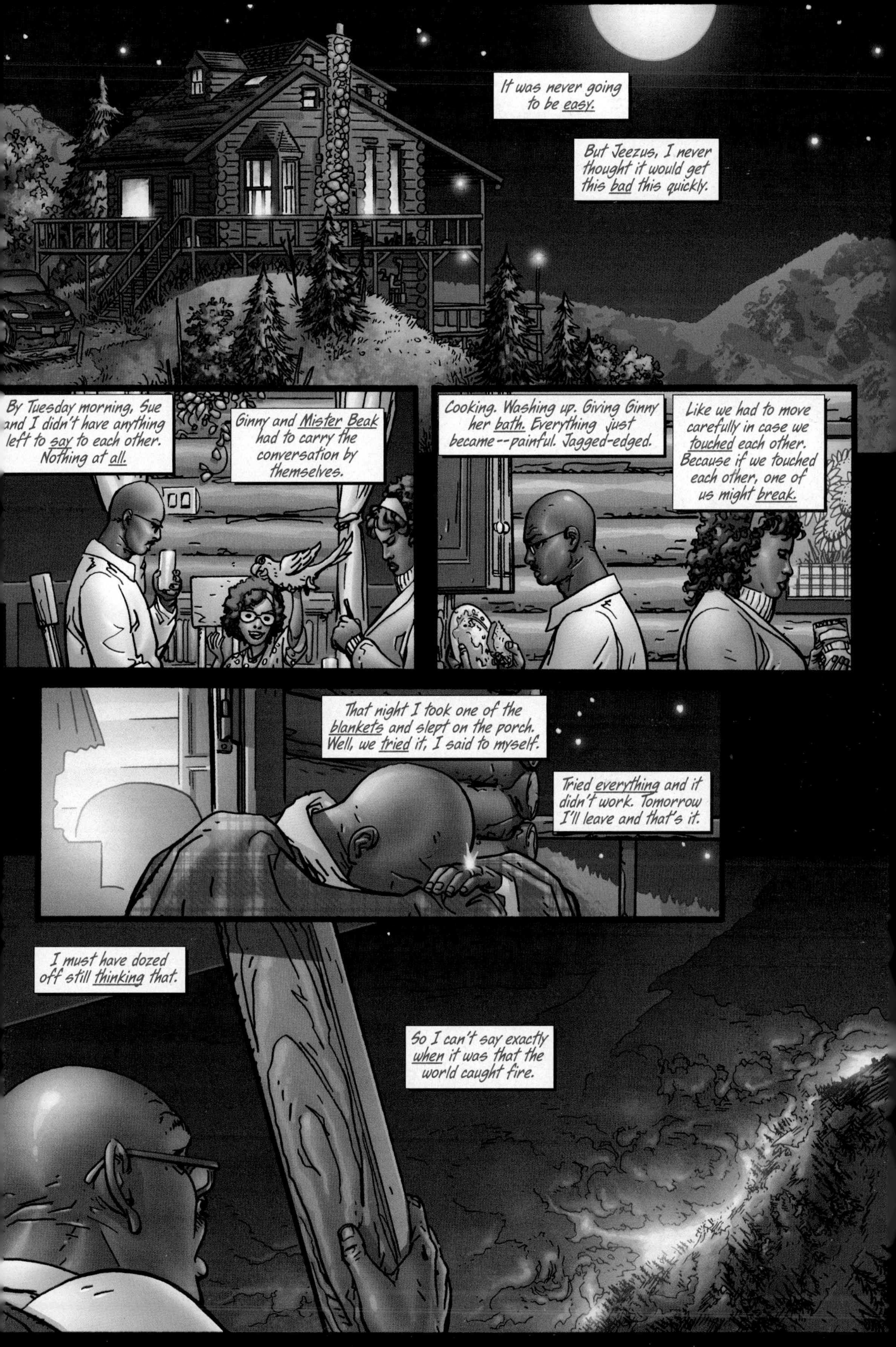
It was never going to be easy.
But Jeezus, I never thought it would get this bad this quickly.
By Tuesday morning, Sue and I didn't have anything left to say to each other. Nothing at all.
Ginny and Mister Beak had to carry the conversation by themselves.
Cooking. Washing up. Giving Ginny her bath. Everything just became--painful. Jagged-edged.
Like we had to move carefully in case we touched each other. Because if we touched each other, one of us might break.
That night I took one of the blankets and slept on the porch. Well, we tried it, I said to myself.
Tried everything and it didn't work. Tomorrow I'll leave and that's it.
I must have dozed off still thinking that.
So I can't say exactly when it was that the world caught fire.

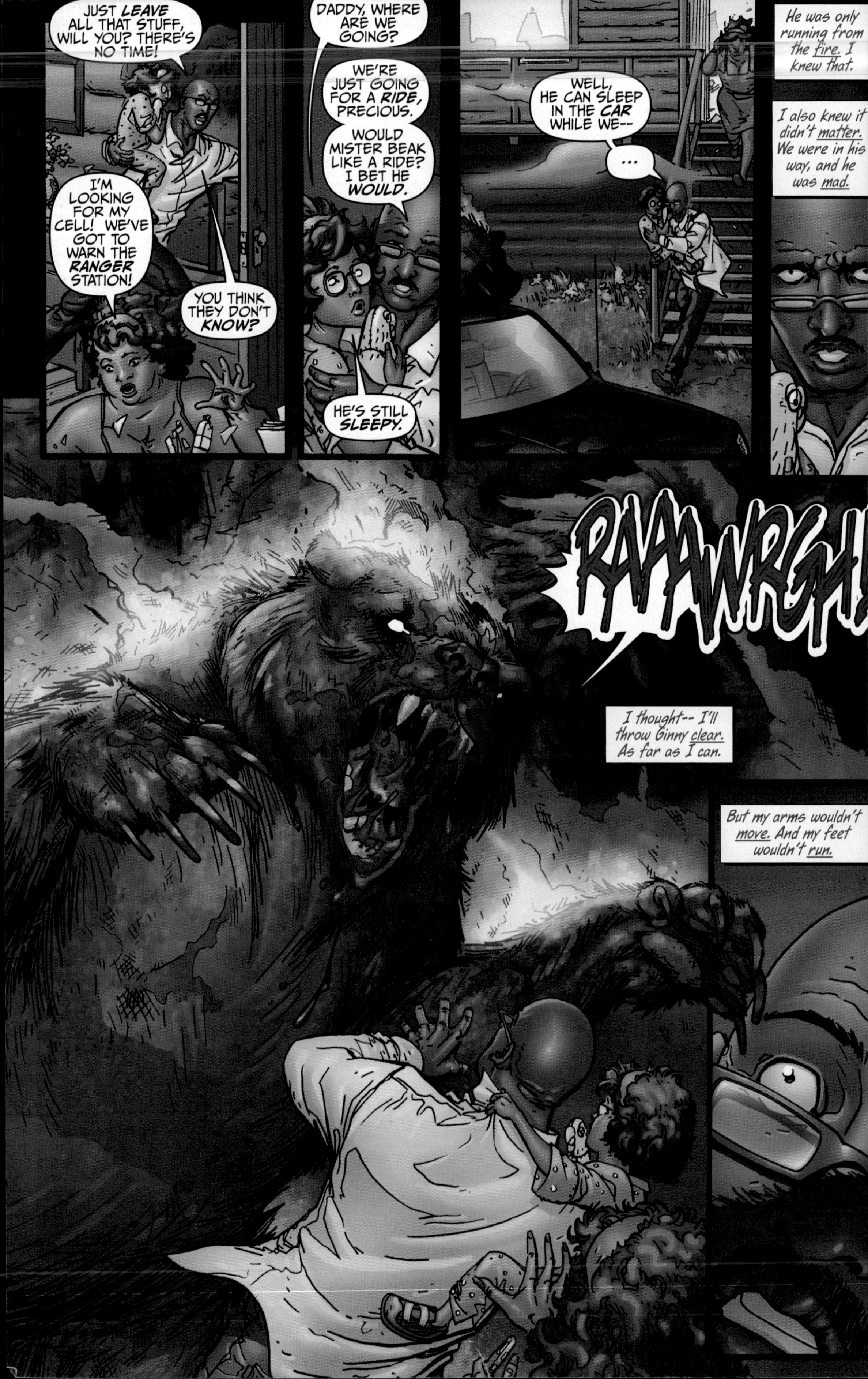
JUST LEAVE ALL THAT STUFF, WILL YOU? THERE'S NO TIME!
I'M LOOKING FOR MY CELL! WE'VE GOT TO WARN THE RANGER STATION!
YOU THINK THEY DON'T KNOW?
DADDY, WHERE ARE WE GOING?
WE'RE JUST GOING FOR A RIDE, PRECIOUS.
WOULD MISTER BEAK LIKE A RIDE? I BET HE WOULD.
HE'S STILL SLEEPY.
WELL, HE CAN SLEEP IN THE CAR WHILE WE--
...
He was only running from the fire. I knew that.
I also knew it didn't matter. We were in his way, and he was mad.
RAAAWRGH!
I thought-- I'll throw Ginny clear. As far as I can.
But my arms wouldn't move. And my feet wouldn't run.

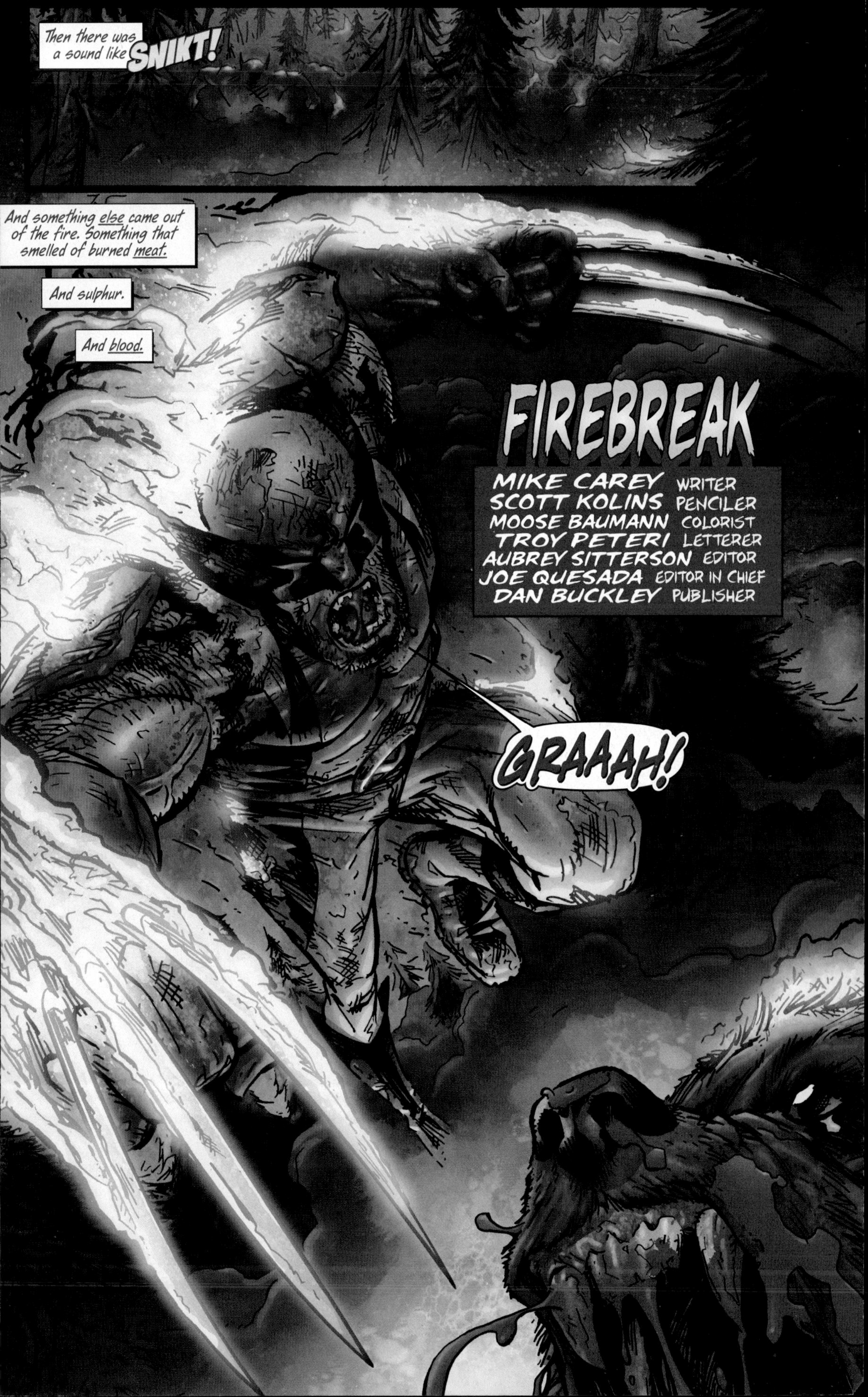

Then there was a sound like SNIKT!
And something else came out of the fire. Something that smelled of burned meat.
And sulphur.
And blood.
FIREBREAK
MIKE CAREY WRITER
SCOTT KOLINS PENCILER
MOOSE BAUMANN COLORIST
TROY PETERI LETTERER
AUBREY SITTERSON EDITOR
JOE QUESADA EDITOR IN CHIEF
DAN BUCKLEY PUBLISHER
GRAAAH!

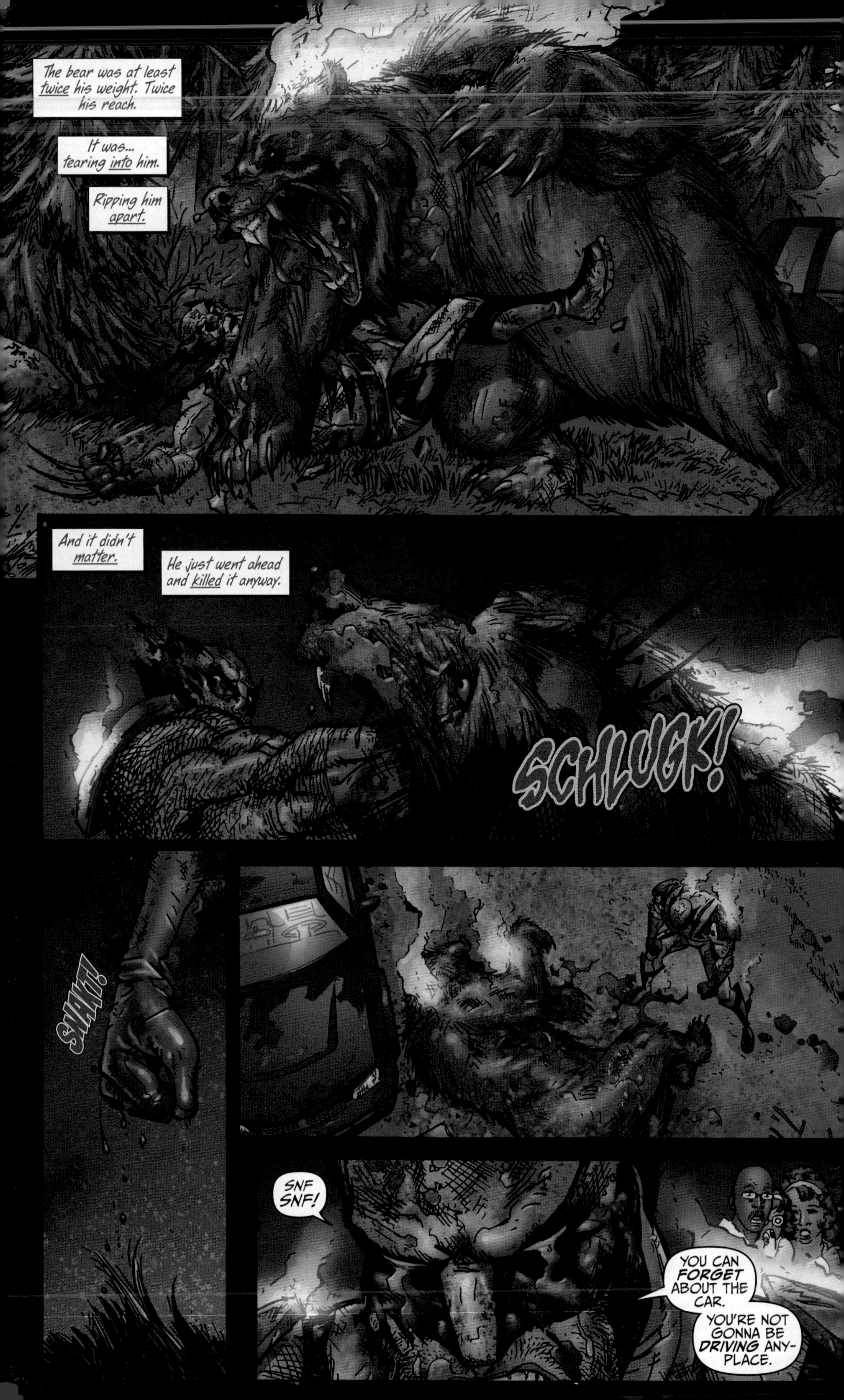

The bear was at least twice his weight. Twice his reach.
It was... tearing into him.
Ripping him apart.
And it didn't matter.
He just went ahead and killed it anyway.
SCHLUCK!
SNIKT!
SNF SNF!
YOU CAN FORGET ABOUT THE CAR.
YOU'RE NOT GONNA BE DRIVING ANY-PLACE.

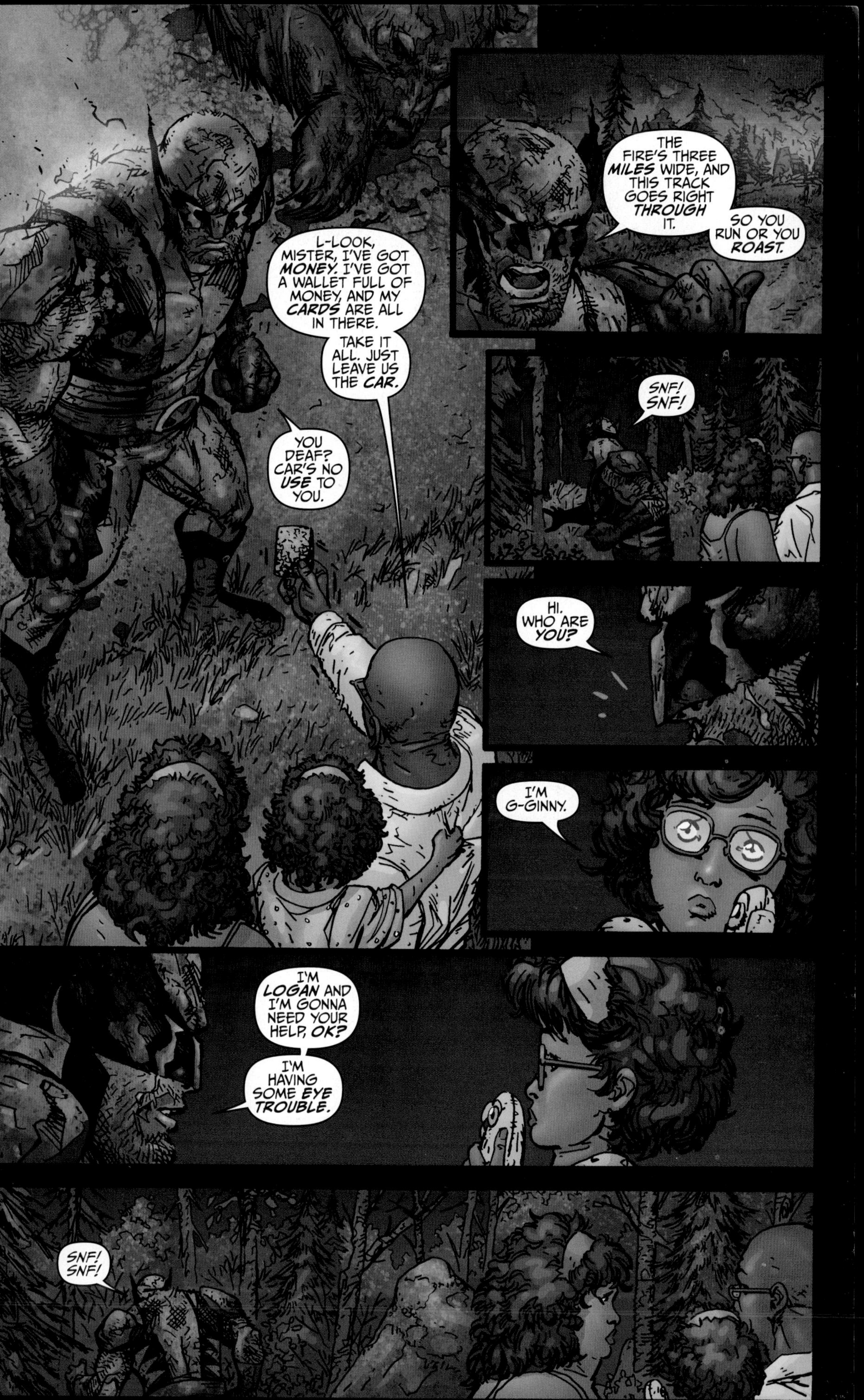

L-LOOK, MISTER, I'VE GOT MONEY. I'VE GOT A WALLET FULL OF MONEY, AND MY CARDS ARE ALL IN THERE.
TAKE IT ALL. JUST LEAVE US THE CAR.
YOU DEAF? CAR'S NO USE TO YOU.
THE FIRE'S THREE MILES WIDE, AND THIS TRACK GOES RIGHT THROUGH IT.
SO YOU RUN OR YOU ROAST.
SNF! SNF!
HI. WHO ARE YOU?
I'M G-GINNY.
I'M LOGAN AND I'M GONNA NEED YOUR HELP, OK?
I'M HAVING SOME EYE TROUBLE.
SNF! SNF!

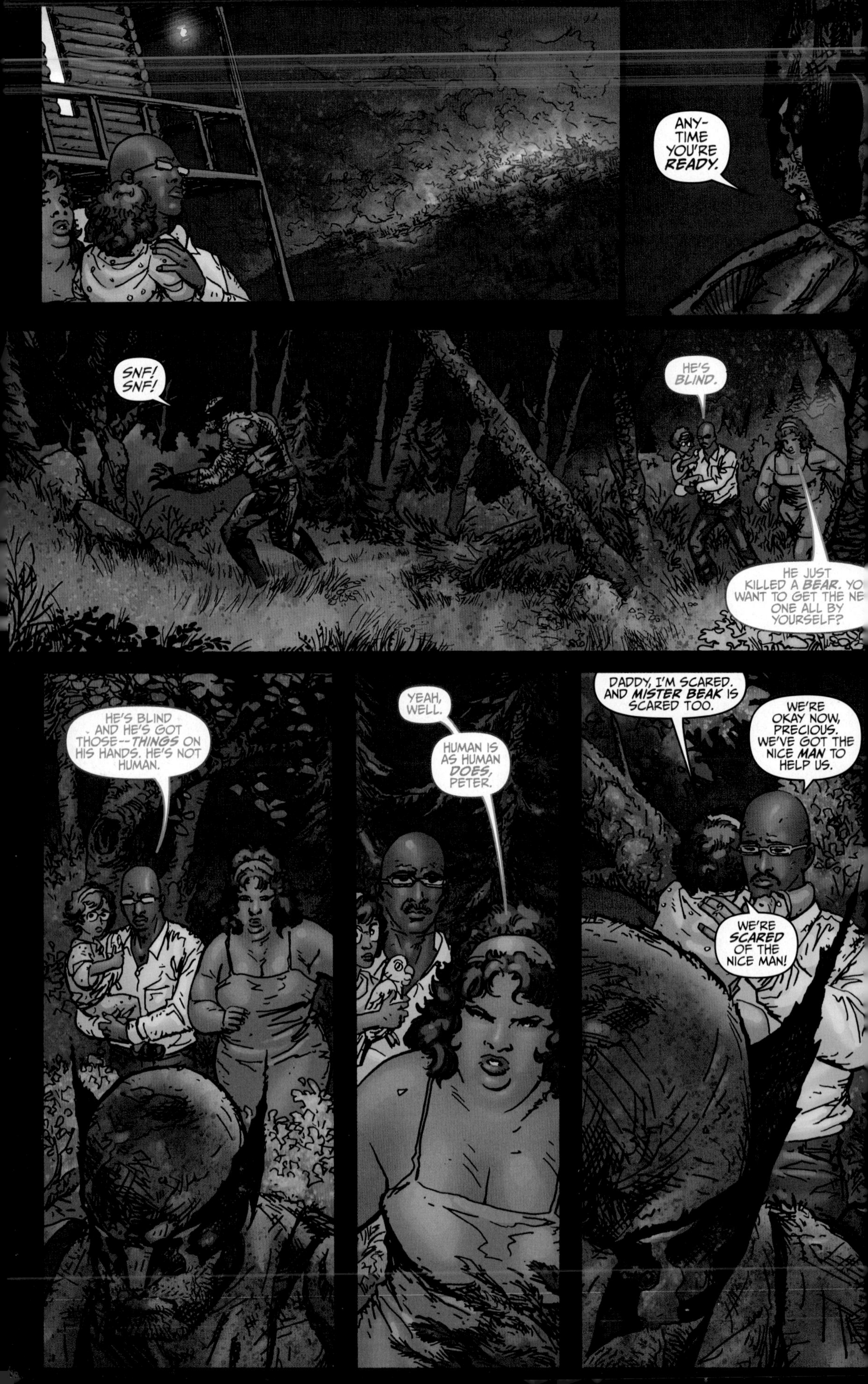
ANY-TIME YOU'RE READY.
SNF! SNF!
HE'S BLIND.
HE JUST KILLED A BEAR. YO WANT TO GET THE NE ONE ALL BY YOURSELF?
HE'S BLIND AND HE'S GOT THOSE--THINGS ON HIS HANDS. HE'S NOT HUMAN.
YEAH, WELL.
HUMAN IS AS HUMAN DOES, PETER.
DADDY, I'M SCARED. AND MISTER BEAK IS SCARED TOO.
WE'RE OKAY NOW, PRECIOUS. WE'VE GOT THE NICE MAN TO HELP US.
WE'RE SCARED OF THE NICE MAN!

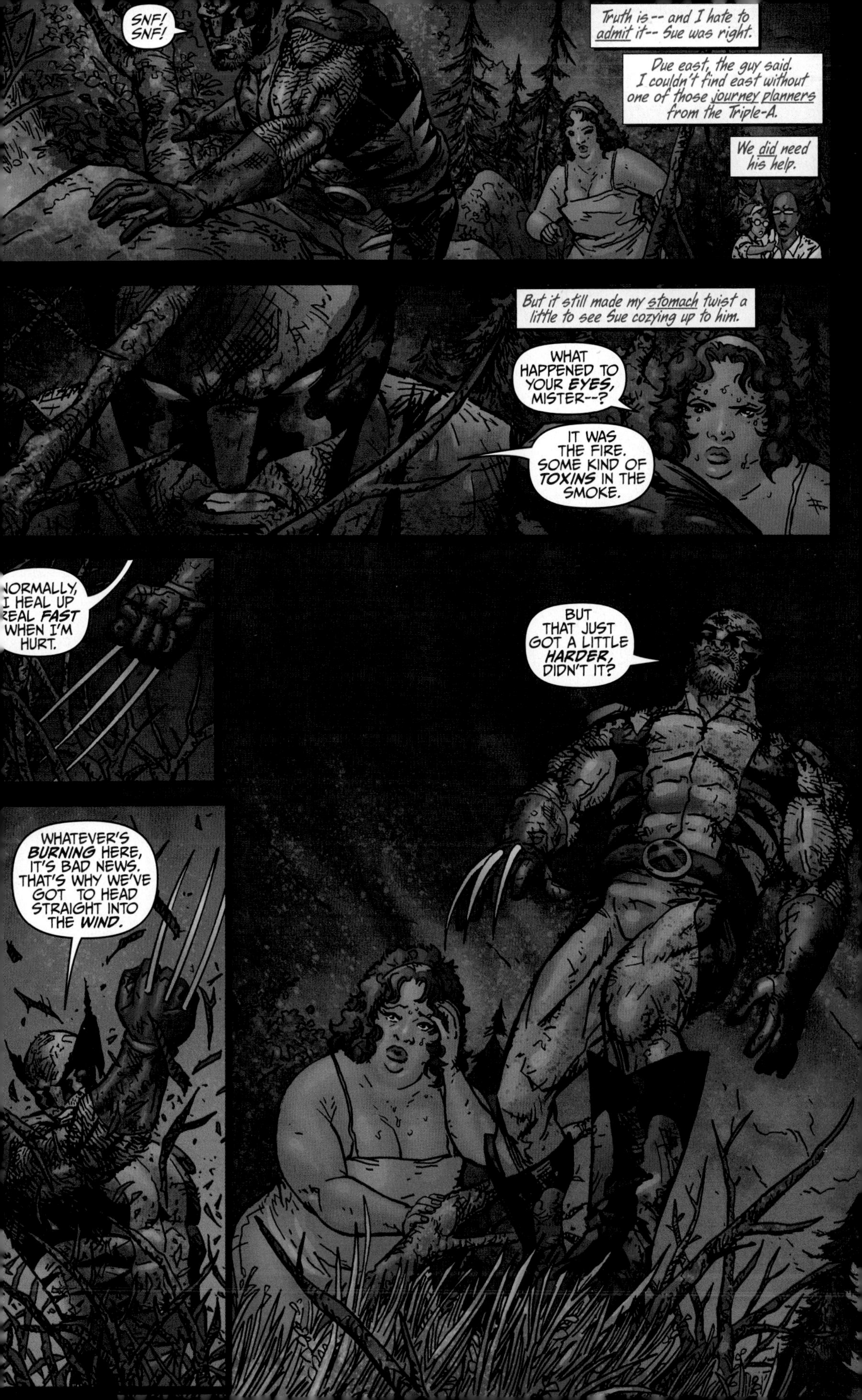
SNF! SNF!
Truth is -- and I hate to admit it-- Sue was right.
Due east, the guy said. I couldn't find east without one of those journey planners from the Triple-A.
We did need his help.
But it still made my stomach twist a little to see Sue cozying up to him.
WHAT HAPPENED TO YOUR EYES, MISTER--?
IT WAS THE FIRE. SOME KIND OF TOXINS IN THE SMOKE.
NORMALLY, I HEAL UP REAL FAST WHEN I'M HURT.
BUT THAT JUST GOT A LITTLE HARDER, DIDN'T IT?
WHATEVER'S BURNING HERE, IT'S BAD NEWS. THAT'S WHY WE'VE GOT TO HEAD STRAIGHT INTO THE WIND.

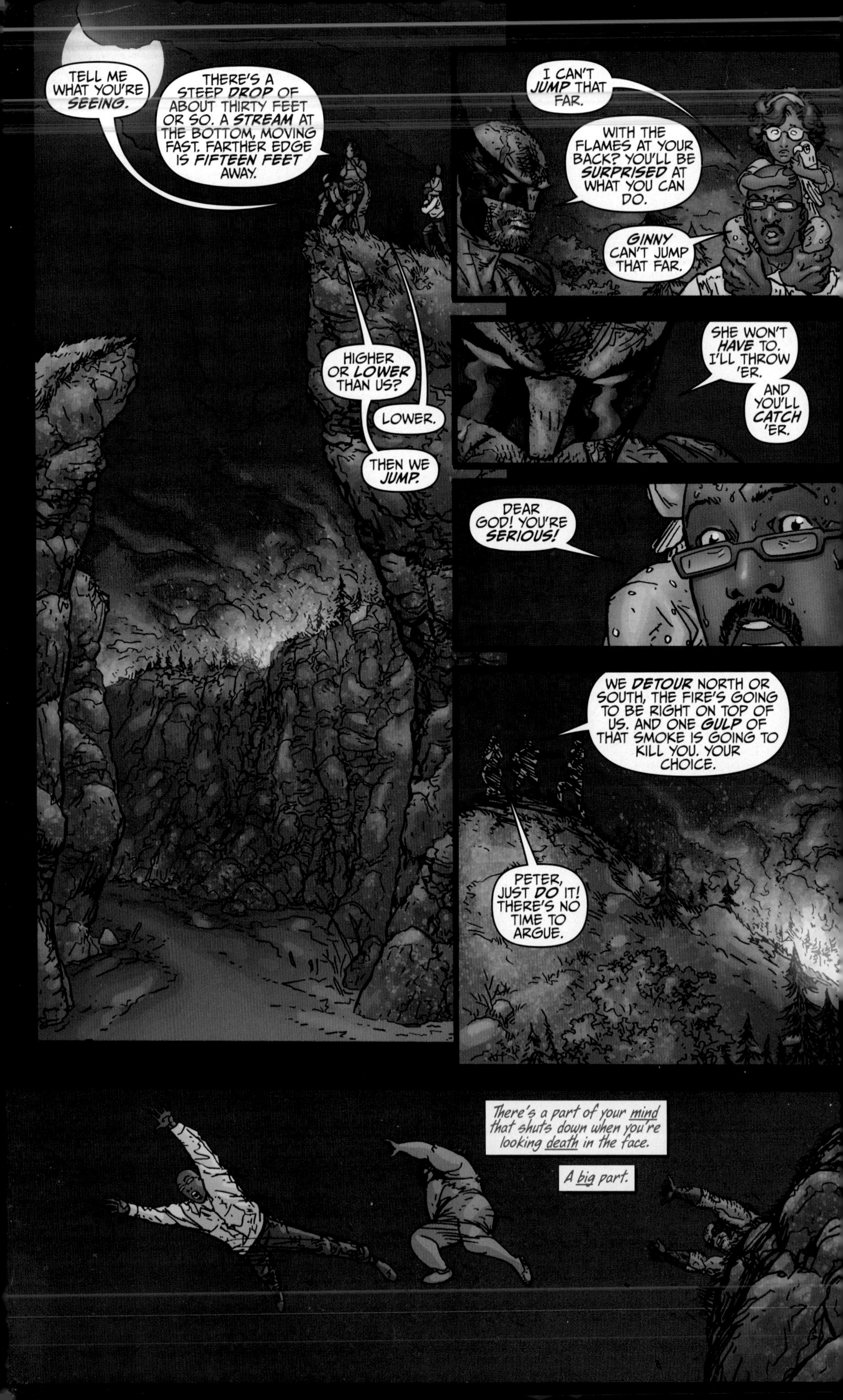
TELL ME WHAT YOU'RE *SEEING.*
THERE'S A STEEP *DROP* OF ABOUT THIRTY FEET OR SO. A *STREAM* AT THE BOTTOM, MOVING FAST. FARTHER EDGE IS *FIFTEEN FEET* AWAY.
HIGHER OR *LOWER* THAN US?
LOWER.
THEN WE *JUMP.*
I CAN'T *JUMP* THAT FAR.
WITH THE FLAMES AT YOUR BACK? YOU'LL BE *SURPRISED* AT WHAT YOU CAN DO.
GINNY CAN'T JUMP THAT FAR.
SHE WON'T *HAVE* TO. I'LL THROW 'ER.
AND YOU'LL *CATCH* 'ER.
DEAR GOD! YOU'RE *SERIOUS!*
WE *DETOUR* NORTH OR SOUTH, THE FIRE'S GOING TO BE RIGHT ON TOP OF US. AND ONE *GULP* OF THAT SMOKE IS GOING TO KILL YOU. YOUR CHOICE.
PETER, JUST *DO* IT! THERE'S NO TIME TO ARGUE.
There's a part of your mind that shuts down when you're looking death in the face.
A big part.

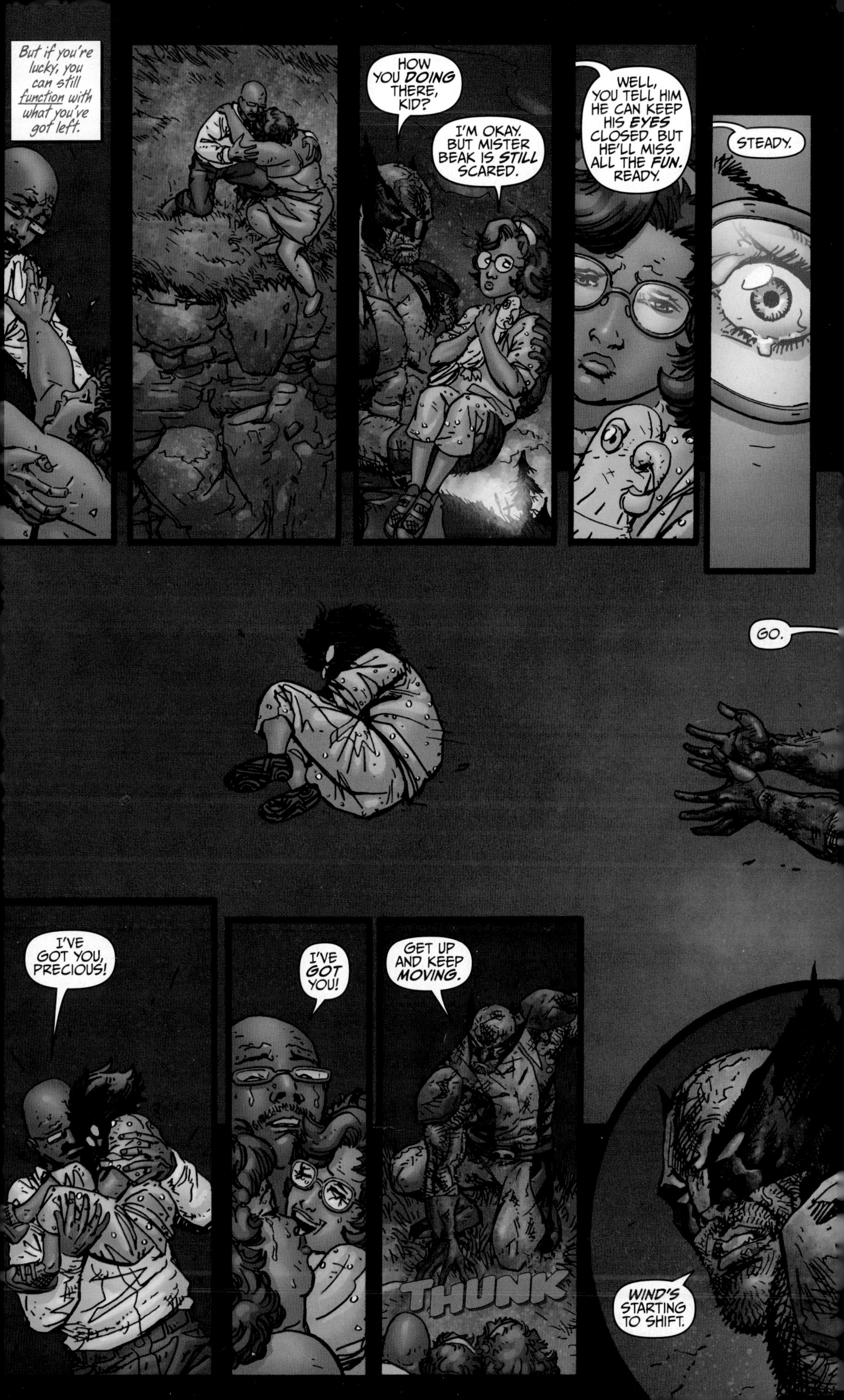
But if you're lucky, you can still function with what you've got left.
HOW YOU DOING THERE, KID?
I'M OKAY. BUT MISTER BEAK IS STILL SCARED.
WELL, YOU TELL HIM HE CAN KEEP HIS EYES CLOSED. BUT HE'LL MISS ALL THE FUN. READY.
STEADY.
GO.
I'VE GOT YOU, PRECIOUS!
I'VE GOT YOU!
GET UP AND KEEP MOVING.
THUNK
WIND'S STARTING TO SHIFT.

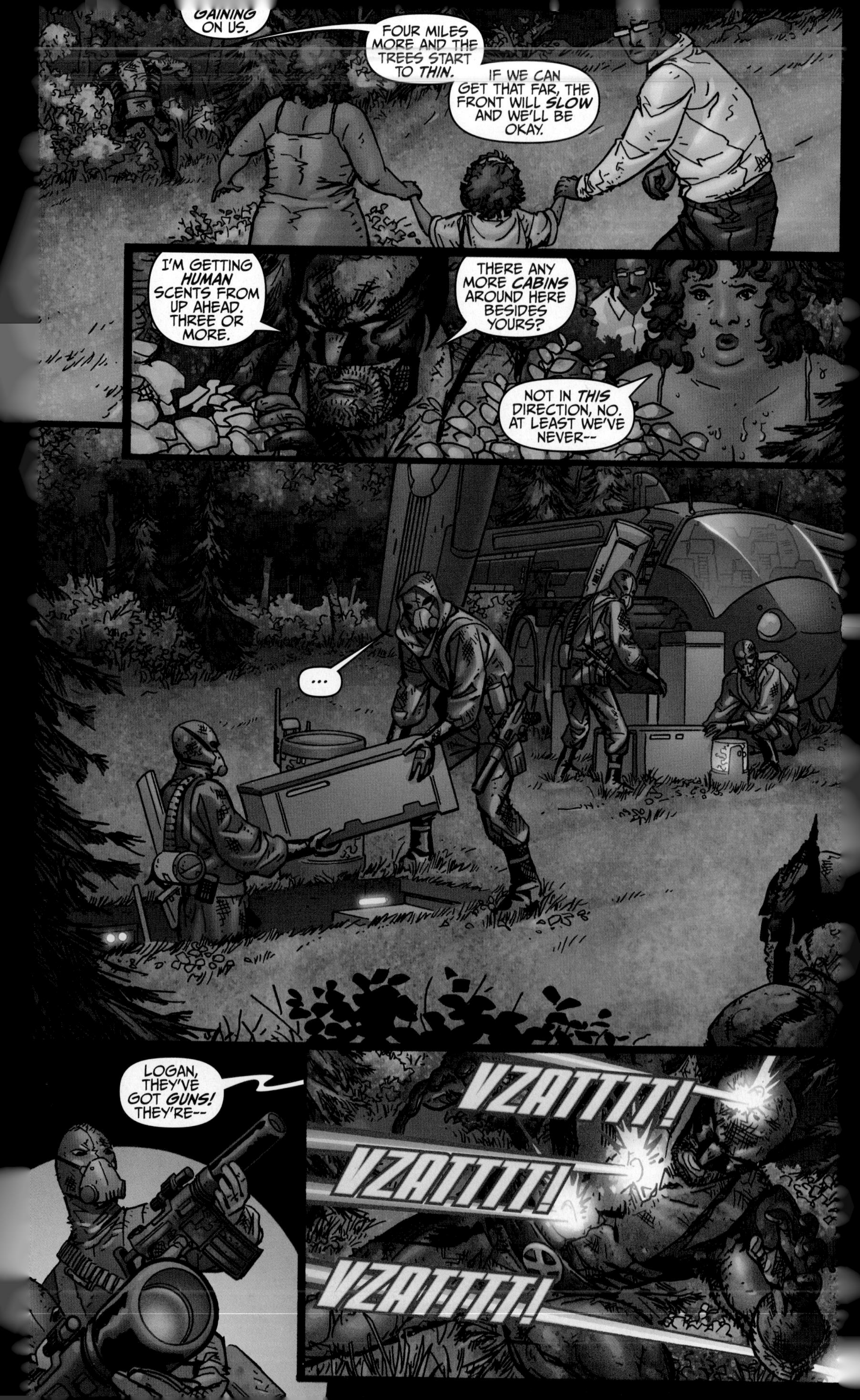
GAINING ON US.
FOUR MILES MORE AND THE TREES START TO THIN.
IF WE CAN GET THAT FAR, THE FRONT WILL SLOW AND WE'LL BE OKAY.
I'M GETTING HUMAN SCENTS FROM UP AHEAD. THREE OR MORE.
THERE ANY MORE CABINS AROUND HERE BESIDES YOURS?
NOT IN THIS DIRECTION, NO. AT LEAST WE'VE NEVER--
...
LOGAN, THEY'VE GOT GUNS! THEY'RE--
VZATTTT!
VZATTTT!
VZATTTT!

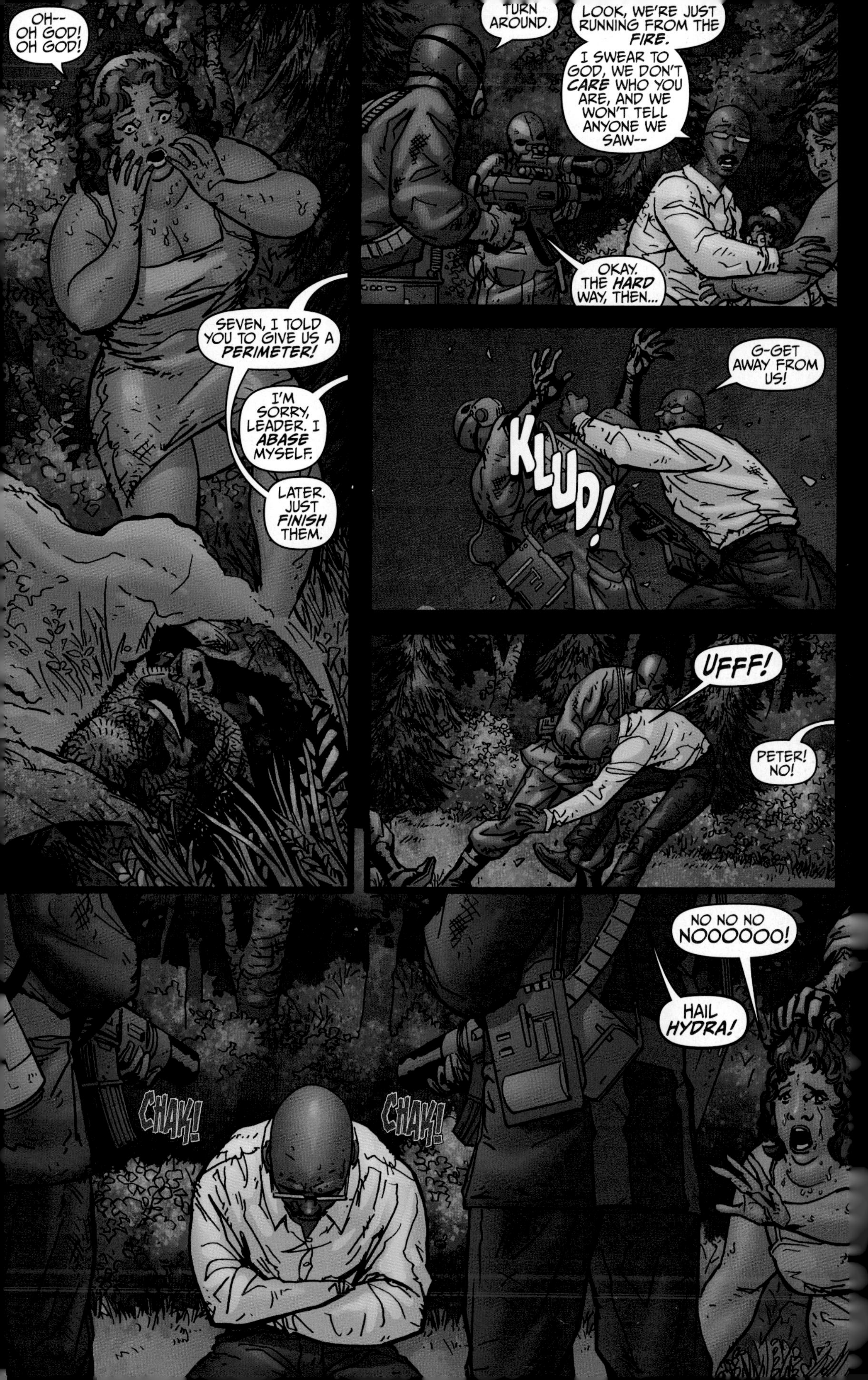

OH-- OH GOD! OH GOD!
TURN AROUND.
LOOK, WE'RE JUST RUNNING FROM THE FIRE. I SWEAR TO GOD, WE DON'T CARE WHO YOU ARE, AND WE WON'T TELL ANYONE WE SAW--
OKAY. THE HARD WAY, THEN...
SEVEN, I TOLD YOU TO GIVE US A PERIMETER!
I'M SORRY, LEADER. I ABASE MYSELF.
LATER. JUST FINISH THEM.
G-GET AWAY FROM US!
KLUD!
UFFF!
PETER! NO!
NO NO NO NOOOOOO!
HAIL HYDRA!
CHAK!
CHAK!

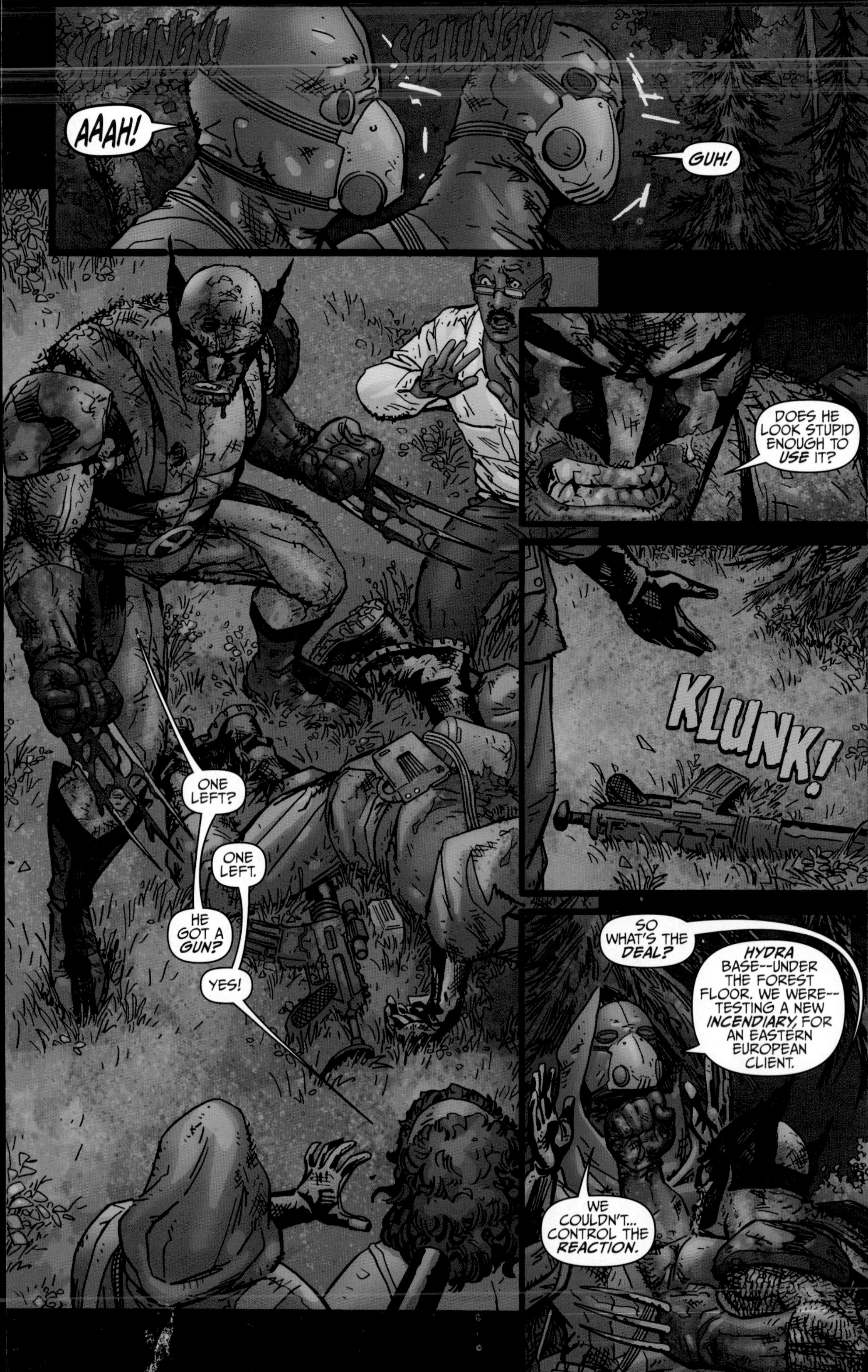
SCHUNGK!
SCHUNGK!
AAAH!
GUH!
ONE LEFT?
ONE LEFT.
HE GOT A GUN?
YES!
DOES HE LOOK STUPID ENOUGH TO USE IT?
KLUNK!
SO WHAT'S THE DEAL?
HYDRA BASE--UNDER THE FOREST FLOOR. WE WERE--TESTING A NEW INCENDIARY, FOR AN EASTERN EUROPEAN CLIENT.
WE COULDN'T... CONTROL THE REACTION.

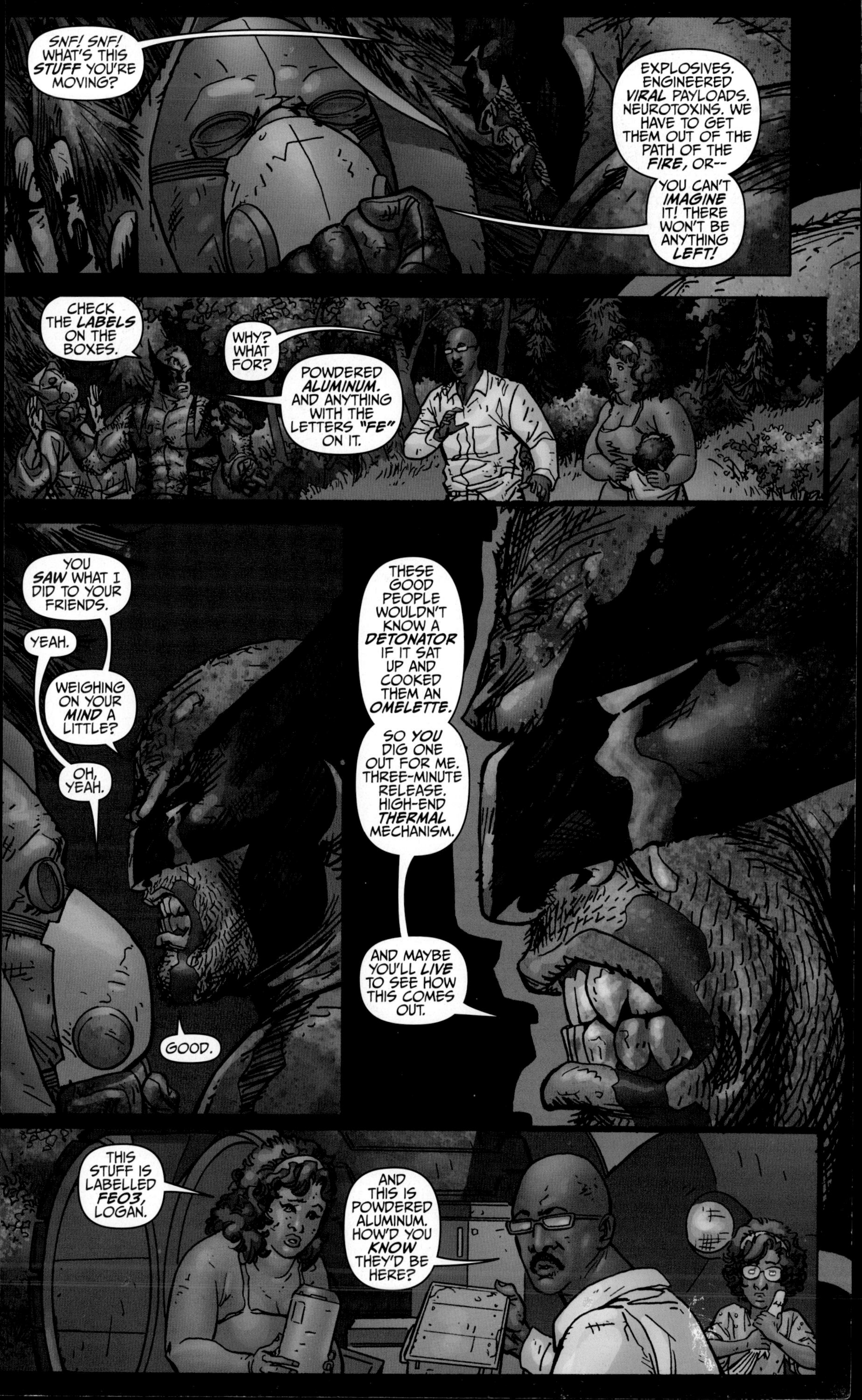
SNF! SNF! WHAT'S THIS STUFF YOU'RE MOVING?
EXPLOSIVES. ENGINEERED VIRAL PAYLOADS. NEUROTOXINS. WE HAVE TO GET THEM OUT OF THE PATH OF THE FIRE, OR--
YOU CAN'T IMAGINE IT! THERE WON'T BE ANYTHING LEFT!
CHECK THE LABELS ON THE BOXES.
WHY? WHAT FOR?
POWDERED ALUMINUM. AND ANYTHING WITH THE LETTERS "FE" ON IT.
YOU SAW WHAT I DID TO YOUR FRIENDS.
YEAH.
WEIGHING ON YOUR MIND A LITTLE?
OH, YEAH.
GOOD.
THESE GOOD PEOPLE WOULDN'T KNOW A DETONATOR IF IT SAT UP AND COOKED THEM AN OMELETTE.
SO YOU DIG ONE OUT FOR ME. THREE-MINUTE RELEASE. HIGH-END THERMAL MECHANISM.
AND MAYBE YOU'LL LIVE TO SEE HOW THIS COMES OUT.
THIS STUFF IS LABELLED FEO3, LOGAN.
AND THIS IS POWDERED ALUMINUM. HOW'D YOU KNOW THEY'D BE HERE?

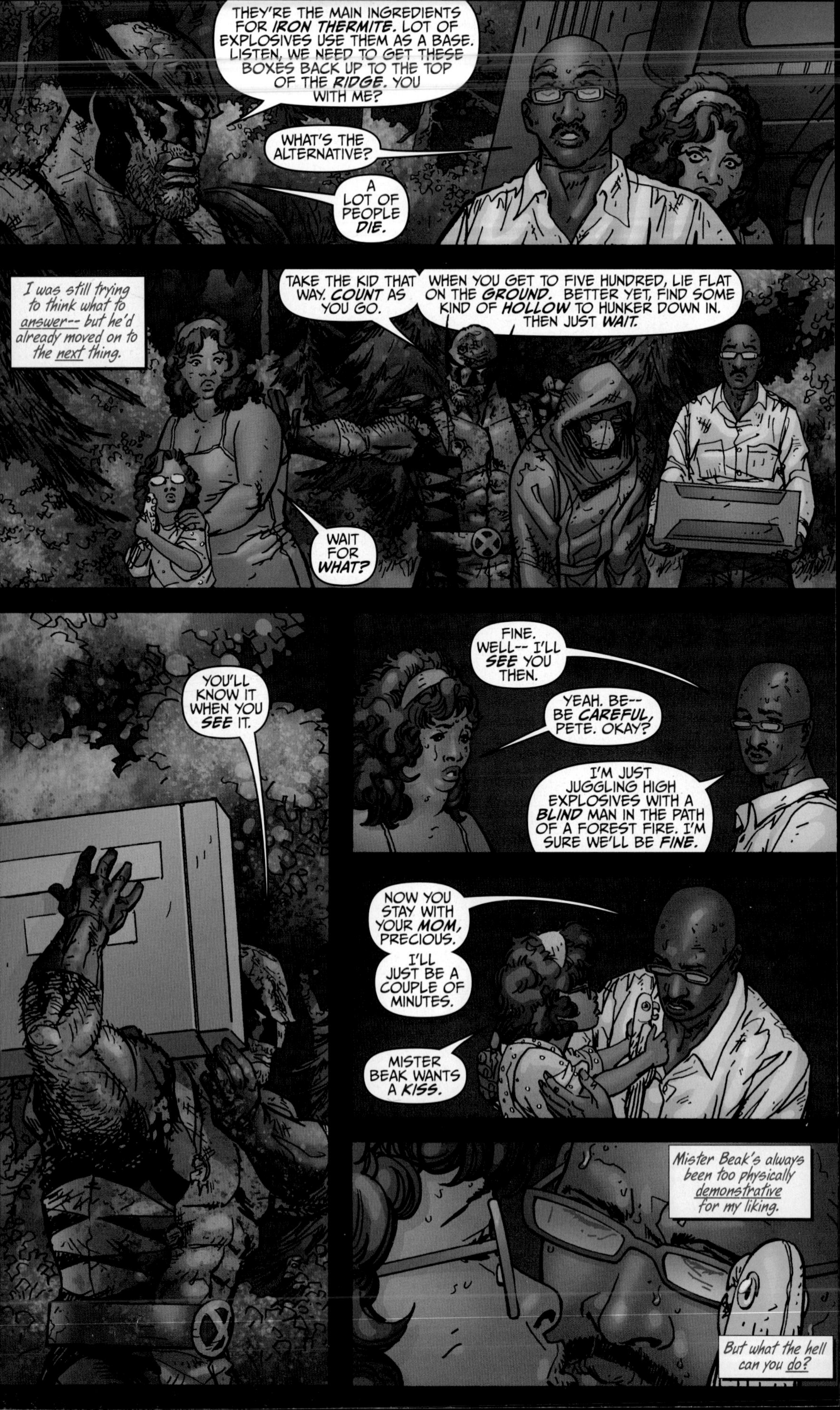
THEY'RE THE MAIN INGREDIENTS FOR IRON THERMITE. LOT OF EXPLOSIVES USE THEM AS A BASE. LISTEN, WE NEED TO GET THESE BOXES BACK UP TO THE TOP OF THE RIDGE. YOU WITH ME?
WHAT'S THE ALTERNATIVE?
A LOT OF PEOPLE DIE.
I was still trying to think what to answer-- but he'd already moved on to the next thing.
TAKE THE KID THAT WAY. COUNT AS YOU GO.
WHEN YOU GET TO FIVE HUNDRED, LIE FLAT ON THE GROUND. BETTER YET, FIND SOME KIND OF HOLLOW TO HUNKER DOWN IN. THEN JUST WAIT.
WAIT FOR WHAT?
YOU'LL KNOW IT WHEN YOU SEE IT.
FINE. WELL-- I'LL SEE YOU THEN.
YEAH. BE-- BE CAREFUL, PETE. OKAY?
I'M JUST JUGGLING HIGH EXPLOSIVES WITH A BLIND MAN IN THE PATH OF A FOREST FIRE. I'M SURE WE'LL BE FINE.
NOW YOU STAY WITH YOUR MOM, PRECIOUS.
I'LL JUST BE A COUPLE OF MINUTES.
MISTER BEAK WANTS A KISS.
Mister Beak's always been too physically demonstrative for my liking.
But what the hell can you do?

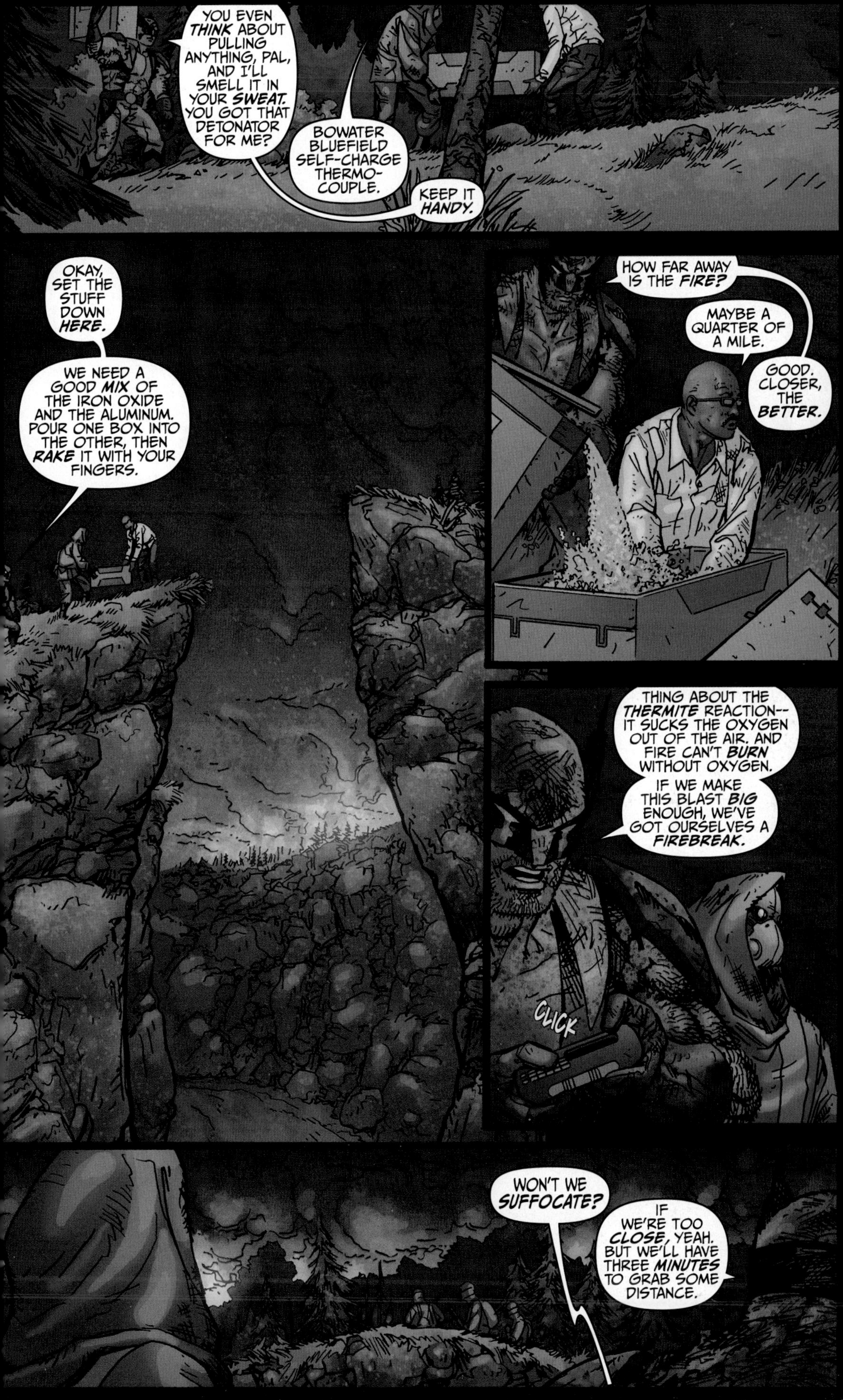
YOU EVEN THINK ABOUT PULLING ANYTHING, PAL, AND I'LL SMELL IT IN YOUR SWEAT. YOU GOT THAT DETONATOR FOR ME?
BOWATER BLUEFIELD SELF-CHARGE THERMO-COUPLE.
KEEP IT HANDY.
OKAY, SET THE STUFF DOWN HERE.
WE NEED A GOOD MIX OF THE IRON OXIDE AND THE ALUMINUM. POUR ONE BOX INTO THE OTHER, THEN RAKE IT WITH YOUR FINGERS.
HOW FAR AWAY IS THE FIRE?
MAYBE A QUARTER OF A MILE.
GOOD. CLOSER, THE BETTER.
THING ABOUT THE THERMITE REACTION-- IT SUCKS THE OXYGEN OUT OF THE AIR. AND FIRE CAN'T BURN WITHOUT OXYGEN.
IF WE MAKE THIS BLAST BIG ENOUGH, WE'VE GOT OURSELVES A FIREBREAK.
CLICK
WON'T WE SUFFOCATE?
IF WE'RE TOO CLOSE, YEAH. BUT WE'LL HAVE THREE MINUTES TO GRAB SOME DISTANCE.

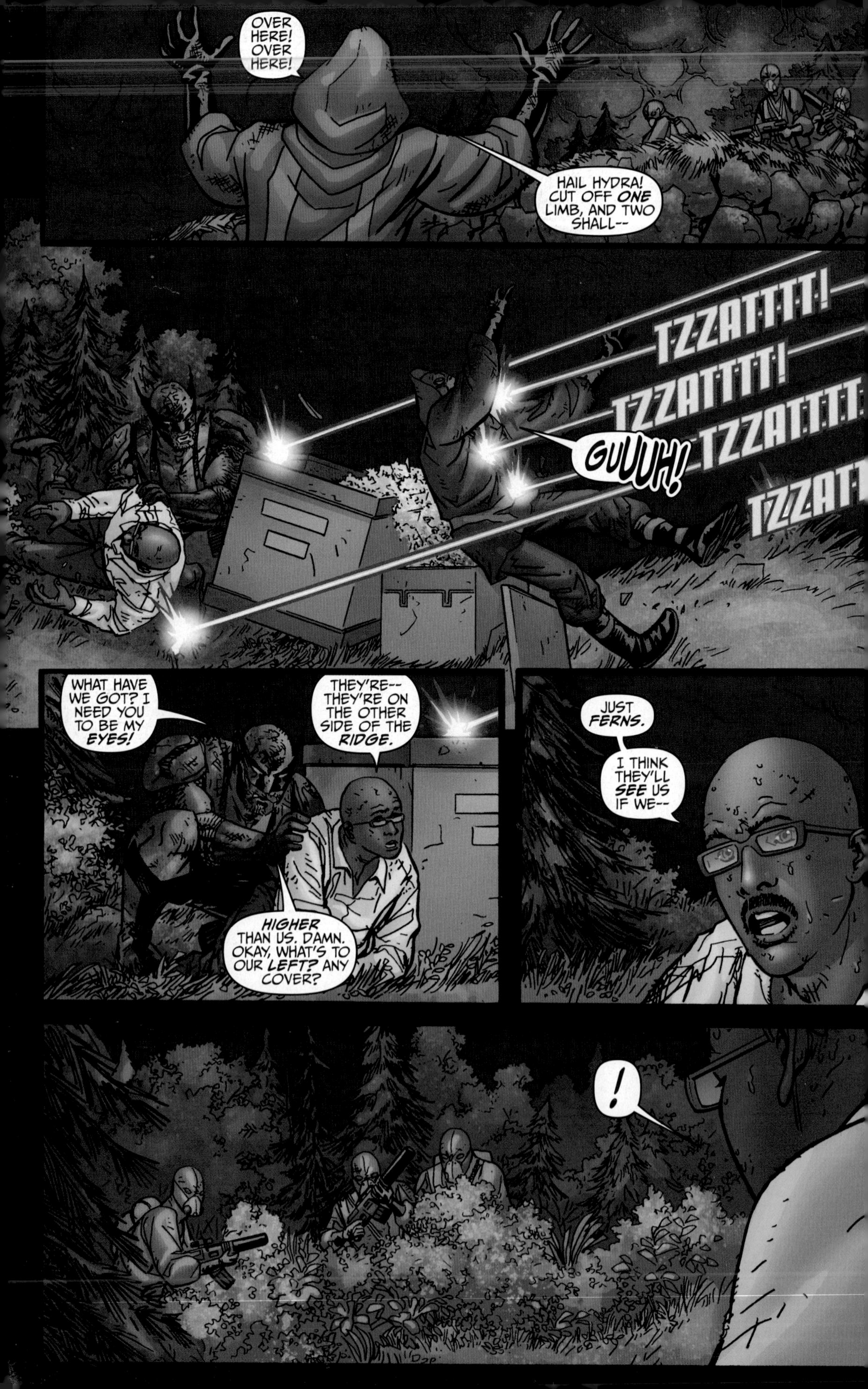
OVER HERE! OVER HERE!
HAIL HYDRA! CUT OFF ONE LIMB, AND TWO SHALL--
TZZATTTT!
TZZATTTT!
TZZATTTT
GUUUH!
TZZATTTT
TZZAT
WHAT HAVE WE GOT? I NEED YOU TO BE MY EYES!
THEY'RE-- THEY'RE ON THE OTHER SIDE OF THE RIDGE.
HIGHER THAN US. DAMN. OKAY, WHAT'S TO OUR LEFT? ANY COVER?
JUST FERNS.
I THINK THEY'LL SEE US IF WE--
!

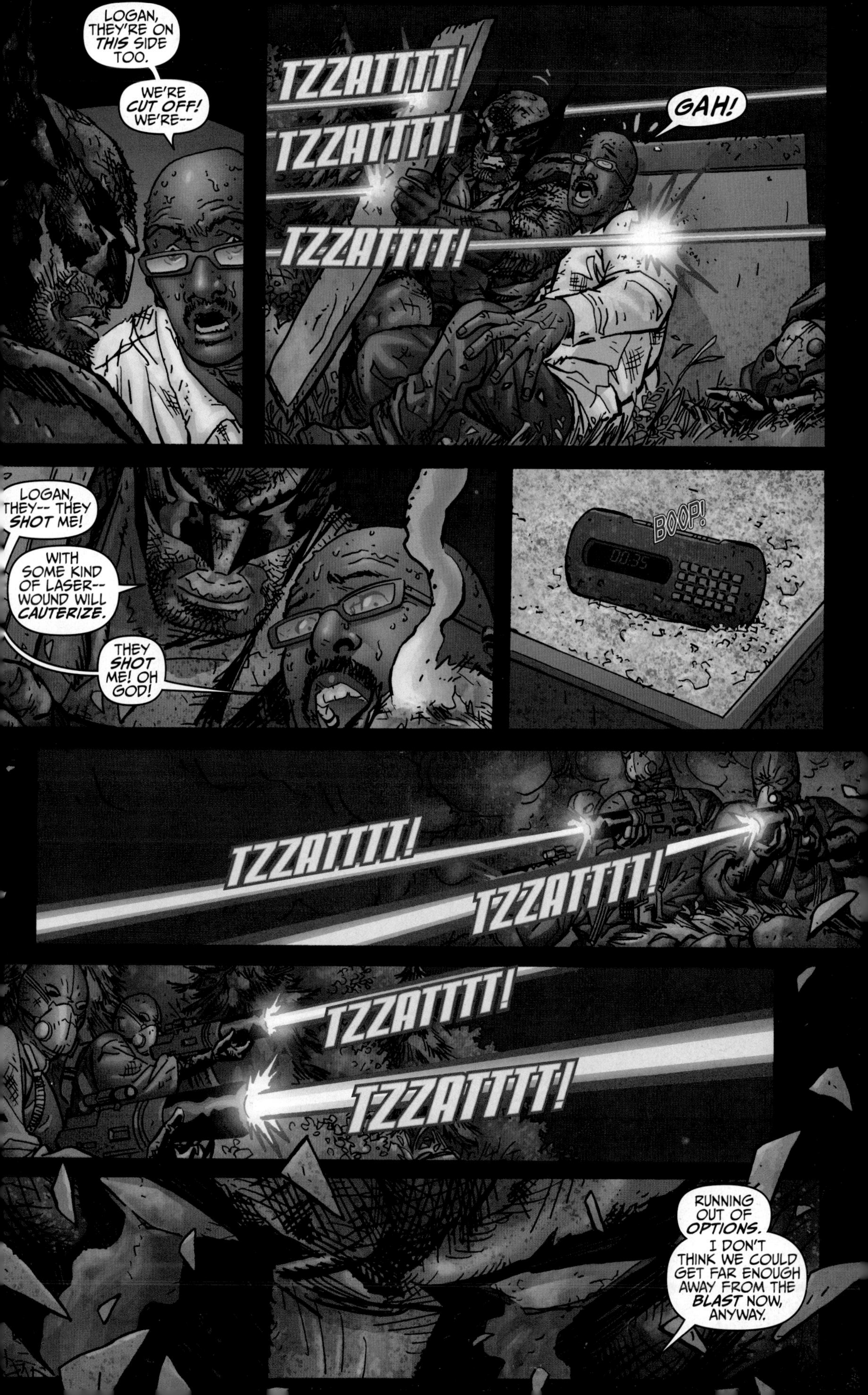
LOGAN, THEY'RE ON THIS SIDE TOO.
WE'RE CUT OFF! WE'RE--
TZZATTTT!
TZZATTTT!
GAH!
TZZATTTT!
LOGAN, THEY-- THEY SHOT ME!
WITH SOME KIND OF LASER-- WOUND WILL CAUTERIZE.
THEY SHOT ME! OH GOD!
BOOP!
00:35
TZZATTTT!
TZZATTTT!
TZZATTTT!
TZZATTTT!
RUNNING OUT OF OPTIONS.
I DON'T THINK WE COULD GET FAR ENOUGH AWAY FROM THE BLAST NOW, ANYWAY.

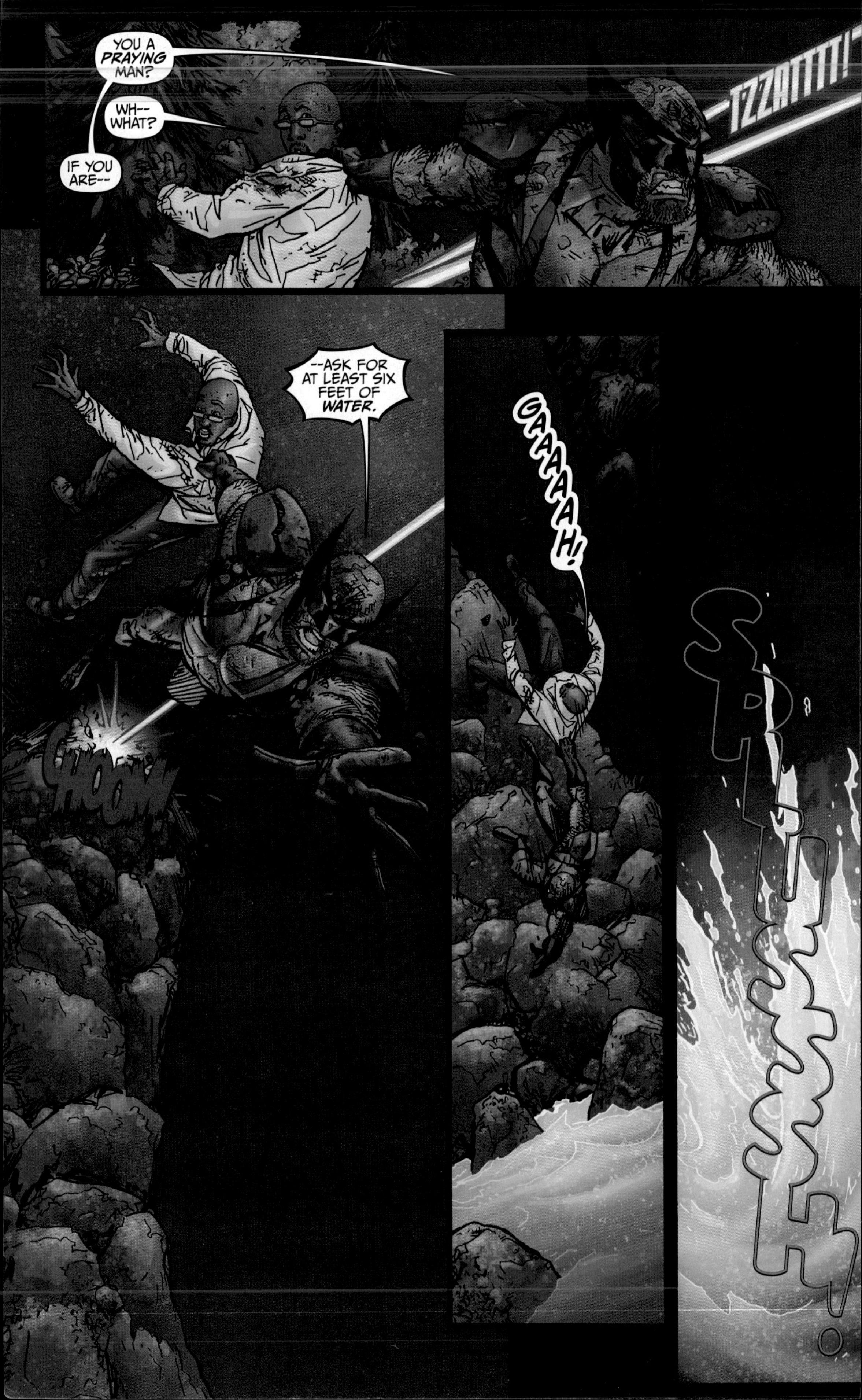
YOU A PRAYING MAN?
WH-- WHAT?
IF YOU ARE--
TZZATTTT!
--ASK FOR AT LEAST SIX FEET OF WATER.
CHOOOM
GAAAAAAH!
SPLOOOOOSH!

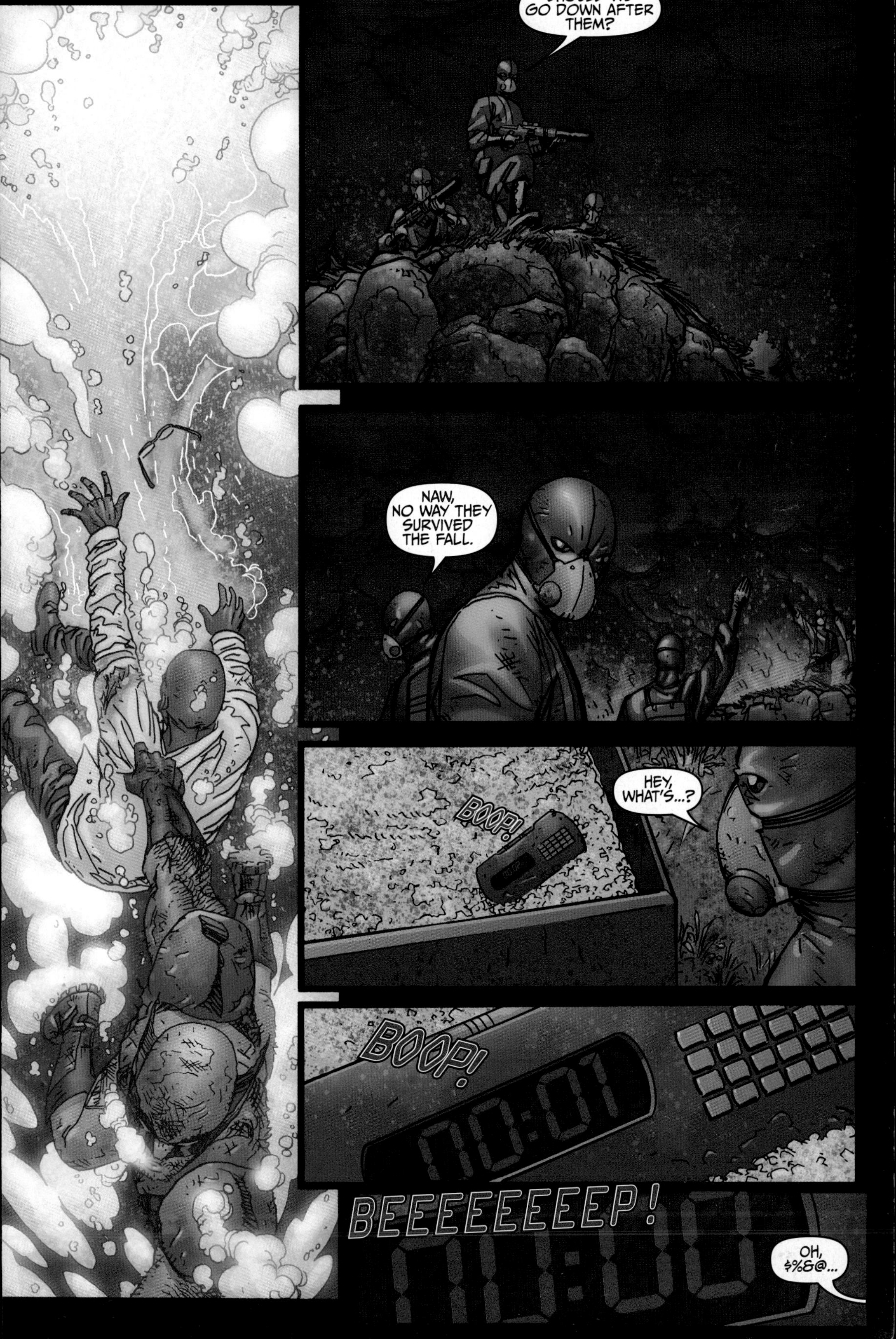
SHOULD WE GO DOWN AFTER THEM?
NAW, NO WAY THEY SURVIVED THE FALL.
BOOP!
HEY, WHAT'S...?
BOOP!
00:01
BEEEEEEEEEP!
00:00
OH, $%&@...

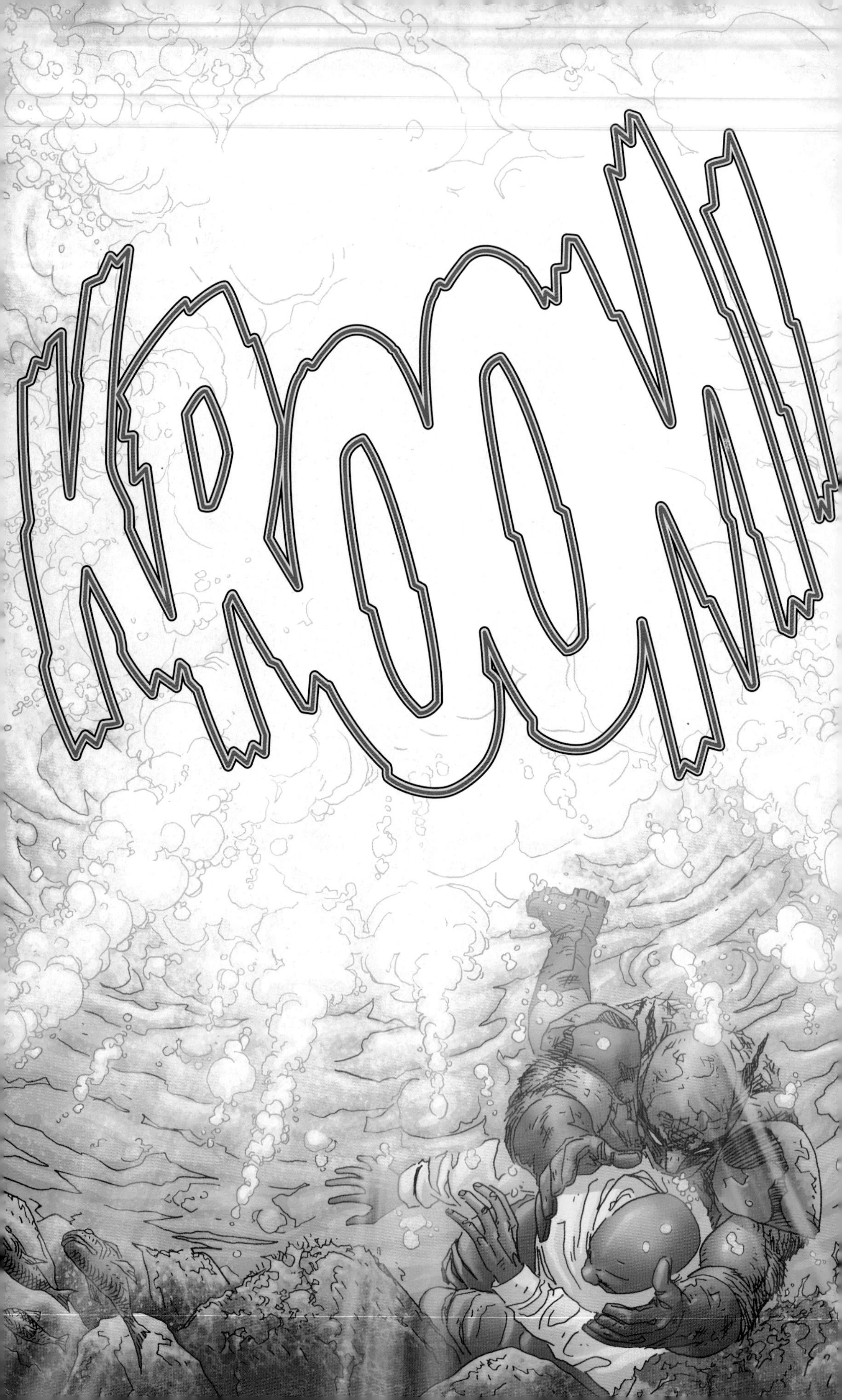
KRROOM!!

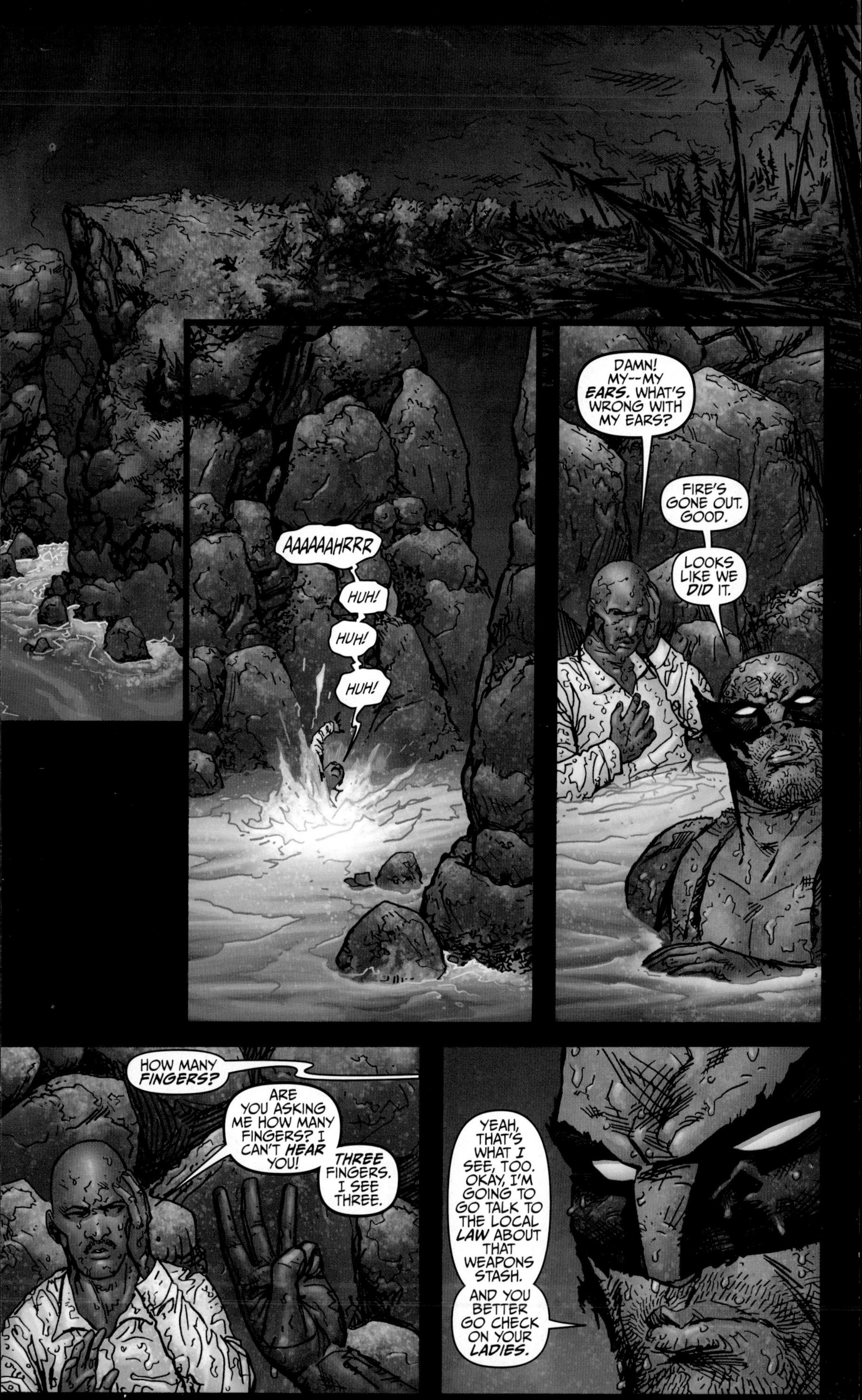

AAAAAAHRRR
HUH!
HUH!
HUH!
DAMN! MY--MY EARS. WHAT'S WRONG WITH MY EARS?
FIRE'S GONE OUT. GOOD.
LOOKS LIKE WE DID IT.
HOW MANY FINGERS?
ARE YOU ASKING ME HOW MANY FINGERS? I CAN'T HEAR YOU!
THREE FINGERS. I SEE THREE.
YEAH, THAT'S WHAT I SEE, TOO. OKAY, I'M GOING TO GO TALK TO THE LOCAL LAW ABOUT THAT WEAPONS STASH.
AND YOU BETTER GO CHECK ON YOUR LADIES.

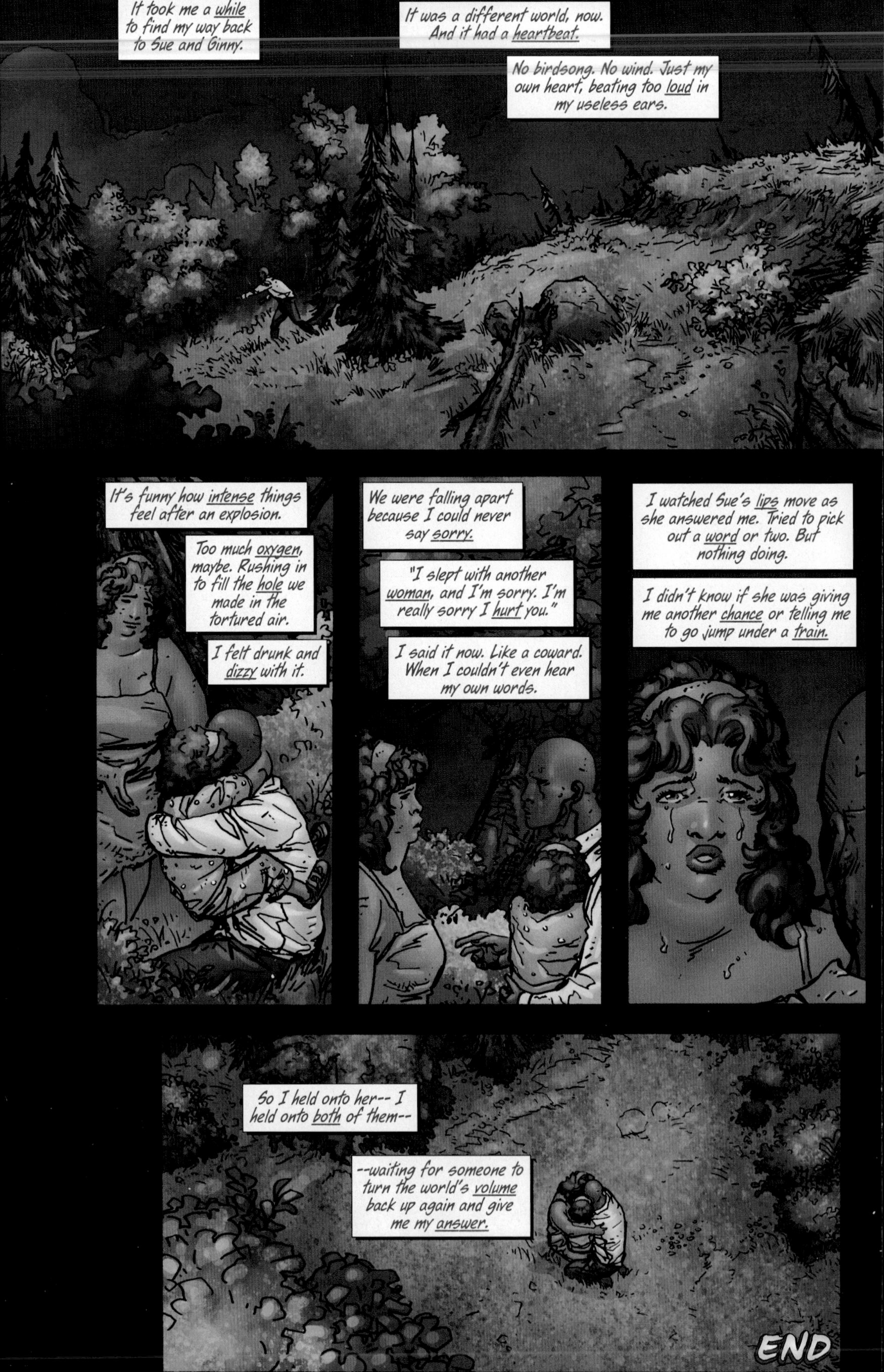
It took me a while to find my way back to Sue and Ginny.
It was a different world, now. And it had a heartbeat.
No birdsong. No wind. Just my own heart, beating too loud in my useless ears.
It's funny how intense things feel after an explosion.
Too much oxygen, maybe. Rushing in to fill the hole we made in the tortured air.
I felt drunk and dizzy with it.
We were falling apart because I could never say sorry.
"I slept with another woman, and I'm sorry. I'm really sorry I hurt you."
I said it now. Like a coward. When I couldn't even hear my own words.
I watched Sue's lips move as she answered me. Tried to pick out a word or two. But nothing doing.
I didn't know if she was giving me another chance or telling me to go jump under a train.
So I held onto her-- I held onto both of them--
--waiting for someone to turn the world's volume back up again and give me my answer.
END

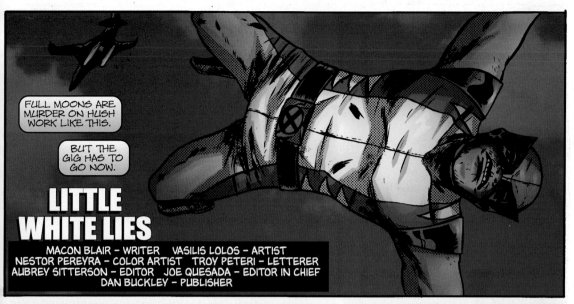

FULL MOONS ARE MURDER ON HUSH WORK LIKE THIS.

BUT THE GIG HAS TO GO NOW.

LITTLE WHITE LIES

MACON BLAIR – WRITER   VASILIS LOLOS – ARTIST
NESTOR PEREYRA – COLOR ARTIST   TROY PETERI – LETTERER
AUBREY SITTERSON – EDITOR   JOE QUESADA – EDITOR IN CHIEF
DAN BUCKLEY – PUBLISHER

POP!

FWOOMP!

CHIEF LACEY CAN'T ABIDE HIS SON IN THE HANDS OF A PSYCHOTIC MONSTER LIKE CARMELO S.S.

HELL, WHO *COULD?*

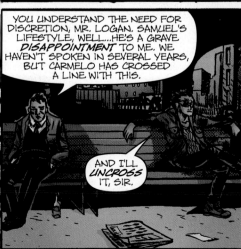

YOU UNDERSTAND THE NEED FOR DISCRETION, MR. LOGAN. SAMUEL'S LIFESTYLE, WELL...HE'S A GRAVE *DISAPPOINTMENT* TO ME. WE HAVEN'T SPOKEN IN SEVERAL YEARS, BUT CARMELO HAS CROSSED A LINE WITH THIS.

AND I'LL *UNCROSS* IT, SIR.

HE NEEDS THE BEST...SO HE GETS *ME.*

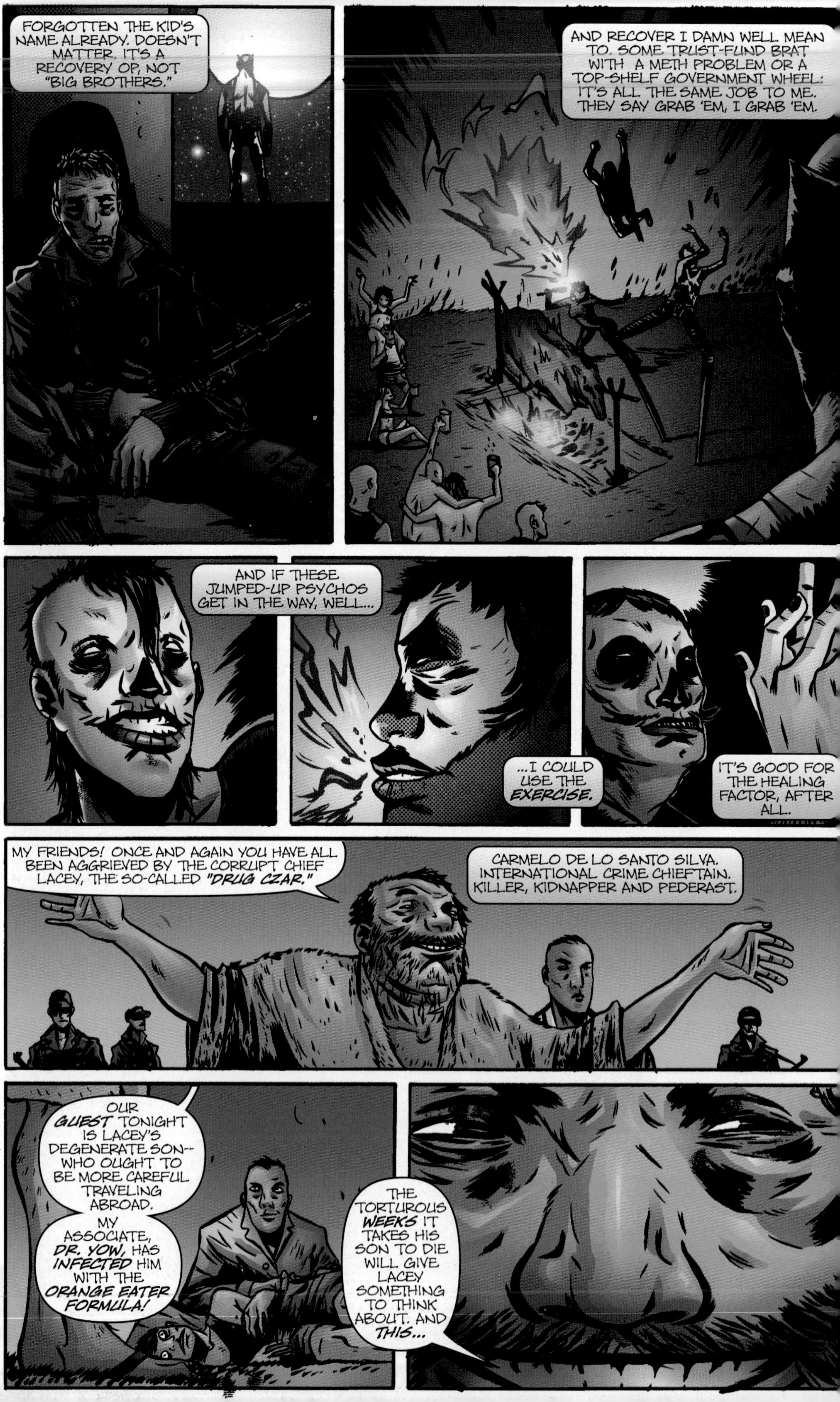
FORGOTTEN THE KID'S NAME ALREADY. DOESN'T MATTER. IT'S A RECOVERY OP, NOT "BIG BROTHERS."
AND RECOVER I DAMN WELL MEAN TO. SOME TRUST-FUND BRAT WITH A METH PROBLEM OR A TOP-SHELF GOVERNMENT WHEEL: IT'S ALL THE SAME JOB TO ME. THEY SAY GRAB 'EM, I GRAB 'EM.
AND IF THESE JUMPED-UP PSYCHOS GET IN THE WAY, WELL...
...I COULD USE THE EXERCISE.
IT'S GOOD FOR THE HEALING FACTOR, AFTER ALL.
MY FRIENDS! ONCE AND AGAIN YOU HAVE ALL BEEN AGGRIEVED BY THE CORRUPT CHIEF LACEY, THE SO-CALLED "DRUG CZAR."
CARMELO DE LO SANTO SILVA. INTERNATIONAL CRIME CHIEFTAIN. KILLER, KIDNAPPER AND PEDERAST.
OUR GUEST TONIGHT IS LACEY'S DEGENERATE SON-- WHO OUGHT TO BE MORE CAREFUL TRAVELING ABROAD.
MY ASSOCIATE, DR. YOW, HAS INFECTED HIM WITH THE ORANGE EATER FORMULA!
THE TORTUROUS WEEKS IT TAKES HIS SON TO DIE WILL GIVE LACEY SOMETHING TO THINK ABOUT. AND THIS...

...THIS IS MY GIFT TO YOU ALL!

HOLA, FELIX, WAKE UP! THE FIESTA IS DONE!

SNIKT!

SNIKT!

SEÑOR DE LO SANTO SILVA WANTS THE NIÑO LOCKED AWAY FOR THE NIGHT.

...AND MAKE SURE THEY DON'T SEE ME COMING.

AND SUDDENLY IT'S A DOUBLE-GRAB: THE TARGET *AND* THE ANTIDOTE. UNFORESEEN COMPLICATIONS REALLY *CHAFE* ME-- I GOTTA PLAY IT SMART...

SHUNGK

UKH--!

CHUNGK

GLUH--!

H-HELP M-ME...

YOU'RE SAFE NOW-- I'VE GOT YOU.

D-DAD...? I'M S-SORRY...

--SPOILED LITTLE *EMBARRASSMENT!* GET *OUT,* SAMUEL!

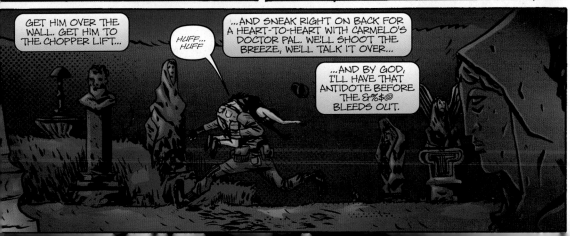

GET HIM OVER THE WALL. GET HIM TO THE CHOPPER LIFT...

HUFF... HUFF...

...AND SNEAK RIGHT ON BACK FOR A HEART-TO-HEART WITH CARMELO'S DOCTOR PAL. WE'LL SHOOT THE BREEZE, WE'LL TALK IT OVER...

...AND BY GOD, I'LL HAVE THAT ANTIDOTE BEFORE THE &%$@ BLEEDS OUT.

TNG

DAMMIT!

WEEoooWEEEoooWEEE...WEEEoooWE

TRIP WIRE ALARM--
STUPID. SLOPPY.

BRAP-AP-AP
BRAP-AP-AP

...OHHH!

TOO LATE FOR
THAT NOW...

SWASHUNGK

PLAYING IT
SMART,
RIGHT?

AGAHH~!

TCHUNK
TCHUNK
TCHUNK

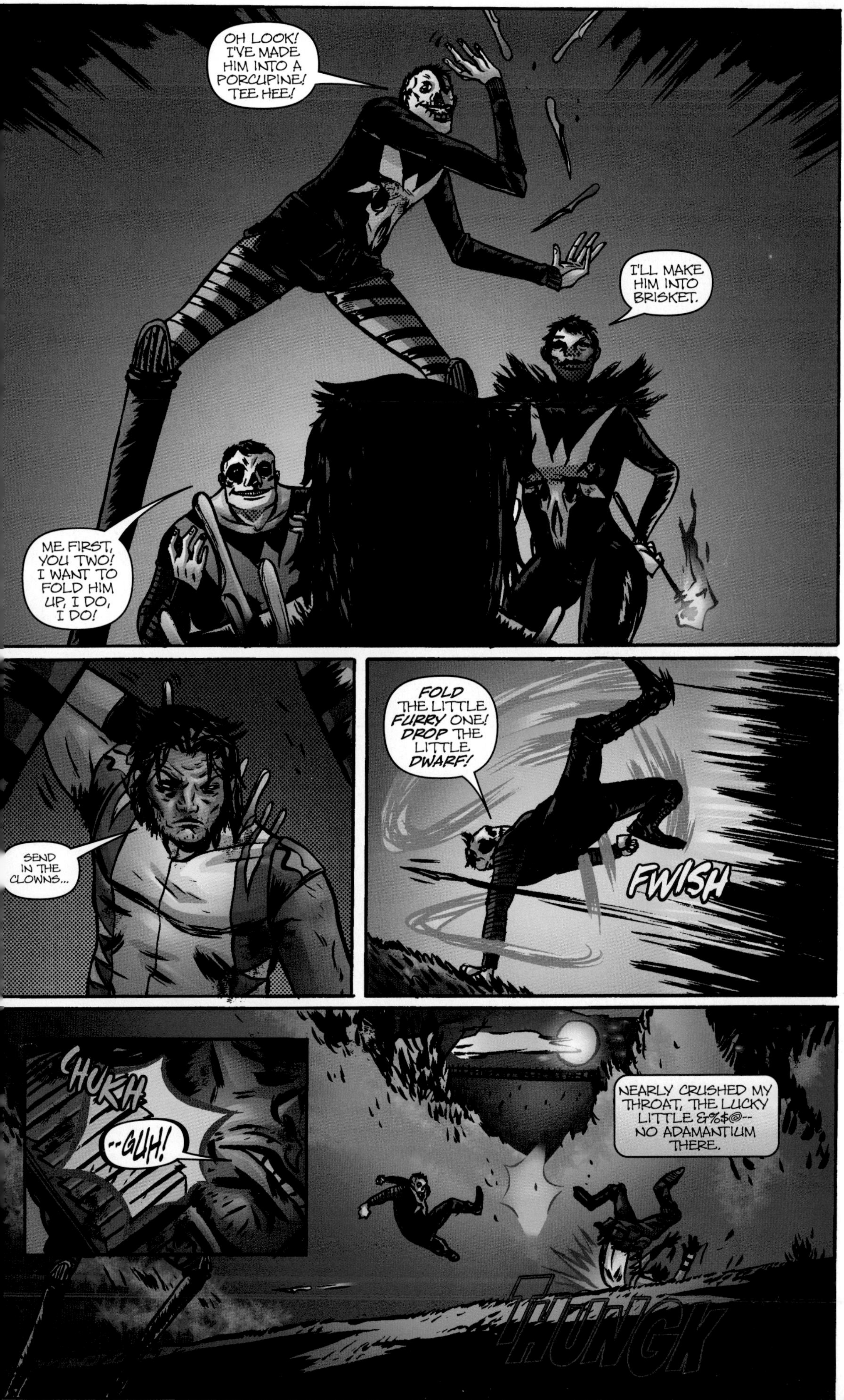
OH LOOK! I'VE MADE HIM INTO A PORCUPINE! TEE HEE!
I'LL MAKE HIM INTO BRISKET.
ME FIRST, YOU TWO! I WANT TO FOLD HIM UP, I DO, I DO!
SEND IN THE CLOWNS...
FOLD THE LITTLE FURRY ONE! DROP THE LITTLE DWARF!
FWISH
CHUKH
--GUH!
NEARLY CRUSHED MY THROAT, THE LUCKY LITTLE &%$@-- NO ADAMANTIUM THERE.
THUNCK

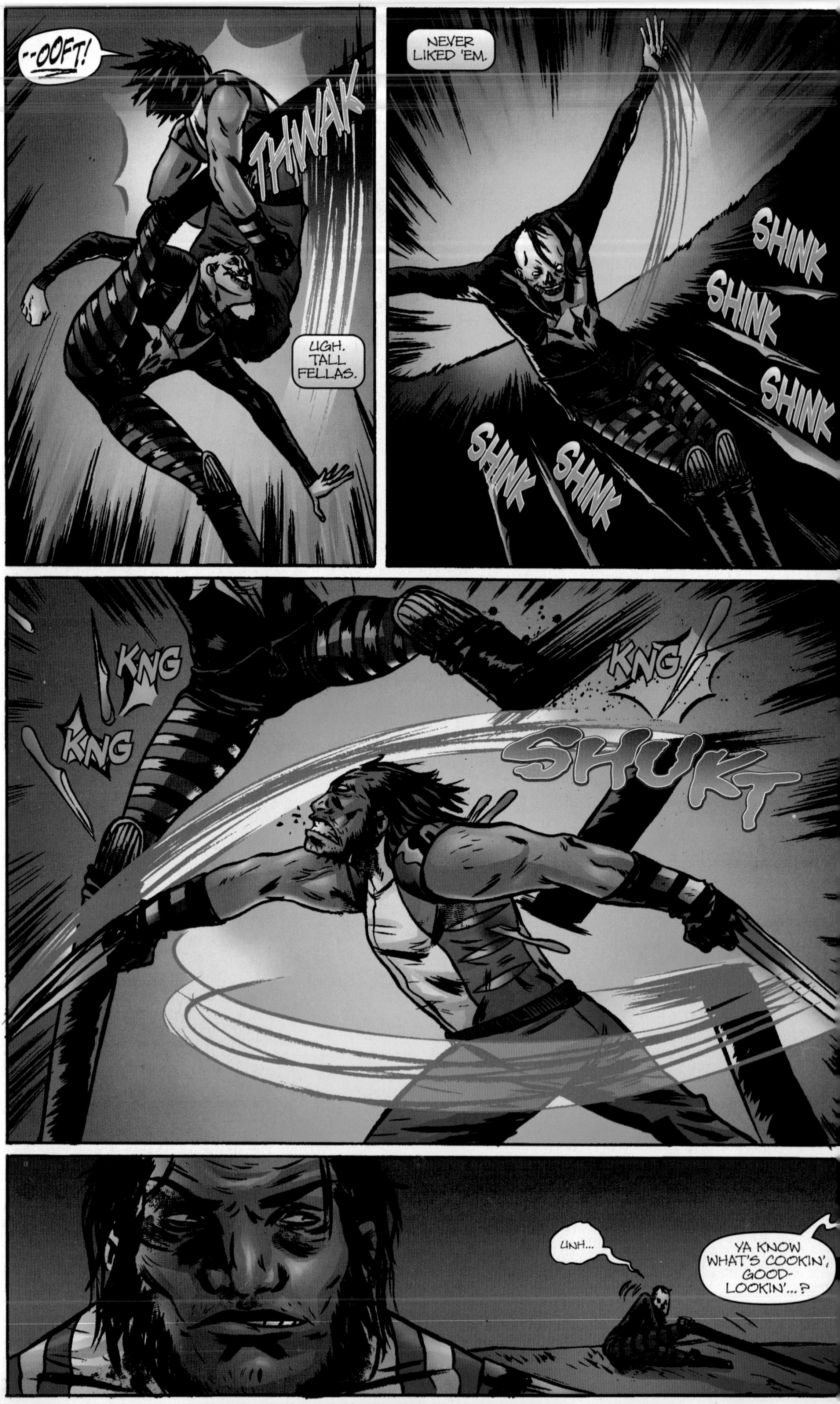
--OOFT!
THWAK
UGH. TALL FELLAS.
NEVER LIKED 'EM.
SHINK
SHINK
SHINK
SHINK
SHINK
KNG
KNG
KNG
SHUKT
UNH...
YA KNOW WHAT'S COOKIN', GOOD-LOOKIN'...?

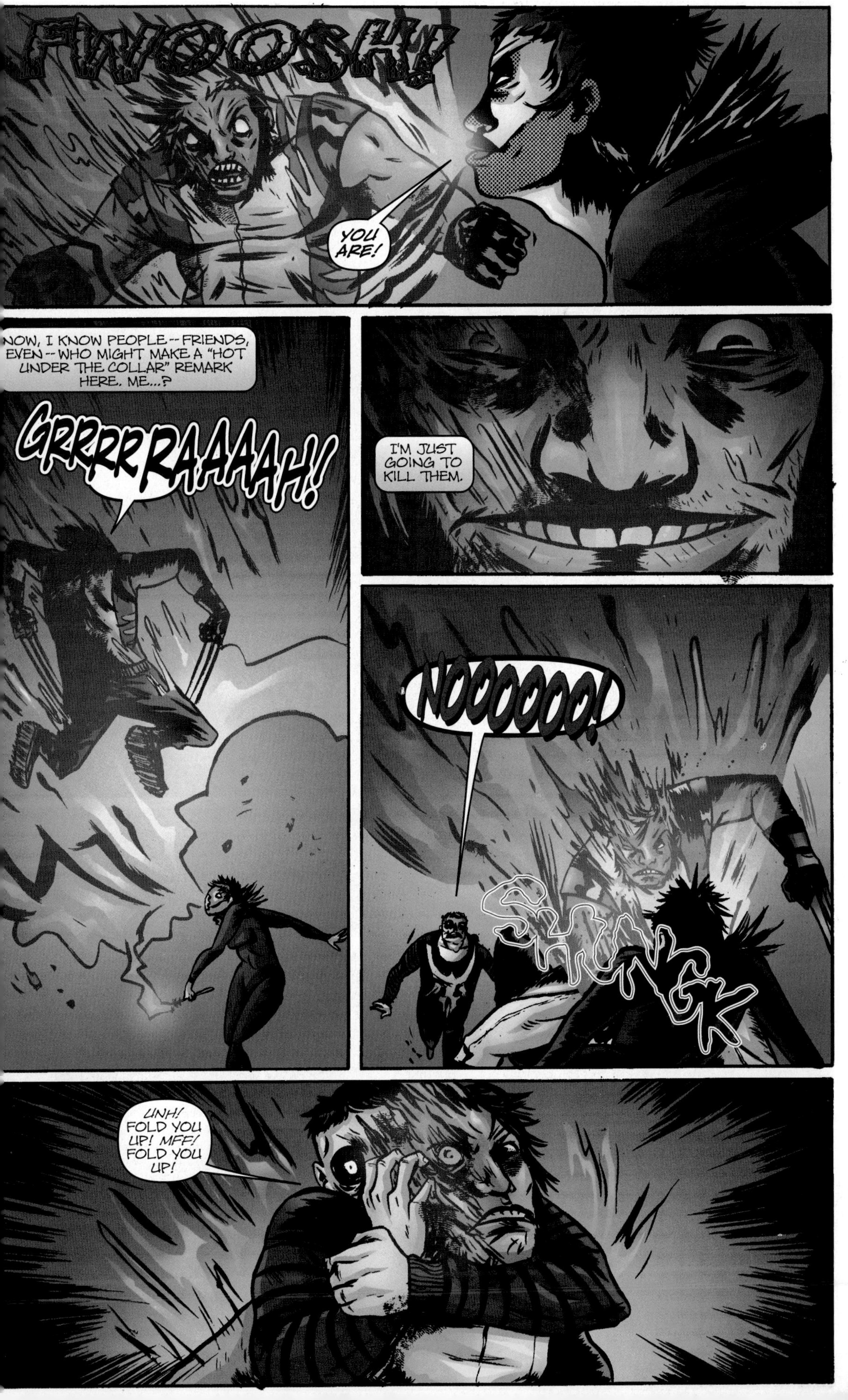
FWOOSH!
YOU ARE!
NOW, I KNOW PEOPLE -- FRIENDS, EVEN -- WHO MIGHT MAKE A "HOT UNDER THE COLLAR" REMARK HERE. ME...?
GRRRRRAAAAAH!
I'M JUST GOING TO KILL THEM.
NOOOOOO!
SHHUNGK
UNH! FOLD YOU UP! MFF! FOLD YOU UP!

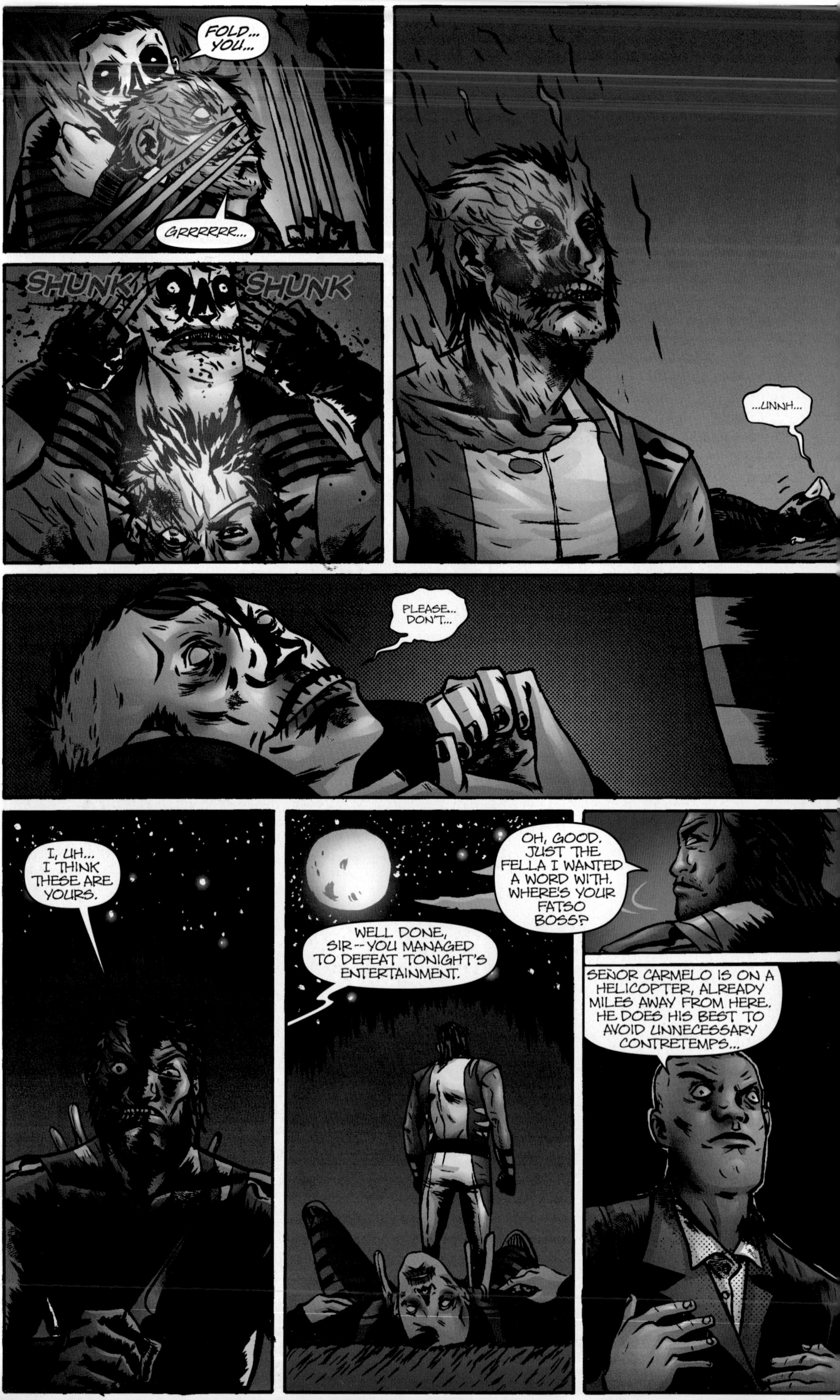
FOLD... YOU...
GRRRRRR...
SHUNK SHUNK
...UNNH...
PLEASE... DON'T...
I, UH... I THINK THESE ARE YOURS.
WELL DONE, SIR--YOU MANAGED TO DEFEAT TONIGHT'S ENTERTAINMENT.
OH, GOOD. JUST THE FELLA I WANTED A WORD WITH. WHERE'S YOUR FATSO BOSS?
SEÑOR CARMELO IS ON A HELICOPTER, ALREADY MILES AWAY FROM HERE. HE DOES HIS BEST TO AVOID UNNECESSARY CONTRETEMPS...

BUT YOU STAYED, 'INTCHA...?

I M-MUST RETRIEVE MY S-SUBJECT. WHERE IS--

I'D BE MORE WORRIED ABOUT *MYSELF* RIGHT NOW, DOC.

YOU-YOU KEEP AWAY FROM ME--!

FLICK A' THE WRIST, DOC--IT'S YOUR CAROTID ARTERY. NOW, THE *ORANGE EATER* ANTIDOTE: SPILL.

CHNGK

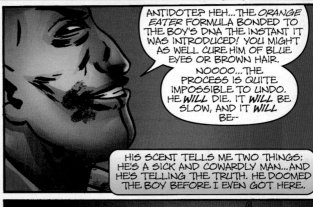

ANTIDOTE? HEH...THE *ORANGE EATER* FORMULA BONDED TO THE BOY'S DNA THE INSTANT IT WAS INTRODUCED! YOU MIGHT AS WELL CURE HIM OF BLUE EYES OR BROWN HAIR. NOOOO...THE PROCESS IS QUITE IMPOSSIBLE TO UNDO. HE *WILL* DIE. IT *WILL* BE SLOW, AND IT *WILL* BE--

HIS SCENT TELLS ME TWO THINGS: HE'S A SICK AND COWARDLY MAN...AND HE'S TELLING THE TRUTH. HE DOOMED THE BOY BEFORE I EVEN GOT HERE.

SHLUNK

...DAD?

I...

...YEAH, I'M HERE.

...PUH... PLEASE... IT HURTS SO BAD... M-MAKE IT STOP...

...OHGOD MAKE IT STOP...

HUSH, NOW.

SNIKT!

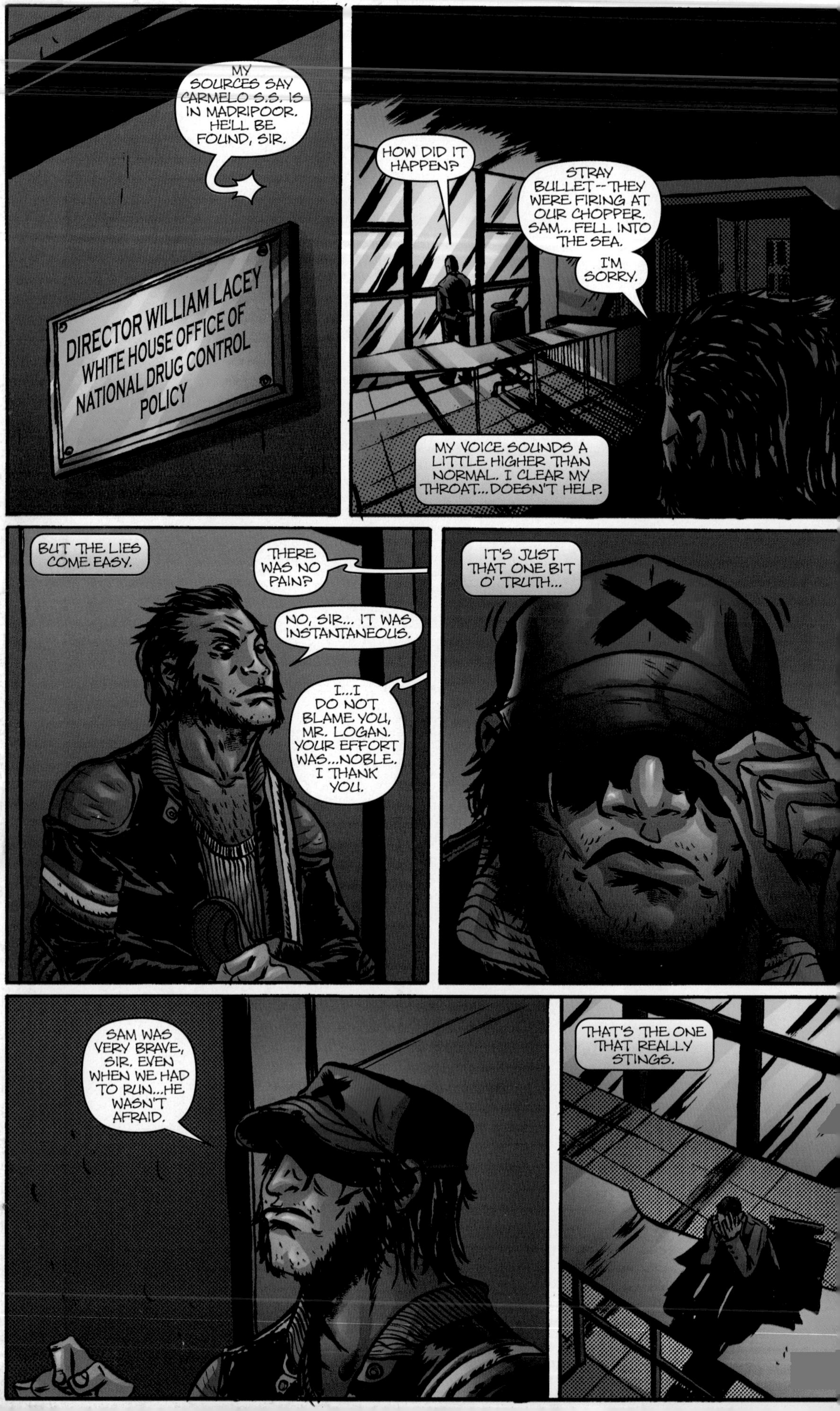
MY SOURCES SAY CARMELO S.S. IS IN MADRIPOOR. HE'LL BE FOUND, SIR.
DIRECTOR WILLIAM LACEY WHITE HOUSE OFFICE OF NATIONAL DRUG CONTROL POLICY
HOW DID IT HAPPEN?
STRAY BULLET--THEY WERE FIRING AT OUR CHOPPER. SAM... FELL INTO THE SEA.
I'M SORRY.
MY VOICE SOUNDS A LITTLE HIGHER THAN NORMAL. I CLEAR MY THROAT...DOESN'T HELP.
BUT THE LIES COME EASY.
THERE WAS NO PAIN?
NO, SIR... IT WAS INSTANTANEOUS.
I...I DO NOT BLAME YOU, MR. LOGAN. YOUR EFFORT WAS...NOBLE. I THANK YOU.
IT'S JUST THAT ONE BIT O' TRUTH...
SAM WAS VERY BRAVE, SIR. EVEN WHEN WE HAD TO RUN...HE WASN'T AFRAID.
THAT'S THE ONE THAT REALLY STINGS.

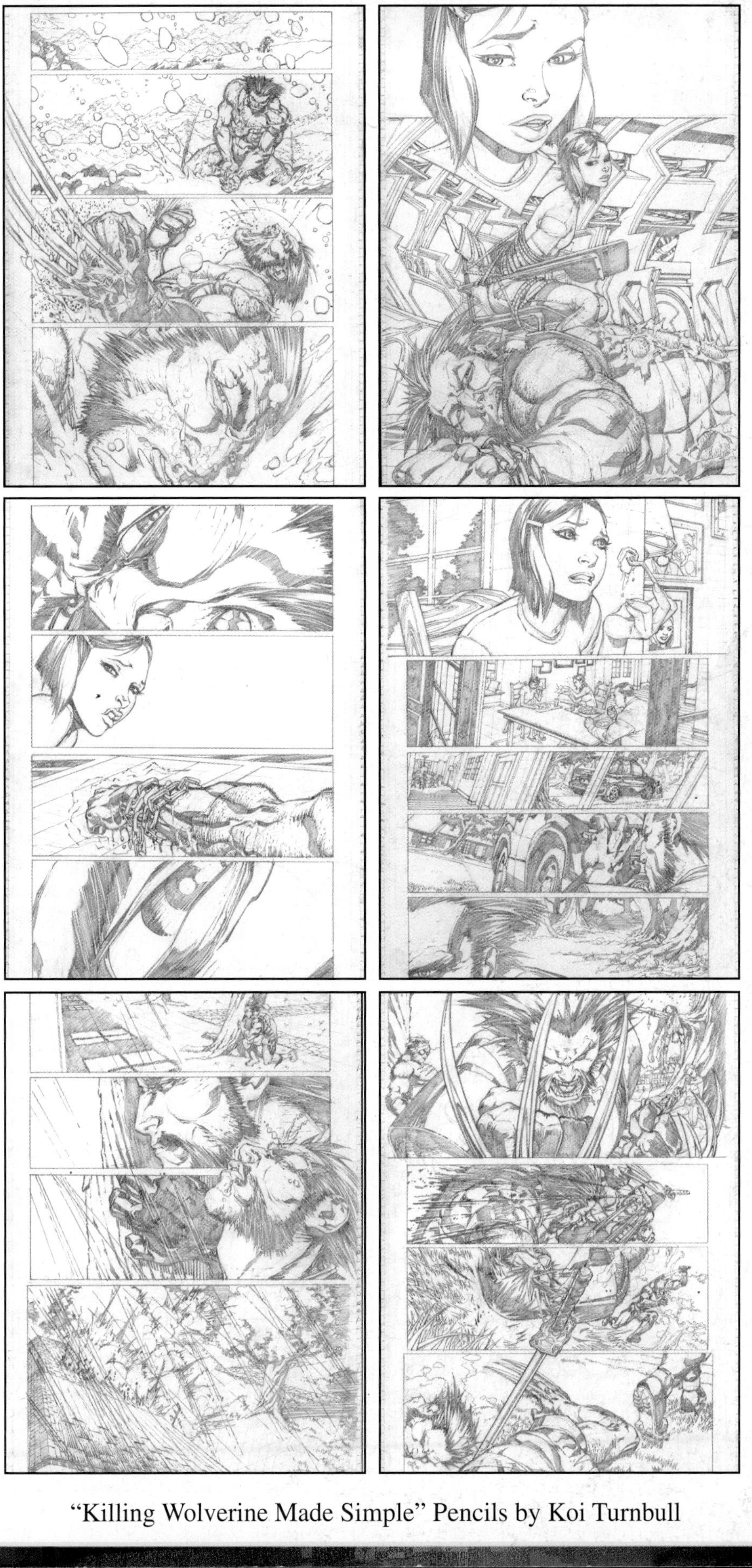

"Killing Wolverine Made Simple" Pencils by Koi Turnbull

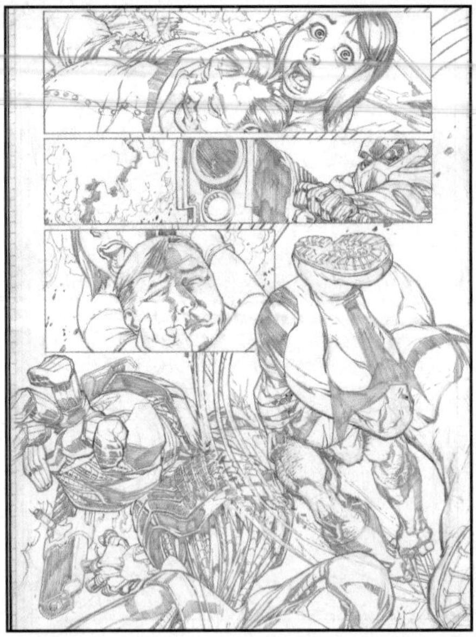
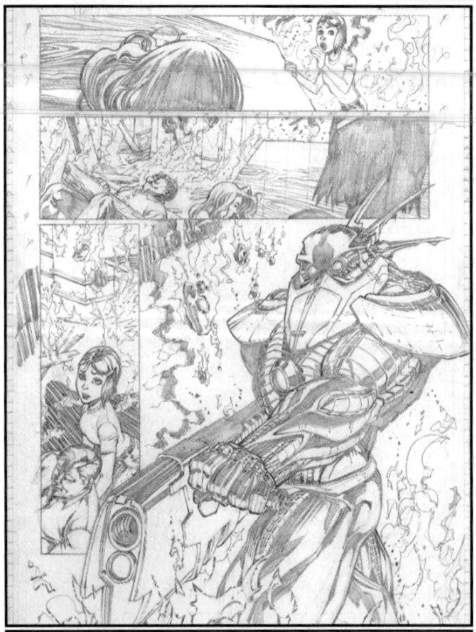
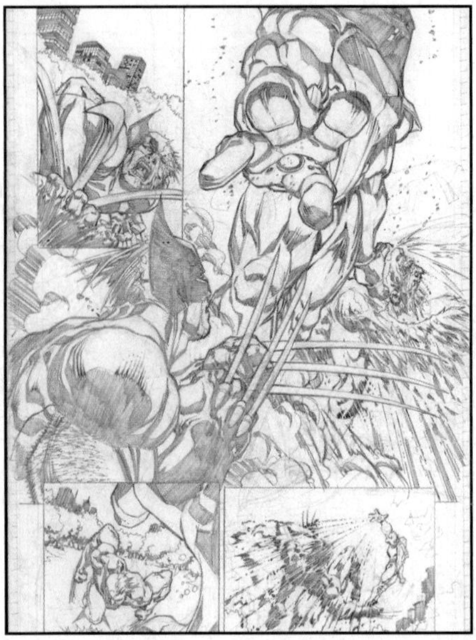
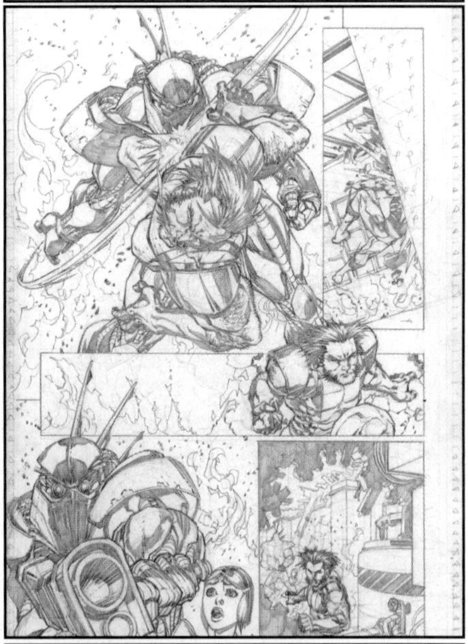
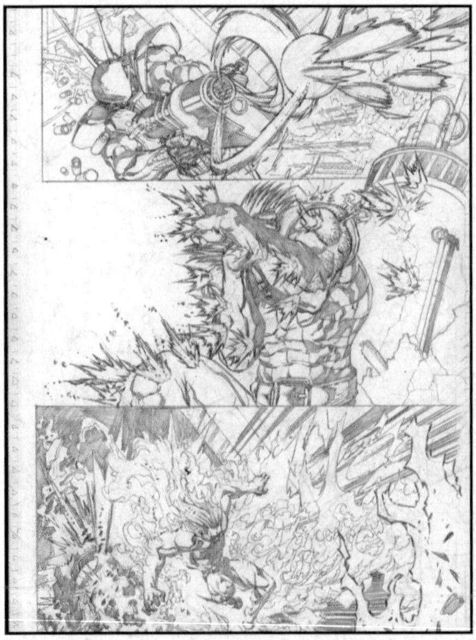
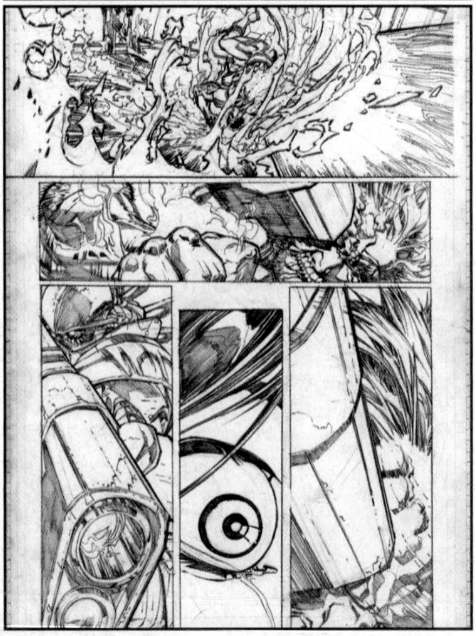

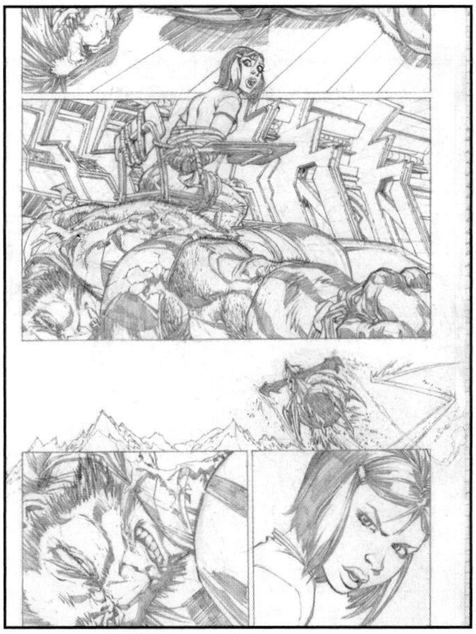
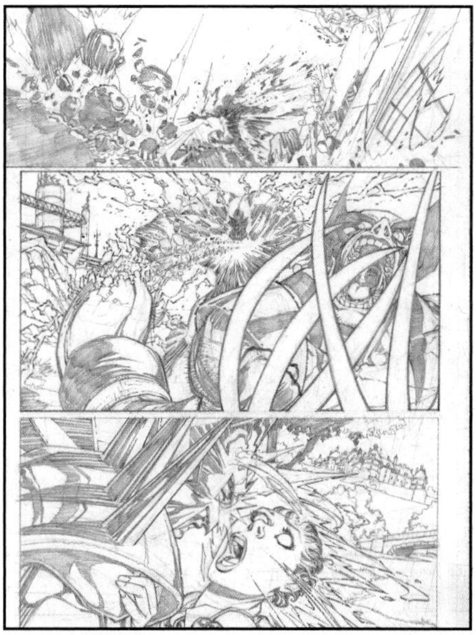
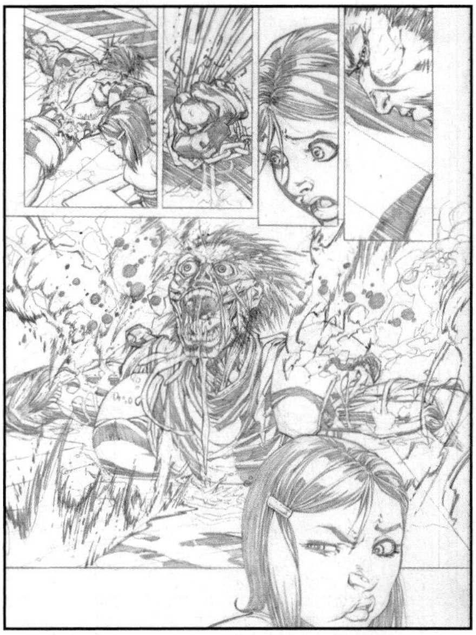
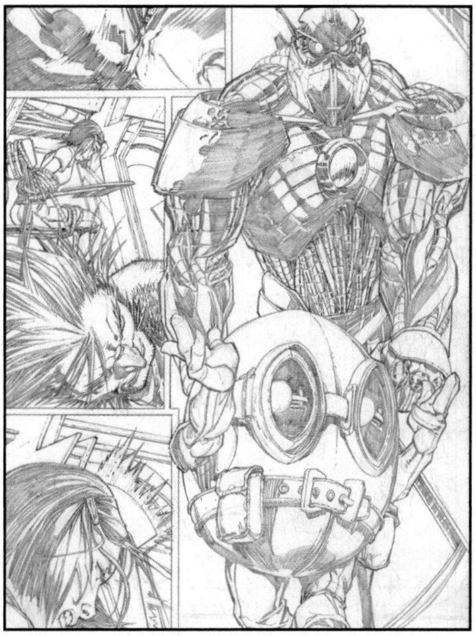
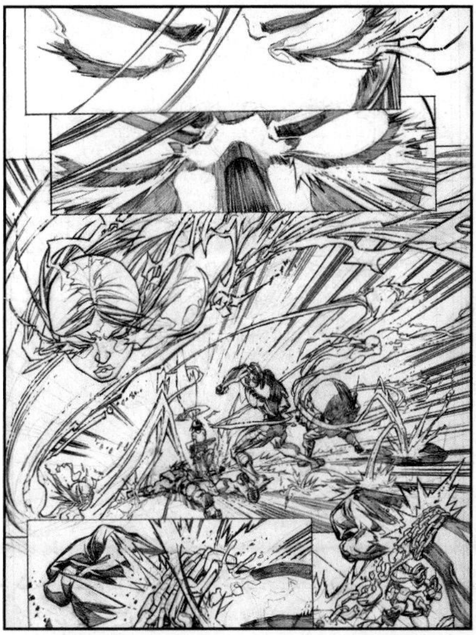
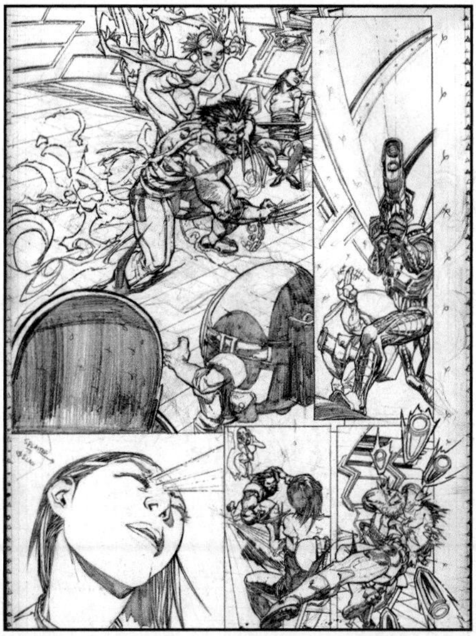